THE
EXPERT ADVANCER

DANNY ROTH is a writer and coach who specializes in teaching bridge to beginners and intermediates. An experienced and successful player at club, country and tournament level, he represented Great Britain in the European Pairs' Championships in 1987. He has written several other books on bridge, and is author of *The Expert Beginner* and *The Expert Improver*, both published by HarperCollins.

COLLINS
WINNING BRIDGE

THE EXPERT ADVANCER

DANNY ROTH

CollinsWillow

An Imprint of HarperCollins*Publishers*

First published in 1993 by
Collins Willow
an imprint of HarperCollins*Publishers*, London

© Danny Roth, 1993

**A CIP catalogue record for this book
is available from the British Library**

ISBN 0 00 218530 X

Printed and bound in Great Britain
by Cox & Wyman Ltd

Contents

Introduction	7
Section 1: Declarer Play at No-trump Contracts	13
Section 2: Declarer Play at Trump Contracts	53
Section 3: Defence against No-trump Contracts	117
Section 4: Defence against Trump Contracts	151
Section 5: Bidding	193
Index	283

Introduction

'A job well begun is a job half done!'

Welcome back again – to stage three. Hopefully, you will have read the first two books in this bridge education series, *The Expert Beginner* and *The Expert Improver*, and will be keen to the take this next step towards club level. Here, and in the sequel, you will be raising your standard of play and knowledge of conventions and procedure to the level at which you can not only play a good social game but can also join in a club event or tournament and hold your own without any worries.

I also have great pleasure in welcoming new readers who will probably have learnt in a circle of family and/or friends or at a club or evening classes. They will already have acquired some playing experience and will want to join at this stage.

I hope that both categories of reader will agree that it will do no harm to briefly review the ground covered in the first two books. I explained that the Expert series constituted something of – to put it in historical language – 'a glorious revolution' against accepted teaching methods. I explained that the bridge teacher, typically at an evening course, was on a hiding to nothing in attempting to teach the game in about a dozen lessons by the 'Let's start playing and we'll learn as we go along' approach. This may well be an enjoyable way of learning but I explained, and demonstrated with countless examples, it is a recipe for failure. There is no greater proof than the thousands of players you will meet all over the world, many of whom proudly boast decades of 'experience' and yet, to this day, can neither bid nor play the simplest of hands.

I explained that, in order to attain even a modest degree of competence, a bridge player must develop a 'platform' of knowledge, consisting of three major elements.

1 Familiarization with the pack of cards.
2 A full understanding of the language and procedure of the game.
3 A complete knowledge and understanding of the scoresheet.

In *The Expert Beginner*, readers were encouraged to develop their platform as solidly as possible and were given a number of exercises to do in respect of (1) and (3) against the stop-watch. The purpose behind timing everything was to ensure that the prospective player had as much knowledge as possible 'at the fingertips' before going anywhere near a bridge table.

There followed an intensive study of winning and losing tricks. We considered the single suit in detail and saw the importance of who won specific tricks and when. The three basic questions to be considered were as follows:

1 How many rounds of a particular suit were likely to be played.
2 How many were likely to be won.
3 How many were likely to be lost, bearing in mind that the answers in (2) or (3) have to total that in (1).

Then we considered the effect of an outside trump suit and saw that suits could now be developed with fewer tricks lost than at no-trumps and that the answers in (2) and (3) did not now have to total that in (1).

Eventually, we played out a few full hands, some in no-trumps and some in suit contracts (with all the cards exposed) to illustrate the application of the platform knowledge and what we had learnt about winning and losing tricks.

We then started basic bidding and heavy emphasis was laid on the overriding importance of considering the final or 'goal' contract. I also insisted that readers should not only find the best bid in a given situation but be able to explain the reasons for it. I explained that bidding can not only be conducted in several different languages or 'systems', but also is very much a question of judgment and that, in many situations, there is scope for considerable difference of opinion, even among experts. You need do no more than pick up a bridge magazine and turn to the 'Bidding Challenge' page for illustration. There are some problems in which a good case could be made for up to half-a-dozen or more different answers. Which one you choose is nowhere near as important as the ability to justify it, i.e. to demonstrate that you understand what you are doing.

A few conventional bids were introduced and there were plenty of tests against the stop-watch to train readers to bid at a speed approaching that expected at the table in a normal game.

The book ended with a short section on leading and defence, although there had already been several references to the approach during the declarer–play section.

Throughout the book, the reader was able to work alone, without the need for other players. Having read the above paragraphs, you can see how much my method differs from that of commonly-accepted teaching. Schools and classes give their students a large number of 'parrot-type' rules in bidding, play and defence. The students proceed to follow them blindly but, as they are not fully understood and, in any case, are inapplicable a fair proportion of the time, results, to put it kindly, are modest.

Worst of all, little attention is paid to scoring and I explained that this amounted to putting a brilliant footballer on to a pitch and expecting him to play without knowing where the goal is! However brilliant his ball skills and fitness may be, he will be of no use whatsoever! It is particularly embarrassing therefore that I must start with an apology and correction.

Literally a few days after *The Expert Beginner* was published, the world's bridge authorities locked the door after the horse had bolted in bringing the scoring for rubber bridge (which I set out in the book) into line with that of duplicate, which we shall learn in the next book. I must therefore record three changes, one large and two very small.

The major alteration is in respect of penalties for doubled contracts, non-vulnerable. You should remember that the old scale read like this:

Number of undertricks	1	2	3	4	5	6	7	8
Penalty		100	300	500	700	900	1100	1300	1500

and so on, increasing by 200 each time. I explained that the formula was to express the penalty in hundreds, multiplying the number of undertricks by two and subtracting one. In an attempt to curb frivolous and disruptive bidding at favourable vulnerability, considered by many to be an abuse of the relatively light penalties in the above table, the scale has been revised as follows:

Number of undertricks	1	2	3	4	5	6	7	8
Penalty		100	300	500	800	1100	1400	1700	2000

and so on, increasing by 300 each time. Thus (still expressing the penalty in hundreds), the revised formula is as follows:

1 For defeats of up to three tricks: multiply by two and subtract one, as before.
2 For defeats of four tricks or more: multiply by three and subtract four.

Thus two down is $(2 \times 2 - 1) \times 100 = 300$
   six down is $(6 \times 3 - 4) \times 100 = 1400$ as in the above table.

The second alteration concerns redoubled contracts which are made (with or without overtricks). The bonus of 50 (for the 'insult') applicable to doubled contracts which are made and which previously applied similarly to redoubled contracts, is now increased to 100.

Finally, in rubber bridge, where a rubber is unfinished, the 50-point bonus for a part-score is increased to 100. In duplicate, the part-score bonus remains at 50 points.

The Expert Beginner should have given the readers who studied it diligently a firm base from which to graduate to playing in realistic conditions and in *The Expert Improver*, I introduced problems in which only two hands were exposed. The declarer play and defence sections were each divided into two subsections, separating no-trump and suit contracts. The use of the 'one-closed-hand' exercise, introduced under the heading of 'familiarization with a pack of cards', was now extended to two hands and, instead of following beginners' parrot rules, we learnt how to place the twenty-six unseen cards with a view to playing effectively 'seeing' all four hands. I explained that the calculations involved a considerable mental effort but that the rewards were incalculable. We then returned to bidding and introduced a number of new conventional bids, illustrating their use, always bearing in mind the uppermost consideration of final contract!

In all sections, there were large numbers of problems to be done against the stop-watch and we are going to continue that set-up in this book. You therefore need the same equipment as before, sitting at a large square table with a pack of cards, pen and paper by your writing hand and a stop-watch by your other hand. You will then be ready to start.

Declarer Play at No-trump Contracts

As was explained in the earlier books, the play at no-trump contracts usually constitutes a race between the two sides to see who can establish its long suit first for winners which obviously cannot be ruffed. However, it is not a straight running race down a clear track. Either side can put obstacles in front of the other in the form of:

1 Blockages in the suit itself.
2 Attacks on side-suit entries.
3 Holding up controls in order to exhaust the partner of the hand with the long suit so that, if he wins a trick, he will have to switch to another suit at the cost of a vital tempo.

Let us start with a simple example:

Hand No. 1
Dealer East
E–W vulnerable

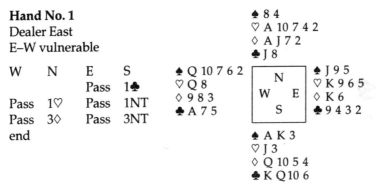

W	N	E	S
		Pass	1♣
Pass	1♡	Pass	1NT
Pass	3◇	Pass	3NT
end			

North hand:
♠ 8 4
♡ A 10 7 4 2
◇ A J 7 2
♣ J 8

West hand:
♠ Q 10 7 6 2
♡ Q 8
◇ 9 8 3
♣ A 7 5

East hand:
♠ J 9 5
♡ K 9 6 5
◇ K 6
♣ 9 4 3 2

South hand:
♠ A K 3
♡ J 3
◇ Q 10 5 4
♣ K Q 10 6

Let us first go through the bidding. South observed the usual rule of bidding the lower-ranking of four-card suits and, over his partner's 1♡ response, rebid 1NT to show 15–16 points. North's 3◇ bid was forcing for one round and offered 4♡, 3NT or possibly 5◇ as candidate goal contracts. With both black suits well stopped, South opted for the nine-trick no-trump game.

West led the usual fourth-highest of his longest suit, the ♠6. Dummy played low, East the ♠J and South correctly played low in an attempt to exhaust East of the suit. South won the second round and saw that he had two spade tricks, at least one heart, three or four diamonds (dependent on the position of the king) and three clubs once the ace had been knocked out. In the meantime, the defenders were threatening to take three spade tricks and the ◇K (if East held it) in addition to the ♣A.

Observing the usual rule of concentrating on the long suit first, South ran the ◇Q, losing to East's ◇K. Back came a third round of spades (but notice that, had East started with only two, he would have now been out of the suit – that was the purpose of declarer's holding up on trick one). South won but, when West got in with the ♣A, he was able to cash two more spades to complete five tricks for one off and +50.

What went wrong? Playing on your long suit first is one rule but knocking out certain losers (here the ♣A) before uncertain losers (here the ◇K, which could be with West and therefore finessable) is another. Let us replay the hand correctly. South should realize that, if West has the ◇K, at least three tricks can be made in the suit without losing the lead. Indeed the lead need only be lost once to the ♣A and the long spades cannot be cashed before South takes at least nine tricks. Thus South should assume that East has the ◇K. On the above line, he lost his first minor-suit trick to the ◇K with East and his second to the ♣A with West. Change the order so that West wins the first trick and East the second, and now East will be out of spades and declarer prevails. Let us play it.

   (i)   A spade, won by East.
  (ii) Another spade, won by South.
 (iii) A club which West ducks (hoping to catch an honour on the next round) won by North's ♣J.
 (iv) Another club won by West.

(v) Another spade, won by South, dummy discarding a heart. West's two remaining spades are now masters.

(vi) A club winner by South, dummy discarding a heart.

(vii) South's last club winner, West discarding a diamond and dummy another heart.

(viii) South now runs the ◊Q, losing to East's ◊K and East has no more spades.

(ix) East switches, say, to a heart to West's ♡Q and dummy's ♡A.

(x-xii) South cashes three more diamonds.

(xiii) The last trick is conceded to East's ♡K.

This way, South has taken nine tricks and conceded four (a trick in each suit) to score +100 and game – a big difference.

So it would appear that it is wise to observe the second rule above in preference to the first. Or is it? All that is needed is a slight change to the above hand and the long-suit rule is right after all:

Hand No. 2

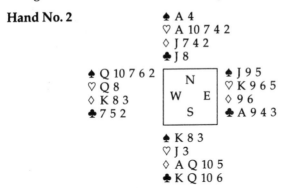

```
              ♠ A 4
              ♡ A 10 7 4 2
              ◊ J 7 4 2
              ♣ J 8

♠ Q 10 7 6 2      N      ♠ J 9 5
♡ Q 8                    ♡ K 9 6 5
◊ K 8 3     W      E     ◊ 9 6
♣ 7 5 2           S      ♣ A 9 4 3

              ♠ K 8 3
              ♡ J 3
              ◊ A Q 10 5
              ♣ K Q 10 6
```

We have kept the distribution unaltered but North-South have exchanged the ◊A and ♠A and East-West the ◊K and ♣A.

Now, on winning the second round of spades, if South starts on clubs, he will be defeated. East wins immediately and plays his last spade to remove South's stop. Later, when West takes his ◊K, he can cash two more spade winners. This time, South must run the ◊J immediately. West wins and plays a spade but later, when East takes his ♣A, he has no more spades and South takes nine tricks.

So much for learning bridge by rules! But indeed there is a rule applicable to this situation. Where you need to lose the lead twice while the opponents are trying to set up a long suit, the entry to the hand with the long suit must be knocked out first (the club in Hand 1 and the diamond in Hand 2). Subsequently, when a trick is lost to the second entry, it will be to the short-spade hand and no harm will be done. Thus you notice that, in Hand 2, if West has both ♣A and ◇K, the contract will be defeated.

Having grasped the idea, can you do these next two problems in match conditions with only two hands on view?

Problem 1
Hand No. 3
Dealer South
N–S vulnerable

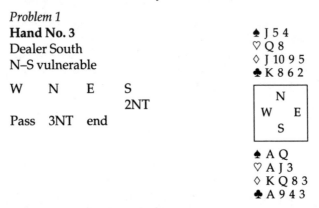

♠ J 5 4
♡ Q 8
◇ J 10 9 5
♣ K 8 6 2

W	N	E	S
			2NT
Pass	3NT	end	

♠ A Q
♡ A J 3
◇ K Q 8 3
♣ A 9 4 3

West leads the ♡5. It costs nothing to try the ♡Q from dummy and indeed it holds, East following with the ♡2. How do you continue?

Problem 2
Hand No. 4
Dealer South
Neither vulnerable

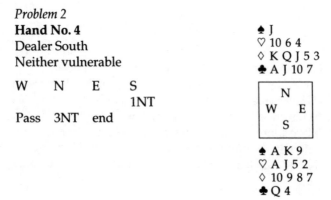

♠ J
♡ 10 6 4
◇ K Q J 5 3
♣ A J 10 7

W	N	E	S
			1NT
Pass	3NT	end	

♠ A K 9
♡ A J 5 2
◇ 10 9 8 7
♣ Q 4

West leads the ♠3 to dummy's jack and East's queen. How do you plan the play?

Solutions

Problem 1

The ♡K appears to be with West so we have two heart tricks, two top clubs, three diamonds (once the ◇A has been knocked out) and two spades. The two spade tricks will be made without losing the lead if East has the ♠K but we will have to lose the lead once if West has it. There is also the possibility of setting up a third club trick if the suit breaks 3–2 but not without losing the lead once.

So nine tricks appear to be available but the defenders are threatening to take the ◇A, the ♠K (if West has it) and possibly three or more heart tricks (unless the suit breaks 4–4).

Look at that heart suit in detail. We now have the ace and jack badly placed under West's king and effectively we have the two-card position of the type we studied in the beginners' book:

```
              8
          ┌───────┐
          │   N   │
    K x   │ W   E │   x x
          │   S   │
          └───────┘
             A J
```

The fact that West actually has more than two cards and North only one is irrelevant. We learnt that, in this position, South can only take one trick unless West leads the suit. We consider the rest of the hand in that light and realize that, as we have to lose the lead twice, once in a black suit and once in diamonds, the first of those two tricks must be lost to West. That would effectively give us an extra heart stop. If we play on diamonds immediately and West holds the ace, there will be no problem but if East has it, he will be able to push a heart through, enabling West to set up the suit. Subsequently, if West takes a trick with a black-suit winner, he may be able to cash two or three more heart tricks to defeat the contract. Thus we should aim to lose a black-suit trick first and there are three possible approaches:

1 We could try playing clubs from the top, hoping that West has the length but, if East has three or more (slightly more likely as we have credited West with the heart length) then East will get in first and we shall be defeated if West has the ◇A.

2 We could try a low club from dummy, intending to put in the nine if East plays low. But now if East has two honours in a trebleton, he can put one of them in, leaving the other well placed behind dummy's ace. Again, East will get in first to push a heart through and we shall be defeated if West has the ◇A.

3 The safe way to lose a trick to West is to take an immediate spade finesse. If it loses, we have two spade tricks and have time to knock out the ◇A before the hearts are cleared. We therefore have two hearts, three diamonds and two clubs in addition for +100.

The deal:

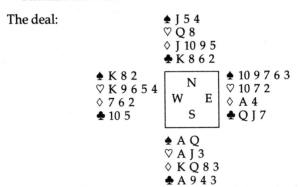

```
                    ♠ J 5 4
                    ♡ Q 8
                    ◇ J 10 9 5
                    ♣ K 8 6 2
   ♠ K 8 2          ┌─────────┐        ♠ 10 9 7 6 3
   ♡ K 9 6 5 4      │    N    │        ♡ 10 7 2
   ◇ 7 6 2          │ W     E │        ◇ A 4
   ♣ 10 5           │    S    │        ♣ Q J 7
                    └─────────┘
                    ♠ A Q
                    ♡ A J 3
                    ◇ K Q 8 3
                    ♣ A 9 4 3
```

You will see that, as the cards lie, the contract can be made if we do start with diamonds. East wins and pushes a heart through. We duck and win the third round. Now three rounds of clubs leave East on play and he has no more hearts. We then make one spade trick, two hearts, three diamonds and three clubs. However, this line would have failed if West had the club length, even with the spade finesse right.

Alternatively, had we played on clubs first, we also would have succeeded as East has the ◇A. However, if West has it, this line would have failed, again even with the spade finesse right. The early spade finesse guarantees the contract, irrespective of the positions of the ◇A, ♠K and the long clubs and is thus the best line.

Problem 2

The first point which we should note is the opening lead. Assuming ♠3 is fourth-highest, West is marked with a four-or five-card suit and thus the nine missing spades are split 5–4, one way or the other. There is therefore no possibility of running either defender out of the suit as South has only three cards. Ducking the first or second round therefore achieves nothing.

I have stressed before that I am very keen that you should get into the habit of picking up these little inferences – I make a point of doing so continually at the table even if they are of little or no relevance to the play. It is a priceless habit to cultivate – helping towards the ultimate goal of be able to play 'seeing' all four hands.

Still considering the spade suit, we notice that, if we win the first round, the king and nine form a tenace against the ten. Thus if East has that card, we have a third stopper in the suit. If West has it, we shall only have a third stopper if he is forced to lead the suit.

Looking at our potential tricks in that light, we can see four in diamonds for one lost, at least two top spades, one heart and three clubs, although we will have to lose the lead once to East if he has the king.

We have learnt that, in this kind of situation, our first loss should ideally be to West as he is the defender who cannot profitably attack spades. We must therefore start on diamonds. Should East have both the ◊A and the ♣K, we are doomed. But playing on diamonds first gains when West has the ◊A, even with the club finesse wrong.

The deal:

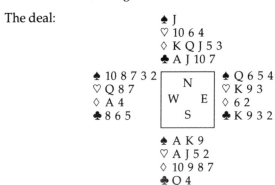

```
                        ♠ J
                        ♡ 10 6 4
                        ◊ K Q J 5 3
                        ♣ A J 10 7
        ♠ 10 8 7 3 2         N          ♠ Q 6 5 4
        ♡ Q 8 7                          ♡ K 9 3
        ◊ A 4            W      E        ◊ 6 2
        ♣ 8 6 5             S            ♣ K 9 3 2
                        ♠ A K 9
                        ♡ A J 5 2
                        ◊ 10 9 8 7
                        ♣ Q 4
```

Satisfy yourself that taking the club finesse first is fatal. East wins and pushes a spade through. Later, when West takes his ◊A, he will have two more spade winners to cash and the defenders will have taken three spade tricks and the two minor-suit winners for one off.

The four examples above have illustrated problems where declarer has to set up tricks in two suits. We now going to look at other complexities in this area. Very often a decision will have to be made as to whether to take a finesse or play to drop a certain card and counting our tricks will be a first priority. Consider this example:

Hand No. 5
Dealer South
Both vulnerable

♠ 8 5
♡ 9 6 4
◊ A K Q
♣ 9 6 5 3 2

W	N	E	S
			1♣
Pass	2♣	Pass	2NT
Pass	3NT	end	

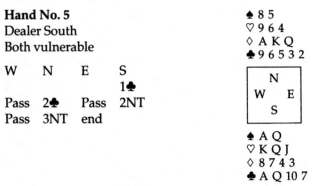

♠ A Q
♡ K Q J
◊ 8 7 4 3
♣ A Q 10 7

Let us first go through the bidding. North has the correct shape and is in the right point range to bid 1NT over 1♣ but, anticipating a final contract of 3NT, he does not want the lead coming round to those very poor major-suit holdings. He therefore prefers 2♣, being maximum in the range for that bid. Ideally South should be covered in all three non-club suits for his 2NT bid but he wants to be declarer in no-trumps to protect his spade holding, the suit being favourite for the opening lead. At least he has some length in diamonds and, with his partner having failed to show a four-card major, it is likely that there will be a reasonable diamond holding on dummy – again note the inference.

West leads the ♠J and East produces the king! So the spade worry was unfounded – virtue is its own reward! Half the time, there would have been a distinct disadvantage in having North as declarer. After winning the first trick, how do you continue?

We have two spade tricks, two hearts (after knocking out the ace), three or four diamonds (depending on the break) and from three to five clubs (depending on the break and positions of the king and jack). So there appear to be plenty of tricks but the defenders are threatening to take at least three spades (four if they are breaking 6–3) as well as the ♡A and possibly a club. So the race is on and the best way to tackle such problems is a series of trial runs in an attempt to combine our chances.

Let us first look at our long suit of clubs. If the suit comes in for five tricks, East having a doubleton king or K x x, we will make the contract easily with five clubs, three diamonds and two spades and will even have time to knock out the ♡A for more overtricks as we still have a spade stopper. However, should it only come in for four (with any 2–2 break) or East having a stiff honour (West having the king), we will still make the contract with four clubs, three diamonds and two spades, again without having to touch the hearts.

The question thus arises whether there is any hope if West has K J x or K J x x. Now the lead would have to be lost twice to establish the long clubs and enemy spades will get in first. There is another chance of working on the red suits. The best line is to cash the ♣A and then try three top diamonds. If they break 3–3, we can count four diamond tricks, two spades and the ♣A and can knock out the ♡A to set up two more in that suit to complete nine tricks. If the diamonds fail to break, then we shall need some luck in clubs and, if no honour has dropped on the first round, will lead a club towards the queen. Note that the cashing of the three diamonds will set up a trick for the defenders if they fail to break evenly but that will not be enough to defeat us. Should the suit break 5–1 or worse, we shall find out in time (i.e. on the second round) and can switch back to clubs immediately.

The deal:

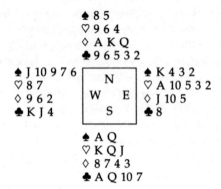

```
                    ♠ 8 5
                    ♡ 9 6 4
                    ◊ A K Q
                    ♣ 9 6 5 3 2
  ♠ J 10 9 7 6        N         ♠ K 4 3 2
  ♡ 8 7                         ♡ A 10 5 3 2
  ◊ 9 6 2      W          E     ◊ J 10 5
  ♣ K J 4          S           ♣ 8
                    ♠ A Q
                    ♡ K Q J
                    ◊ 8 7 4 3
                    ♣ A Q 10 7
```

Indeed it is a good general guide to play for a drop (in diamonds in the above case) before trying finesses, the reason being that playing winners enables you to hold the lead and reassess your tactics, while finessing allows the opponents the lead, probably to their advantage. You can apply the principle to this next example.

Hand No. 6
Dealer North
E–W vulnerable

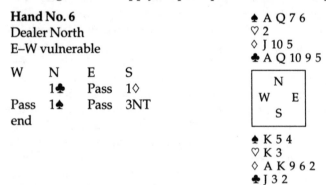

```
                    ♠ A Q 7 6
                    ♡ 2
                    ◊ J 10 5
                    ♣ A Q 10 9 5
                        N
                  W          E
                        S
                    ♠ K 5 4
                    ♡ K 3
                    ◊ A K 9 6 2
                    ♣ J 3 2
```

W	N	E	S
	1♣	Pass	1◊
Pass	1♠	Pass	3NT
end			

A good case can be made for bidding 3NT direct over 1♣ on the South hand and indeed, many good players would do so. However, with plenty of top controls, life would be very difficult for a slam-minded partner with three levels of bidding lost. Furthermore, if partner were to produce a rebid in hearts rather than spades, it could be preferable to have him as declarer in no-trumps should his spade holding prove to be Q x.

I am putting these discussions in because I want you to continue to think in this way. My style is to favour the above auction with a view to accurate bidding while others, including many world-class names, would describe me as a 'daisy picker' and prefer the direct game bid rather than giving the defence a long lecture on what to lead. As I mentioned in a previous book, the debate continues!

West leads the ♡Q to his partner's ace and East returns the ♡5 to your king. How do you continue?

It is clear that we will lose at least three further heart tricks if the opponents get in again (and then only on an optimistic 5–5 split – it could be more) so we must run home now or never. We have the heart trick and three top spades, with the possibility of a fourth should the suit break 3–3. Thus it is clear that one of the minors must be brought in for five tricks without loss and it is a question of whether we can have two bites at the cherry. Clearly we cannot take both finesses because, if the first one loses, we shall be down before we have a chance to take the second. So we observe the guide of 'Drop first; then finesse.'

The choice must obviously depend on probabilities and there is clearly a better chance of dropping the ◊Q (which would need to be singleton or doubleton) than the ♣K (which would need to be specifically a singleton). Thus we cash the ace and king of diamonds, intending to run the ♣J if the ◊Q does not fall.

The deal:

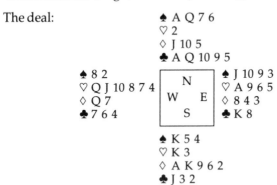

```
               ♠ A Q 7 6
               ♡ 2
               ◊ J 10 5
               ♣ A Q 10 9 5
  ♠ 8 2              N        ♠ J 10 9 3
  ♡ Q J 10 8 7 4              ♡ A 9 6 5
  ◊ Q 7        W       E      ◊ 8 4 3
  ♣ 7 6 4            S        ♣ K 8
               ♠ K 5 4
               ♡ K 3
               ◊ A K 9 6 2
               ♣ J 3 2
```

Having grasped the idea, you should be able do the following couple of problems under match conditions and it is time the stop-watch was brought into action. You should be able to give a complete analysis of each hand in under one minute, approaching the time expected at the table.

Problem 3
Hand No. 7
Dealer South
Both vulnerable

W	N	E	S
			2NT
Pass	3NT	end	

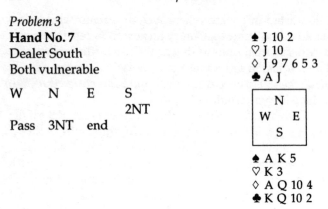

♠ J 10 2
♡ J 10
◊ J 9 7 6 5 3
♣ A J

♠ A K 5
♡ K 3
◊ A Q 10 4
♣ K Q 10 2

West leads the ♡4 to his partner's ♡A and East returns the ♡5 to your ♡K and West's ♡2. How do you continue?

Problem 4
Hand No. 8
Dealer East
Neither vulnerable

W	N	E	S
		Pass	2NT
Pass	3♣	Dble	3◊
Pass	3NT	end	

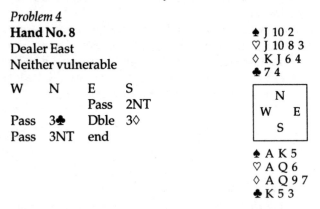

♠ J 10 2
♡ J 10 8 3
◊ K J 6 4
♣ 7 4

♠ A K 5
♡ A Q 6
◊ A Q 9 7
♣ K 5 3

After North's Stayman enquiry, East doubled for a club lead and West leads ♣6 to his partner's ♣10. You hold off in case West started with a doubleton but East persists with the ♣Q, which you take with your king, West confirming a trebleton by playing the nine. How do you continue?

Solutions

Problem 3
The play to the first two tricks indicates that West started with five

hearts and East four. Therefore, if a trick is lost in another suit, we shall lose four heart tricks and suffer immediate defeat. We count our tricks in that light. In addition to the heart, there are four top clubs, two top spades and the ◊A to total eight. Both the diamond and spade finesses are available and the problem is how to combine the chances. The possible lines of play are:

1 Play for the drop in diamonds and, if it fails, try the spade finesse.
2 Play for the drop in spades and, if it fails, try the diamond finesse.

Let us work out the percentages. The two finesses are each 50:50 (actually slightly better as East has four hearts to West's five). The drop of the ♠Q requires the spades to split 5:2 (30.5%) with the queen among the doubleton (⅖ x 30.5%) = 8.7% plus the small chance of a 6:1 split with the queen as the singleton or East having all seven when the finesse will be marked after West discards on the first round: say about 9% in all. The drop of the ◊K requires a 2:1 split (78%) with the king as the singleton (⅓ x 78%) = 26%, which is obviously a far better chance.

Thus the correct technique is to cash one top spade (just in case the queen drops or West shows out) and then play the ◊A. If the king does not appear, cross to dummy with a club and try the spade finesse.

The deal:

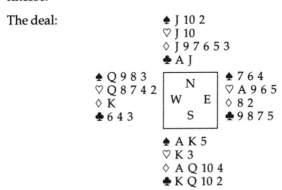

```
              ♠ J 10 2
              ♡ J 10
              ◊ J 9 7 6 5 3
              ♣ A J
  ♠ Q 9 8 3            ♠ 7 6 4
  ♡ Q 8 7 4 2    N     ♡ A 9 6 5
  ◊ K         W    E   ◊ 8 2
  ♣ 6 4 3        S     ♣ 9 8 7 5
              ♠ A K 5
              ♡ K 3
              ◊ A Q 10 4
              ♣ K Q 10 2
```

Problem 4

The spade position is identical to that in Problem 3 but the rest of the hand is altered to the degree that the suit may have to be played differently. We have already lost one club trick and are threatened with three more and therefore cannot afford to lose a trick in a non-club suit. In addition to the club already won, we have four top diamonds, two top spades and a heart to total eight and the ninth must come from one of the majors. Again both finesses are available but we can take only one. Our first try must be a drop and it is clearly more likely that we can drop a doubleton ♠Q (about 9% as demonstrated above) than a singleton ♡K, which would need a 5–1 split (15%) with the king singleton (⅙ x 15% = 3%). Therefore we cash the two top spades and, if the queen does not appear, we cross to dummy in diamonds to try the heart finesse.

The deal:

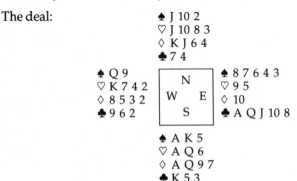

```
                    ♠ J 10 2
                    ♡ J 10 8 3
                    ◊ K J 6 4
                    ♣ 7 4
    ♠ Q 9                         ♠ 8 7 6 4 3
    ♡ K 7 4 2          N          ♡ 9 5
    ◊ 8 5 3 2      W     E        ◊ 10
    ♣ 9 6 2           S           ♣ A Q J 10 8
                    ♠ A K 5
                    ♡ A Q 6
                    ◊ A Q 9 7
                    ♣ K 5 3
```

These last two examples illustrated a point emphasized in the previous books – that suit combinations need to be handled according to the demands of the hand as a whole rather than as a separate entity. I also mentioned that availability of entries, always an important consideration, will be relevant. This is an excellent lead-in to a further study of these two factors. This next hand illustrates a position often mishandled through lack of foresight.

Hand No. 9
Dealer North
Both vulnerable

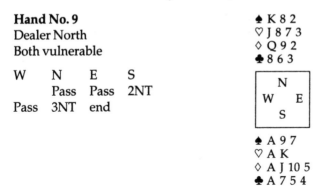

♠ K 8 2
♡ J 8 7 3
◊ Q 9 2
♣ 8 6 3

W	N	E	S
	Pass	Pass	2NT
Pass	3NT	end	

♠ A 9 7
♡ A K
◊ A J 10 5
♣ A 7 5 4

West leads the ♣K and you hold up the first round. On the ♣Q, East discards the ♠5, so there is little point in holding up again. You therefore win. How do you continue?

The clubs have split badly and West is threatening to take four tricks in that suit. Even if he is kept out of the lead, we have only four tricks in the majors (unless the ♡Q drops in two rounds) in addition to the ♣A. This almost certainly means that the diamonds will have to be brought in for four tricks without loss, implying that the ◊K must be credited to East. If it is among three or fewer, there will be no problem but what happens if East has four or more? Now three finesses will need to be taken and there is a problem in that there is only one entry to dummy.

The deal:

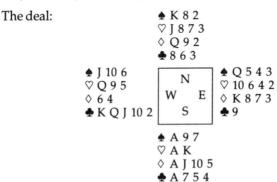

♠ K 8 2
♡ J 8 7 3
◊ Q 9 2
♣ 8 6 3

♠ J 10 6
♡ Q 9 5
◊ 6 4
♣ K Q J 10 2

♠ Q 5 4 3
♡ 10 6 4 2
◊ K 8 7 3
♣ 9

♠ A 9 7
♡ A K
◊ A J 10 5
♣ A 7 5 4

Suppose we cross to dummy in spades and lead the ◊Q. East will play low and so does South. Dummy now leads a low diamond and

East plays low again. This time, South is left with A J 10 and has to win, leaving himself in the wrong hand to take another finesse. We must arrange for North to be on lead after two rounds and this can only be achieved by starting with the nine. When that holds, we shall be in a position to play the queen now and underplay our jack or ten, leaving dummy on lead for the third finesse.

As a connoisseur of such situations, you should be able to do this next example in under one minute. Start your stop-watch.

Hand No. 10
Dealer West
N–S vulnerable

♠	A 4 3 2		
♡	Q 9		
◊	A J 10 8		
♣	A Q J		

W	N	E	S
Pass	1◊	Pass	1NT
Pass	2NT	Pass	3NT
end			

```
        N
   W         E
        S
```

♠ J 8 6
♡ A 5 4
◊ 9 6 4
♣ K 10 6 2

West leads the ♡2; you try the queen from dummy but East produces the king. How do you plan the play?

The hearts appear to be breaking 4–4 and there is therefore little to be gained by holding up the ace. Indeed, it might be fatal to do so if the defenders are unkind enough to switch to spades. In that event, we might well lose three spade tricks in addition to the heart and at least one diamond. We have four club tricks (remembering to overtake the third round) and the two major aces, implying the need for three diamond tricks. Thus West must be credited with at least one honour and we must play with care in case he has length (four or more) in the suit.

On winning the first heart, we start with a *low* diamond and put in the jack or ten, losing to East (say the queen). They will presumably cash their hearts (while we discard useless low spades from both hands) and switch to spades. We take the ace on dummy, cash the ace and queen of clubs, overtake the jack with the king and cash the ten. Now, in hand for the last time, we are in a position to pick up the diamonds:

A J 8

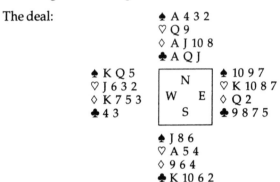

K x x | N
W   E
S | x

9 6

We play the nine and, when West plays low, underplay the eight so that the lead remains in hand. Now it remains to take a simple finesse against the king.

The deal:

     ♠ A 4 3 2
     ♡ Q 9
     ◇ A J 10 8
     ♣ A Q J

♠ K Q 5   ♠ 10 9 7
♡ J 6 3 2   N   ♡ K 10 8 7
◇ K 7 5 3   W   E   ◇ Q 2
♣ 4 3   S   ♣ 9 8 7 5

     ♠ J 8 6
     ♡ A 5 4
     ◇ 9 6 4
     ♣ K 10 6 2

You should satisfy yourself, by trial and error, that no other handling of the diamond suit succeeds and therefore this is the only route to nine tricks.

The consideration of entries and communication brings another clash of two rules into the limelight. We learnt at great length in the earlier books that, in order to be able to cash winners in a suit which had honours on both sides of the table, it is necessary to cash high cards from the short hand first. Thus with:

A K 7
Q 6 5 4 2

we should cash the ace and king first before leading low to the queen.

We learnt that playing the queen earlier would result in blocking the suit and we would then need an entry in a side-suit to be able to enjoy the two long cards. On the other hand, we also learnt that it is necessary to keep entries to the hand with a long suit intact as long as possible. The conflict is highlighted here:

Hand No. 11
Dealer North
Neither vulnerable

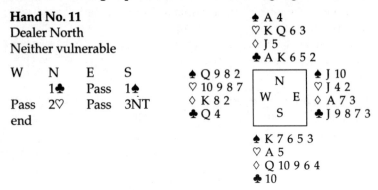

W	N	E	S
	1♣	Pass	1♠
Pass	2♡	Pass	3NT
end			

North hand: ♠ A 4 ♡ K Q 6 3 ◇ J 5 ♣ A K 6 5 2

West hand: ♠ Q 9 8 2 ♡ 10 9 8 7 ◇ K 8 2 ♣ Q 4

East hand: ♠ J 10 ♡ J 4 2 ◇ A 7 3 ♣ J 9 8 7 3

South hand: ♠ K 7 6 5 3 ♡ A 5 ◇ Q 10 9 6 4 ♣ 10

First, let us go through the bidding. With 17 points and at least tolerance for spades, North has easily enough to reverse and South then knows that the partnership has sufficient points for game. There are now two approaches. It is reasonable to bid 3NT outright but many experts would recommend a fourth-suit-forcing 3◇, giving North the opportunity to bid 3♠ with a 3415 shape, after which 4♠ may be the better contract. The case against 3◇ on this occasion lies in the possibility of North being 1426 or 2416 with no diamond feature. Having been asked to describe his hand further, he might justifiably feel obliged to bid 4♣, particularly if his clubs are very strong and hearts very poor. Now the best contract of 3NT will certainly be missed.

Notice again the importance of thinking ahead when planning the auction. Expert teachers and authors continually emphasize the necessity of working through the whole play and defence at trick one but the application of this principle to bidding tends to be sadly neglected in much of bridge literature. If players of all standards thought ahead before bidding, many of the idiocies in this branch of the game would be avoided.

West leads the ♡10. Let us count our tricks. There are two tops in spades, three in hearts and two in clubs to total seven so far. Were the spades to break 3–3, two more tricks could be established in that suit. That would mean keeping the ♡A intact in the South hand as entry. A better line, however, is to set up the diamonds. Looking at the suit in detail, we note that, as the defenders are not obliged to win the first round, we shall need two entries to the South hand to set up and then cash the long suit. These will obviously have to be the ♡A and ♠K.

Looking at the heart suit in more detail, we note that, in the context of the suit considered alone, we should win the first trick in the short hand, i.e. South, so that we can enjoy the other two top winners without disruption. However, we just agreed that the ♡A must be held as entry to the diamonds so the 'short-hand first' rule must be waived.

We therefore win the first heart in dummy and play the ◊J (this time, we do play high from the short hand first!). Trying to make communications difficult, the defenders allow the jack to hold and we continue the suit, losing to West. If West continues hearts, we *now* use the ♡A (at the proper time) and continue with the ◊Q, losing to East. If East continues hearts, we win in dummy, cross to hand with the ♠K and cash two more diamonds, followed by the two clubs and the ♠A for ten tricks and game (100 under the line and 30 over).

So important is this exercise in entries and communication that it is worth trying a few variations in the defence to illustrate how careful declarer must be. Remember that we have blocked the heart suit on trick one and there could be consequent disruption in that area.

Suppose that, after winning the second round of diamonds, West switches to a spade. How do we play now? It is best to win in dummy with the ♠A, keeping the ♠K as entry to the diamonds, cross to the ♡A, unblocking the hearts in the process, and then continue with a high diamond. The club honours now serve as entry to the last high heart while the ♠K is kept for the diamonds. Alternatively, we can win the spade in hand, knock out the diamond and, while East can knock out either the ♠A or the club entry to dummy, he cannot knock out both and we still make the ten tricks. What we should obviously not do is to win the spade switch in dummy and then cross to hand in spades to knock out the diamond. Not only does this risk losing spade tricks (as we have removed our stoppers and East would have two winners waiting, or even more on a bad split, which he could cash if he had both diamond honours) but East could also switch to a club, prematurely removing our entry to the last heart honour. We will still make nine tricks but there will be many hands in which a mistake like that could cost a contract.

If West switches to a club, after winning the second diamond, we win in dummy and again it is advisable to use the ♡A (unblocking the suit) as first entry to the diamonds, keeping the ♠K intact. If we use the ♠K first, East, on winning his diamond, could play a second spade, again cutting us off from the third winning heart. We should now be advised to cash the second club before crossing to the ♡A for the winning diamonds, again being held to nine tricks.

I strongly advise you to play this hand out, over and over again in various orders, to satisfy yourselves which of them lead to the correct result of ten tricks, which give you only nine and which result in defeat. The hand illustrates the difficulty of playing with something of a misfit and why you should demand a higher point-count for a no-trump game when it is clear that you will have serious communication problems. Careful study of situations like this will save you many headaches in the future.

Having seen the idea, try your hand at a couple of problems in match conditions. You should be able to give a full analysis in under one-and-a-half minutes each. Start your stop-watch.

Problem 5
Hand No. 12
Dealer West
E–W vulnerable

				♠ A 8 2
				♡ A K J 7
				◊ 5 2
				♣ A K 6 5

W	N	E	S
Pass	1♣	1♠	1NT
Pass	3NT	end	

```
        N
   W        E
        S
```

♠ K J 4
♡ 5 4
◊ Q J 10 9 6
♣ 9 7 3

With your spade honours well placed over the bid and the solidity of the diamond suit, you are entitled to value this hand at least a point or two above its seven high-card points.

West leads the ♠3 and you note that East has come in, at adverse vulnerability, on a suit which is, at best, queen high. It is obvious therefore, that the lead is a singleton. How do you plan the play?

Problem 6
Hand No. 13
Dealer East
Both vulnerable

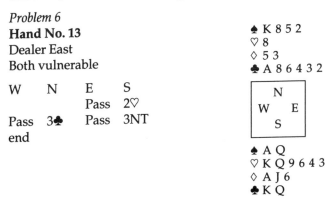

W	N	E	S
		Pass	2♡
Pass	3♣	Pass	3NT
end			

♠ K 8 5 2
♡ 8
♢ 5 3
♣ A 8 6 4 3 2

♠ A Q
♡ K Q 9 6 4 3
♢ A J 6
♣ K Q

West leads the ♢7 to the ♢3 and East's ♢Q. How do you plan the play?

Solutions

Problem 5
We have three obvious spade tricks and two tops each in hearts and clubs. There are possibilities for extra tricks in the heart finesse (unlikely to succeed on the bidding – the drop is probably a better chance) or a 3–3 club split (again unlikely in view of the known 6–1 spade split). To be realistic, therefore, the diamonds will have to be established for three more tricks. When we saw this situation in Hand 11, we learnt that the defenders will try to avoid winning the first round of the suit so that we will need two entries to be able to establish and cash the long winners.

They can only come from spades and thus to play the obvious 'second-hand low', accepting the free finesse, is fatal as we should then be using one of those entries too early.

The correct play to keep them intact is to win the first spade in dummy with the ace. East will take the second round of diamonds to exhaust dummy of the suit and continue spades. Now we use the first of our two entries to knock out the remaining high diamond. Subsequently, the third round of spades is won in the correct hand, South, after which we can cash our remaining diamonds to complete ten tricks for the loss of two diamonds and a heart or club at the end.

The deal:

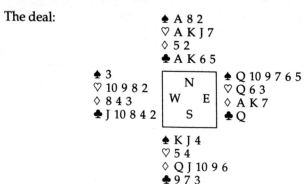

♠ A 8 2
♥ A K J 7
♦ 5 2
♣ A K 6 5

♠ 3
♥ 10 9 8 2
♦ 8 4 3
♣ J 10 8 4 2

♠ Q 10 9 7 6 5
♥ Q 6 3
♦ A K 7
♣ Q

♠ K J 4
♥ 5 4
♦ Q J 10 9 6
♣ 9 7 3

Play the hand over again and satisfy yourself that, if we play a low spade from dummy on the first round, we cannot make the contract.

Problem 6

Looking at top tricks, we have three in spades, three in clubs and the ♦A and we can set up one more in hearts by knocking out the ace; but that is only eight tricks. Playing on hearts is unlikely to be successful: two tricks in the suit will have to be lost and, by that time, the defenders may well have set up three diamond tricks to complete five. It looks as though the whole club suit will be needed. That implies a 3–2 split but even then, we still have to reach dummy to cash the long cards.

    The only entry outside clubs is the ♠K, which means that we shall have to sacrifice one of our top spade tricks by overtaking our own ♣Q. Recounting our tricks in that light, we have six club tricks (given a friendly 3–2 break), two spades and the ♦A to total nine and we may have time to knock out the ♥A for an overtrick.

The deal:

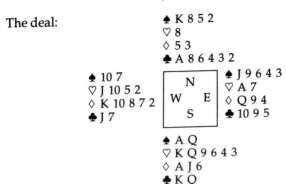

```
                    ♠ K 8 5 2
                    ♡ 8
                    ◊ 5 3
                    ♣ A 8 6 4 3 2
   ♠ 10 7                          ♠ J 9 6 4 3
   ♡ J 10 5 2          N           ♡ A 7
   ◊ K 10 8 7 2    W       E       ◊ Q 9 4
   ♣ J 7               S           ♣ 10 9 5
                    ♠ A Q
                    ♡ K Q 9 6 4 3
                    ◊ A J 6
                    ♣ K Q
```

Our plan is to cash the two club honours in hand, then overtake the ♣Q with the ♣K and cash the ♣A and the remainder of the suit, finishing with the ♠A.

From the point of view of the contract, it does not matter whether we win the first diamond or hold it up but it should be realized that, if we decide to hold it up and East cunningly switches to a spade, attempting to attack our entry, we must win this with the ♠A, keeping our ♠Q intact for when it is needed. Satisfy yourself that, if we put on the ♠Q, we cannot make the contract.

Sometimes a declarer must disrupt the attempt of the defenders to set up their suit by ruining their communications. Consider this example, an excellent illustration of the importance of the order in which tricks are won and lost.

Hand No. 14
Dealer East
Neither vulnerable

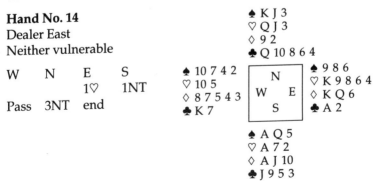

```
                                    ♠ K J 3
                                    ♡ Q J 3
                                    ◊ 9 2
                                    ♣ Q 10 8 6 4
W     N     E     S      ♠ 10 7 4 2              ♠ 9 8 6
            1♡    1NT    ♡ 10 5        N         ♡ K 9 8 6 4
                        ◊ 8 7 5 4 3  W    E      ◊ K Q 6
Pass  3NT   end         ♣ K 7            S       ♣ A 2
                                    ♠ A Q 5
                                    ♡ A 7 2
                                    ◊ A J 10
                                    ♣ J 9 5 3
```

West leads the ♡10. The heart position is typical of the sort of suit combination we studied at great length in *The Expert Beginner*. We are now going to understand why. Let us look at it in isolation.

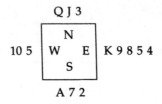

We can see that, with the king conveniently sandwiched between the solid Q J and the A, North-South will win two tricks out of the first three for one lost but how does the play go after West has led the ten? There are a number of possible orders:

(1) Dummy covers with an honour, East puts on the king and South wins.
(2) Dummy covers with an honour, East puts on the king and South holds up.
(3) Dummy covers with an honour, East and South play low.
(4) Dummy and East play low and South wins.
(5) Dummy and East play low and South holds up.

In view of the importance of this kind of position, it will be worth setting out the two-card positions resulting in each case:

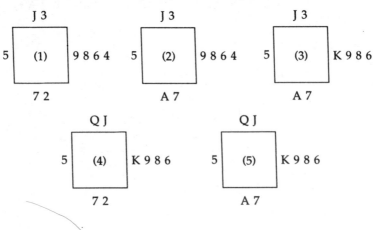

(1) North–South have won the first round and will have the option of whether to win the second or third.

(2) East–West have won the first round and North–South will win both the second and third.

(3) North–South have won the first round and have the option of whether they win the second or third.

(4) North–South have won the first round but East–West will have the option as to whether they win the second or third.

(5) East–West have won the first round and North–South will win the second and third.

We can see three spade tricks, two hearts, at least one diamond, probably two as the honours are likely to be well placed under our tenace and thus the long clubs will need to be established for three tricks after the ace and king have been knocked out. Again, which defender wins these top club tricks will be crucial. The first point to realize is that, if East has both ace and king, there is no hope as the defenders are a move ahead. On winning his first club, East will knock out our second heart stopper and, on winning his second club, he will be able to cash three more hearts for one down – and this all applies irrespective of how the heart play goes.

The critical case thus arises when West has one of the club honours and is able to win the first round of that suit while his partner's entry is kept intact – in other words when the clubs are breaking 2–2 as above. If West is able to lead a second heart, then the contract will be defeated. However, if he has been exhausted of hearts before taking his club trick, we are a move ahead and our clubs will come in first, allowing us nine tricks. We reconsider the possible heart procedures above in that light:

(1) West will have a heart to play on winning the first round of clubs and the defence prevails.

(2) East will win the first heart and will continue the suit, exhausting West. West will therefore not have another heart on winning his club trick and the declarer prevails.

(3) The same applies as in (1) and the defence prevails.

(4) It is as in (1) and (3) and again the defence prevails.

(5) West will win the first trick and continue the suit, exhausting his hand and the position will be similar to (2).

So we see that, in situations where the declarer won the first trick, the defence prevails and vice versa and therefore appreciate that, in (2), East has defended incorrectly. If an honour is played from dummy, he should duck and now the defence prevails. However, we can insist on losing the first trick while still keeping our double stop intact by ducking the first round completely in both hands, leaving the defenders with no answer.

I would strongly recommend that you go through every variation until you fully understand each one and that you do not proceed further until you are completely familiar with this type of situation. All future studies depend on this method of reasoning and it can only become more complicated when we introduce the trump element and/or consider defence. This example, above all others, should drive home, once and for all, the importance of understanding the work we did on two-and three-card positions in *The Expert Beginner* and why scores of pages were devoted to it. A full understanding of these positions is a vital part of your platform.

Note that, if we juggle the heart position to:

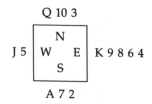

and West leads the ♡J, it must be allowed to hold. It seems so obvious to cover with the ♡Q, setting up the ♡10, but East will duck and down we go. Allow the ♡J to hold, however, and the double stop remains intact, the two tricks being taken at the correct time!

Having grasped the idea, you should have no difficulty with this next problem in match conditions. You should now be aiming to get under a minute. Start your stop-watch.

Problem 7
Hand No. 15
Dealer West
Neither vulnerable

♠ Q J 7
♡ K 9
◊ 10 5 3
♣ Q J 8 6 4

W	N	E	S
Pass	Pass	1♠	1NT
Pass	3NT	end	

```
        N
    W       E
        S
```

♠ A 4 2
♡ A 10 4
◊ A K 9
♣ 9 7 5 3

West leads the ♣9. How do you plan the play? For full credit, you should not only discuss in detail what will happen in the spade suit but also the play of the rest of the hand.

We have two top tricks in each of the red suits, with the faint chance of a third if a defender holds Q J doubleton in either, in addition to two spade tricks – eight tricks in total at best. Therefore the clubs will have to be established, which will involve losing the lead twice. The lead is probably the higher of a doubleton and the defenders are threatening to take three spade tricks in addition to the inevitable two clubs. We can see that, if East has both club honours, we have no chance as he is a move ahead. West must therefore be credited with one of them and we must observe the guide of losing the first round of the spade suit so that West has to play his second card immediately, exhausting himself of the suit while our double stop remains intact. We must therefore play low from both hands.

On the second round, we play an honour from dummy and now the spotlight turns on East. In the context of the spade suit, considered in isolation, it makes no difference whether he covers or not. However, in the context of the whole hand, it may be worth reconsidering. Two tricks must be lost to North-South but East can dictate whether the first is lost to South and the second to North or vice versa. A thoughtful East will prefer to play low at trick two, allowing dummy to win. Now before reading on, can you say why?

How did you intend to play the club suit, assuming that North was allowed to hold the second trick? If you proposed to start with a low card, you would lose if the layout were like this:

```
            Q J 8 6 4
           ┌─────────┐
           │    N    │
   K 2     │ W     E │   A 10
           │    S    │
           └─────────┘
             9 7 5 3
```

Now *East* could win both rounds of the suit and can set up and cash his spades.

On the other hand, if you intended to start with an honour, you would lose in the actual layout:

The deal:

```
                      ♠ Q J 7
                      ♡ K 9
                      ◊ 10 5 3
                      ♣ Q J 8 6 4
      ♠ 9 6          ┌─────────┐    ♠ K 10 8 5 3
      ♡ 8 7 6 5 2    │    N    │    ♡ Q J 3
      ◊ J 8 7 6 4    │ W     E │    ◊ Q 2
      ♣ K            │    S    │    ♣ A 10 2
                     └─────────┘
                      ♠ A 4 2
                      ♡ A 10 4
                      ◊ A K 9
                      ♣ 9 7 5 3
```

Now East's ♣ A 10 would form a tenace over dummy and he would have a third stopper. The correct procedure in the club suit is to lead from weakness to strength by starting with a low club from hand and see which card West plays. You should thus have crossed to hand with the ◊A (slightly safer than the ♡A as North-South have more diamonds than hearts between them and it is less likely that you will lose too many tricks if the defenders turn their attention to the red suit you choose) and played a low club from hand. West's ♣K now *drops on air* and you can play low from dummy, leaving the ♣ Q J solid against the ace. Note again (it is worth stressing) how East gave you a chance to go wrong by playing low to the second round of spades. Thus you should only take full credit if you appreciated the above points in *both* black suits.

We are going to conclude the section on no-trump declarer play with five miscellaneous examples which I should like you do in match conditions against the stop-watch. You should be speeding up by this stage and aiming to break the one-minute barrier for each example, thus completing the test in under five minutes. For full credit, you should give a complete analysis, stating all problems that are likely to arise, the likely layout of the unseen cards and how you expect the play to go from start to finish. Start your stop-watch.

Problem 8
Hand No. 16
Dealer West
N–S vulnerable

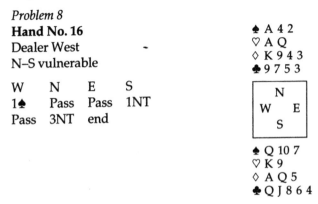

♠ A 4 2
♡ A Q
◇ K 9 4 3
♣ 9 7 5 3

W	N	E	S
1♠	Pass	Pass	1NT
Pass	3NT	end	

♠ Q 10 7
♡ K 9
◇ A Q 5
♣ Q J 8 6 4

Your 1NT bid in the protective position showed 12–14 points. West leads the ♣5 to dummy's ♣2 and East's ♣J. Plan the play.

Problem 9
Hand No. 17
Dealer South
Both vulnerable

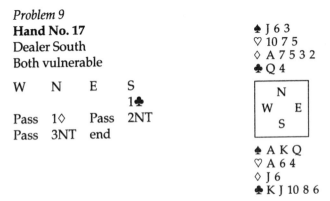

♠ J 6 3
♡ 10 7 5
◇ A 7 5 3 2
♣ Q 4

W	N	E	S
			1♣
Pass	1◇	Pass	2NT
Pass	3NT	end	

♠ A K Q
♡ A 6 4
◇ J 6
♣ K J 10 8 6

West leads the ♡3 and East puts on the ♡Q. You may assume that, if you hold up the ace, East will continue the suit. You therefore have the option to win the first, second or third round. Plan the play, giving clear reasons for the timing of the ♡A.

Problem 10
Hand No. 18
Dealer South
N–S vulnerable

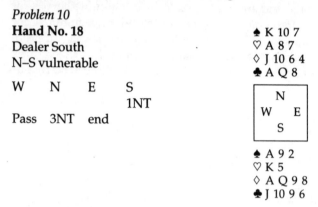

W	N	E	S
			1NT
Pass	3NT	end	

♠ K 10 7
♡ A 8 7
◇ J 10 6 4
♣ A Q 8

♠ A 9 2
♡ K 5
◇ A Q 9 8
♣ J 10 9 6

West leads the ♡3. You have the option to refuse completely, win in hand, after which you may win or refuse the second round, or win the first round in dummy. Which is it to be and how do you plan the play of the rest of the hand?

Problem 11
Hand No. 19
Dealer East
N–S vulnerable

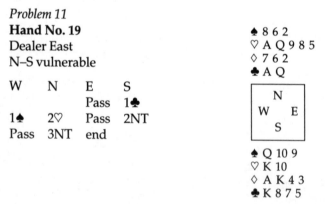

W	N	E	S
		Pass	1♣
1♠	2♡	Pass	2NT
Pass	3NT	end	

♠ 8 6 2
♡ A Q 9 8 5
◇ 7 6 2
♣ A Q

♠ Q 10 9
♡ K 10
◇ A K 4 3
♣ K 8 7 5

West leads the ♠A, all following, and switches to the ◇J. Plan the play.

Problem 12
Hand No. 20
Dealer South
N–S vulnerable

♠ K 7
♡ J 9 8 5
◇ Q 8 5
♣ J 9 6 4

W	N	E	S
			2♣
Pass	2◇	Pass	3NT
Pass	4NT	Pass	6NT
end			

```
      N
  W       E
      S
```

♠ Q J
♡ A K Q
◇ A J 10 9 7
♣ A K Q

Let us first go through the bidding. After South's game force, North showed a negative response and South about 25–27 points. Within the negative range (say 0–7 points), North has a maximum hand and therefore, confident that the partnership will make at least ten tricks, almost certainly eleven, he can make a try for a slam. 4NT in this situation is quantitative, showing about 6–7 points. As I have mentioned many times before, but it can hardly be repeated too often, nothing could be less appropriate than Blackwood in this situation. Firstly, no suit has been agreed and secondly, after South's reply, North, the weak hand, would have to take the decision on the final contract based on number of aces alone, with little idea of the big hand opposite – a clear case of the tail wagging the dog!

With 26 points and a five-card suit with good intermediates, South may be entitled to consider his hand maximum but he should note that the ace-king-queens are not pulling their full weight in trebletons and the spade holding should be devalued by at least a point. He decides to accept the invitation but his actual choice of 6NT is not the best. He could have offered the alternative of 6◇, either by bidding it directly or merely trying 5◇, allowing the partnership to stop there or in 5NT. In fact, North would have been entitled to value up his diamond holding and possible spade ruff and 6◇ would have been the final contract. As it proves, the pair are lucky in that there is no spade ruff available!

West leads the ♡4. Plan the play.

Solutions

Problem 8

Well, really, this is getting boring! Not a couple of pages back, I carefully explained that, in order to exhaust East while keeping the double stop intact, the ♠J had to be allowed to hold. So did you refuse the trick? If you did, you are down, and possibly heavily! Before reading on, can you give *two* good reasons why?

First, did you do a one-closed-hand exercise on this hand, particularly in regard to points? There are 14 in the South hand and 13 in the North, totalling 27 so far and East has already shown up with the ♠J. That leaves 12 unaccounted for and they must surely all be with West; in any case he will certainly have both club honours. Holding up the first trick in an attempt to exhaust East is therefore inapplicable here and there is the further bonus that, if we win the first trick, we are left with this two-card position:

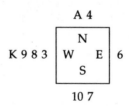

A 4

K 9 8 3 |N / W E / S| 6

10 7

We have established that East will never get on play and thus only West can touch the suit. In that case, our split tenace gives us a *third* stop in the suit, enabling us to set up and enjoy the clubs despite both top honours being in the hand with the long spades. We have two spade tricks, two hearts and three (possibly four) diamond tricks outside, totalling eight at most.

The deal:

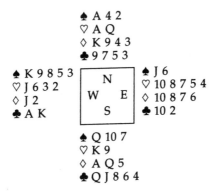

```
                    ♠ A 4 2
                    ♡ A Q
                    ◇ K 9 4 3
                    ♣ 9 7 5 3
  ♠ K 9 8 5 3        ┌─────┐      ♠ J 6
  ♡ J 6 3 2          │  N  │      ♡ 10 8 7 5 4
  ◇ J 2            W │     │ E    ◇ 10 8 7 6
  ♣ A K              │  S  │      ♣ 10 2
                    └─────┘
                    ♠ Q 10 7
                    ♡ K 9
                    ◇ A Q 5
                    ♣ Q J 8 6 4
```

For full credit, however, you should also have mentioned that holding up the spade gives East a chance to switch to hearts and now you will lose the original spade, three heart tricks and two clubs to go two down. Admittedly, it is most unlikely that East will find the switch; if his ♠J holds, he will surely be encouraged to continue his partner's suit but it is a point worth noting and the possibility of a switch of this kind is an important factor when considering whether to win or refuse a specific trick. At least one whole book has been written on this subject alone!

Problem 9
On the reasonable assumption that West has led his longest suit, we first notice that his card was the ♡3, which must be the lowest of a four-card suit or the fourth of five. Counting our tricks, we see four club tricks, after knocking out the ace, three top spades and the two red aces to total nine. Therefore the first point to realize is that, if the hearts are 4–3, we can win immediately and knock out the ♣A, starting with a low card to the ♣Q (high from the short hand first) and the contract is in no danger. At worst, we shall lose three heart tricks and the club.

The dangerous position thus arises when the lead is from a five-card suit. We are now in danger of losing four heart tricks in addition to the club. If West has the ♣A with his long hearts, there is no hope, so that card must be credited to East.

The deal:

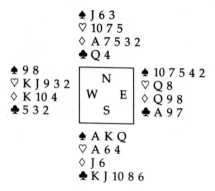

```
                    ♠ J 6 3
                    ♡ 10 7 5
                    ◇ A 7 5 3 2
                    ♣ Q 4
      ♠ 9 8                        ♠ 10 7 5 4 2
      ♡ K J 9 3 2      N           ♡ Q 8
      ◇ K 10 4     W     E         ◇ Q 9 8
      ♣ 5 3 2         S            ♣ A 9 7
                    ♠ A K Q
                    ♡ A 6 4
                    ◇ J 6
                    ♣ K J 10 8 6
```

So we have established that we must exhaust East of hearts by refusing the first round. But does it make any difference if we win the second or third? Indeed it does because West, on winning the second round, will realize that, lacking a quick entry, he has no hope of enjoying his long hearts and must look elsewhere. A switch to diamonds ensures two tricks for the defenders in that suit in addition to the two hearts already won and the ♣A for one off. We must not allow this and it is therefore correct to win the *second* round of hearts and play on clubs. Remember that, if East has a third heart, we shall only lose three tricks in that suit.

Problem 10

Assuming West has chosen his longest suit, the lead could come from a four-or five-card suit. If it is four, we can never lose more than two tricks in the suit together with the two minor-suit kings (being prepared for both finesses to be wrong) and the contract is in no danger. In this case, how we play to the hearts is irrelevant. We must therefore credit West with five hearts and now the defenders are threatening to take three heart tricks and the two minor-suit kings. We have four top tricks in the majors and at least three in each minor but both kings will have to be knocked out if we are to make nine tricks.

The dangerous situation therefore arises when West has the ◇K and East the ♣K:

The deal:

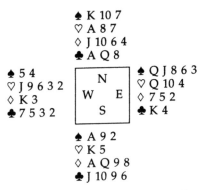

♠ K 10 7
♡ A 8 7
◊ J 10 6 4
♣ A Q 8

♠ 5 4
♡ J 9 6 3 2
◊ K 3
♣ 7 5 3 2

♠ Q J 8 6 3
♡ Q 10 4
◊ 7 5 2
♣ K 4

♠ A 9 2
♡ K 5
◊ A Q 9 8
♣ J 10 9 6

The order of losing tricks is now crucial. First, let us consider the hearts. We have, effectively, a three-card situation and we obviously cannot win both the first and second rounds as that would leave East with another card and communications between the defenders open. Thus winning the first round in dummy (which would force us to win the second in hand) is ruled out. We have a choice between refusing the first round or winning the first round in hand, intending to refuse the second.

Once we win a heart, we must consider which minor-suit finesse we should try first. The aim must be to lose a trick to East when he has run out of hearts and to knock West's entry out early, i.e. before the hearts are established. Therefore diamonds must be played first. The question then arises as to how to get to dummy to take the finesse. We cannot use the ♣A as that would mean foregoing the club finesse. This could be right all the time, in which case we would lose an unnecessary club trick to West, who would have his long hearts waiting for us. It is less obvious that it is also dangerous to use the ♠K. On taking his ◊K, West should realize that there is now no hope for the hearts and would turn to spades, setting up three tricks for his partner, who has the ♣K as entry.

It is therefore wise to forego the diamond finesse completely as we are not worried who wins a trick in that suit while the hearts are still guarded. We can win the first or second round of hearts in hand and play the ace and another diamond, losing to East. He now clears the hearts (if we won the first round, we must refuse the second) and we cross to hand in diamonds to take the club finesse (starting with the jack, ten or nine to hold the lead), losing to the now safe hand, East. We are now assured of three tricks in each minor and two in each major to total ten tricks against a heart and two minor-suit kings lost.

I strongly recommend that you play and replay this everyday hand with every possible lie of the cards and satisfy yourself that the above arguments hold and are understood. You should also note that, if there is reason to believe that East has the long hearts, (say he had bid them) the order must be reversed and clubs must be played first; we can now safely try the finesse.

Problem 11

We have three club tricks and two diamonds on top. There will be no spade trick unless West leads them again, which implies the need for four heart tricks of which we have three on top. Before deciding our line of play, let us look at each suit in more detail. In spades, West's overcall has suggested at least five and we note that, if he has six, East will have played a singleton to the first trick and our queen cannot profitably be attacked. The dangerous position arises when West has five and East a doubleton. Now, if East ever gets on play, a spade from his side will ensure four more tricks in the suit.

For that reason, we can almost rule out the possibility of a third trick in diamonds. The suit would need to break 3–3 and West would have to win the third round, implying that he would have to be credited with Q J 10 (or that he misdefends by failing to unblock his high cards from a weaker holding – the switch suggests that the queen is with East). We should therefore concentrate on that heart suit. If it breaks 3–3, there is no problem – we have five tricks automatically. However, if it breaks unevenly and the jack is with the length, a trick will have to be lost before the long card can be enjoyed. It will be safe to lose a heart trick, provided it is to West. For that reason, on winning the diamond, we should cross to dummy in clubs and play a heart, intending to insert our ten if East plays low.

The deal:

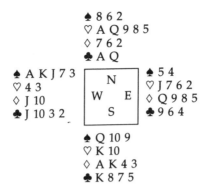

♠ 8 6 2
♥ A Q 9 8 5
♦ 7 6 2
♣ A Q

♠ A K J 7 3
♥ 4 3
♦ J 10
♣ J 10 3 2

♠ 5 4
♥ J 7 6 2
♦ Q 9 8 5
♣ 9 6 4

♠ Q 10 9
♥ K 10
♦ A K 4 3
♣ K 8 7 5

On the above layout, the ten will hold and we can now cash the king, cross back to dummy in clubs and cash the rest of the suit, followed by the other top diamond and the ♣K to total ten tricks. If West proves to have the ♥J and he plays a second club, dummy wins and now we avoid blocking the heart suit by playing the ace, swallowing our king, and the remainder of the suit is good.

The alert student will thus note that, because of the shortage of entries to dummy, the safety play in hearts is not available if we exchange the positions of the ace and king of hearts. The expert reader will also note that, even if he plays hearts in the normal manner, starting with the king and then the ace and queen, he can, as the cards lie, still save himself. However, anyone good enough to see how will have played the hearts in the correct way in the first place. We must discuss this one in a more advanced book!

Problem 12

Having recovered from the shock of the spade duplication, we see that we are in a very poor contract. The ♣A is a certain loser and the ♦K will have to be with West if we are to have any chance. Even then, there will still be problems.

As so often happens when one partner is markedly stronger than the other, there are entry problems and we have to be able to get to hand to take the diamond finesse. Both clubs and hearts are blocked and the only hope is in spades. We have a typical two-card position of the type discussed in *The Expert Beginner*.

There is no doubt that, in either case, it will be one trick each but it is a question of who wins the one for North-South.

On the left, East is in charge. If South starts with the queen and North plays low, East simply refuses to win and the North hand is dead. If North overtakes the queen with the king, East wins and the second round is won by South; again the North hand is dead. The contract cannot now be made except in the unlikely event of the ◊K turning out to be a singleton.

On the right, however, South has a chance. The queen is led from hand. Now if West wins, North plays low and the king will win the next round, allowing the diamond finesse. If West plays low, North overtakes with the king and again is in the correct hand for the finesse.

So our first hurdle is to assume that West has the ◊A. On winning the first heart, we lead the ♣Q from hand and, if West plays low, overtake with the king. If West wins, take his assumed club or heart return and cross to dummy with the ♣K.

The second hurdle is the diamond suit. There will be no problem if West has king as a singleton or in a doubleton or trebleton. If he has all five, there is no chance. The critical case arises when he has exactly four.

The deal:

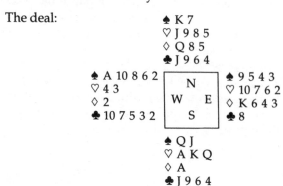

Now three finesses need to be taken and we must play with care. There are two satisfactory approaches, bearing in mind that North must win the first two rounds. Either start with the eight and underplay the seven, following with the queen, underplaying the nine, ten or jack; or start with the queen, underplaying the nine, ten or jack and follow with the eight, underplaying the seven. In either case, the third lead can come from North and another finesse taken. The ace will then pick up the king.

It shouldn't need repeating but you should play these hands over again until you fully understand everything in the solutions and appreciate why alternative lines fail. Once you feel completely at home with these hands, you can then proceed to the next section when we introduce the complication of the trump suit.

SECTION 2:

Declarer Play at Trump Contracts

We are now going to introduce the trump element and learn how similar principles apply, bearing in mind that the trump suit can act as a number of extra 'stops'.

Very often, a trump contract will have been preferred to one in no-trumps because North-South are weak in a particular side-suit. Where their only control is a weak tenace position, the fate of the contract will very often depend on keeping a specific defender off lead. We learnt countless examples in *The Expert Beginner*:

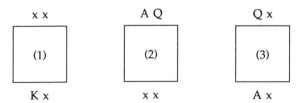

In (1), particularly if the bidding and/or early play suggests that West has the ace, it will be important to keep East off lead. If West has to attack the suit, it will cost his side a trick.

In (2), the converse applies if East has the king and we will have to lose the lead more than once during the course of play. Here we will be keen to keep West off play.

In (3), the position is less clear. It will be all right for the defender who has the king to be left on play but his *partner* is the dangerous hand and, if possible, should be prevented from winning a trick.

Let us illustrate with a simple example overleaf:

Hand No. 21
Dealer North
Both vulnerable

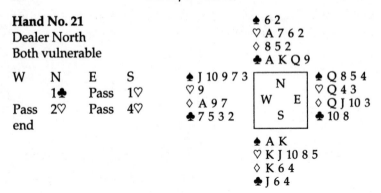

W	N	E	S
	1♣	Pass	1♡
Pass	2♡	Pass	4♡
end			

West leads the ♠J, won by South's ♠A. Counting tricks available to both sides, we see that we have at least four heart tricks, two top spades and four top clubs to total ten (even allowing for the loss of the queen of trumps). However, the defenders could take three diamond tricks, if the ace is with West, and the queen of trumps before we can discard a losing diamond on the fourth round of clubs.

There are three ways to play the trump suit:

1 Bang down the ace and king, hoping for the drop of the queen but holding the lead if she does not appear.
2 Cash the king and take a finesse through West round to East.
3 Cash the ace and take a finesse through East round to West.

Which is it to be? In terms of percentages, there is little to choose between the three lines, (1) being the slight favourite. But that is considering the trump suit in isolation. In the context of the whole hand, it is a very different matter. We have established that, if East holds the ◊A, our ◊K will score and the contract is never in danger. However, if West has that card, it is essential to prevent East from leading the suit.

Therefore, if we fail to catch the queen of trumps, we must see to it that the trick is lost to West. Clearly, therefore (3) is the correct line. West cannot profitably attack diamonds and we will have time to cash four clubs, discarding a diamond on the last round, conceding only two diamonds and the heart.

But let us juggle the above hand around to show that the correct line in trumps can alter according to the diamond position. Exchange the positions of the ◊8 and ◊K so that we now have:

K 5 2

```
┌─────────┐
│    N    │
│ W     E │
│    S    │
└─────────┘
```

8 6 4

Now we are in trouble if East has the ◊A. West has 'missed the boat' by failing to lead the suit at trick one and must certainly not be given another chance. This time, (2) is the correct line in trumps, losing to East, the safe hand in the context of the diamond suit.

Finally, let us give the ◊K to the opponents in exchange for the jack:

J 5 2

```
┌─────────┐
│    N    │
│ W     E │
│    S    │
└─────────┘
```

8 6 4

This time (barring a blockage, someone having two honours in a doubleton or a singleton honour) the suit is wide open for three tricks to the defenders, irrespective of who leads it (again they have missed the boat at trick one) and our prime necessity is to hold the lead. Now (1) is the correct line for the trumps. If the queen fails to drop, we still have the chance that the defender holding her also has as at least three clubs. In that case, he will follow three times, allowing us a fourth round, on which we discard a losing diamond, whether he ruffs or not. Now we will lose the trump and two diamonds only.

Having grasped the idea, I should like you to do three problems in match conditions, aiming for under one minute in each case. State clearly your line of play, giving good reasons for your choice. Start your stop-watch.

Problem 1
Hand No. 22
Dealer East
E–W vulnerable

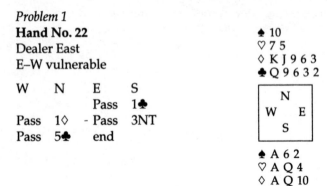

♠ 10
♡ 7 5
◇ K J 9 6 3
♣ Q 9 6 3 2

♠ A 6 2
♡ A Q 4
◇ A Q 10
♣ K 10 7 5

W	N	E	S
		Pass	1♣
Pass	1◇	- Pass	3NT
Pass	5♣	end	

We could discuss the bidding of this hand at some length but that is best left for some other time. For the moment, it will be sufficient to say that, had North bid 4♣ after South's game bid, that would have been forcing and slam invitational, leaving more room for discussion, typically by cue-bidding. A direct game bid in this situation, on what is known as the 'principle of fast arrival' expresses a desire to play there and certainly denies an ace.

West leads the ♠Q. How do you plan the play?

Problem 2
Hand No. 23
Dealer West
Neither vulnerable

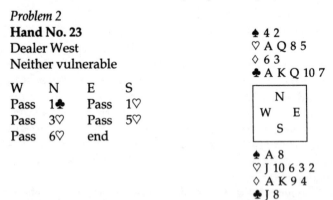

♠ 4 2
♡ A Q 8 5
◇ 6 3
♣ A K Q 10 7

♠ A 8
♡ J 10 6 3 2
◇ A K 9 4
♣ J 8

W	N	E	S
Pass	1♣	Pass	1♡
Pass	3♡	Pass	5♡
Pass	6♡	end	

South's 5♡ bid indicates controls in the unbid suits and specifically asks partner about the quality of his trumps. With two of the three top honours (having promised no more than four small cards at the time he bid 3♡), North is happy to accept the slam invitation.

West leads the ♠K. Plan the play.

Problem 3
Hand No. 24
Dealer East
Both vulnerable

♠	K Q 10		
♡	10 7		
◊	K Q J 8		
♣	8 7 3 2		

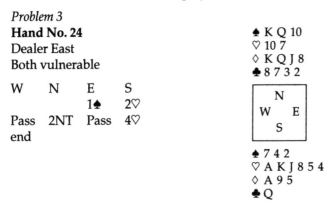

W	N	E	S
		1♠	2♡
Pass	2NT	Pass	4♡
end			

♠ 7 4 2
♡ A K J 8 5 4
◊ A 9 5
♣ Q

South's 4♡ bid is dubious, to say the least. In this kind of position, 3NT is very often the better contract, especially if North turns out to have a 'slow' spade stopper, say ♠ Q J x x when West is bound to be short and will be ruffing. Against that, there is a danger from clubs, even on the expected initial spade lead and, on this occasion, South, seeing the dummy, is pleased to observe that he has made the right choice.

West leads the ♣9. When you put on dummy's ♠K, East plays an encouraging ♠8. How do you continue?

Solutions

Problem 1
In trumps, we could lose two tricks and there is also a danger of losing to the ♡K if it is in the West hand. The heart finesse can be avoided if the diamonds can be brought in as we can discard our losing hearts on the fourth and fifth rounds – but not before trumps are drawn.

We consider our play in the trump suit in that light. Assuming that West does hold the ♡K (we are obviously not in danger otherwise), East is the dangerous hand and thus we must try to avoid losing trump tricks to that hand. We cannot argue with the ace but we have options regarding how we are going to try and catch the jack. Again we have a number of possibilities:

1 Lead a low card towards the queen, intending to finesse on the next round.
2 Lead a low card towards the queen, intending to play for the drop on the next round.
3 Lead a low card and finesse the nine.
4 Cross to dummy and lead a low card towards the king, intending to finesse on the next round.
5 Cross to dummy and lead a low card towards the king, intending to play for the drop on the next round.
6 Cross to dummy and lead a low card, intending to finesse the ten.

The way to decide our choice is to mentally hold a series of 'trial runs'. The crucial consideration is that, if we must lose two tricks, it is desirable that the first is lost to West, who cannot profitably attack hearts. Let us try each line above bearing that in mind.

1 If the queen loses to East's ace, he can play a heart. We can then try the finesse, but if it loses, we still have to catch the jack of trumps – no certainty of success.
2 Same applies as in (1).
3 The nine could lose to East's jack and now a heart will force us to try the finesse. If that fails, we are doomed, irrespective of the position of the ace of trumps. We should look very silly if East's ♣J turned out to be singleton!
4 If the king loses to West's ace, we shall be successful, irrespective of the position of the jack, as West cannot profitably attack hearts. However, if the king holds and East turns out to have ♣ A J x, we will have to lose our first trick in the suit to him. He will then be able to attack hearts and we are defeated if the finesse is wrong.
5 Same applies as in (4).
6 This looks better. If we must lose to the jack, it will be to West, who cannot profitably attack hearts. We now have time to knock out the ace of trumps. If this should be with East, he can play a heart but now we rise with the ace, draw any outstanding low trump and play five rounds of diamonds to discard our two heart losers. If West does hold a singleton ♣J, we are quite happy to look silly because we still make the contract!

The deal:

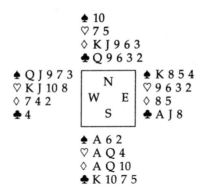

```
                    ♠ 10
                    ♡ 7 5
                    ◇ K J 9 6 3
                    ♣ Q 9 6 3 2
    ♠ Q J 9 7 3                    ♠ K 8 5 4
    ♡ K J 10 8        N            ♡ 9 6 3 2
    ◇ 7 4 2       W       E        ◇ 8 5
    ♣ 4               S            ♣ A J 8
                    ♠ A 6 2
                    ♡ A Q 4
                    ◇ A Q 10
                    ♣ K 10 7 5
```

Thus the correct line is to win the first spade, cross to dummy by ruffing a spade (better than using diamonds as, if there is a 4–1 split in that suit, there may be a ruff against us) and lead a low club, finessing the ten if East plays low. Satisfy yourself that (barring a 4–0 split), this guarantees the contract, irrespective of the positions of the ace and jack. East can, of course, rise with the ♣A to push a heart through but that means our two trump honours remain intact and the ♣J can never score, even if East has all four trumps.

Problem 2
Obviously we shall win the first round of spades and we see that, even if a trick has to be lost to the ♡K, we have four trump tricks, five clubs, two diamonds and the spade to total twelve, even without considering possible diamond ruffs in dummy. The danger, however, lies in losing a spade trick. Clearly the spade loser must be discarded on clubs and there are therefore two possible lines of play:

1 Take the trump finesse – a straight 50% chance.
2 Cash the ace of trumps, holding the lead, and then play clubs, hoping to discard the spade loser on the third round before we are interrupted.

Let us work out the odds this time. We shall succeed if the ♡K is a singleton. That implies a 3–1 split (50%) with the ♡K as the singleton (¼ x 50% = 12.5%). We shall also succeed if the clubs are 3–3 (36%) and in many of the 4–2 splits, viz. where the hand with the club length has ♡ x x (when his partner will have to ruff the third club with the king of trumps while we discard our spade, effectively coalescing two losers into one) or any three or all four hearts. Also, if East has the club shortage and ♡ x x, he can ruff our third club but now we overruff and may be able to cash two top diamonds and return to dummy with a diamond ruff. Now we lead a fourth high club and East, exhausted of trumps, must discard while we throw our spade loser and West is still following suit.

There is no need to bother you with the intricate calculation combining these percentages. It will suffice to say that the total is way over 50% and the finesse line only gains when West has the king, among three or four hearts, and two or fewer clubs.

Line 2 therefore should be taken and is rewarded with an overtrick here:

The deal:

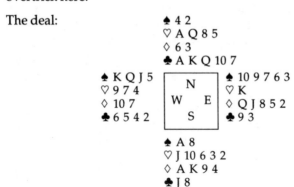

```
                    ♠ 4 2
                    ♡ A Q 8 5
                    ◊ 6 3
                    ♣ A K Q 10 7
   ♠ K Q J 5                      ♠ 10 9 7 6 3
   ♡ 9 7 4          N             ♡ K
   ◊ 10 7       W       E         ◊ Q J 8 5 2
   ♣ 6 5 4 2        S             ♣ 9 3
                    ♠ A 8
                    ♡ J 10 6 3 2
                    ◊ A K 9 4
                    ♣ J 8
```

Problem 3

The spade position is typical of the type of three-card layout discussed in *The Expert Beginner:*

```
            K Q 10
              N
      5   W       E   A J 6 3
              S
            7 4 2
```

The fact that West has only two cards and East has two to spare is neither here nor there. West is on lead and, when the nine is played to the king, East realizes that, if he takes his ace, he cannot profitably continue the suit and now North's queen will remain in dummy as a stop. He therefore plays well to refuse the first trick, merely encouraging with the eight. Now, if West can get on play again, the five gives the defenders two immediate tricks in this two-card position:

```
            Q 10
          ┌───────┐
          │   N   │
       5  │ W   E │  A J 6 3
          │   S   │
          └───────┘
            7 4
```

Again, the fact West has only one card and East two to spare is purely of academic interest.

Therefore we can see that, whereas in Problem 1, we had to keep East off play at all costs, here it is West who has to be kept out of mischief. Counting our tricks, we see five trumps (assuming that a trick has to be lost to the queen), four diamonds and the spade already won, totalling ten, but there is the danger of losing two spades, the trump and a club. Thus the trumps must be played with a view to keeping West off lead. With eight cards between our two hands, the finesse offers a superior percentage to the drop but we know better by now.

The best play is to cash the ace and king and then play on the diamonds. Even if the ♡Q fails to fall, there is still the chance that the hand holding her has at least three diamonds. We can then discard a black-suit loser on the fourth round, restricting our losses to the other two black-suit losers and the trump.

The deal:

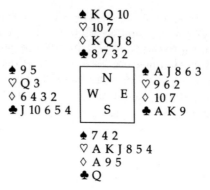

```
                        ♠ K Q 10
                        ♡ 10 7
                        ◇ K Q J 8
                        ♣ 8 7 3 2
        ♠ 9 5              N          ♠ A J 8 6 3
        ♡ Q 3                         ♡ 9 6 2
        ◇ 6 4 3 2     W       E       ◇ 10 7
        ♣ J 10 6 5 4       S          ♣ A K 9
                        ♠ 7 4 2
                        ♡ A K J 8 5 4
                        ◇ A 9 5
                        ♣ Q
```

This line of play only loses against the finesse line if East has ♡ Q x x and two or fewer diamonds.

Note that, had East won the first spade and returned the suit, taking the view that the only hope was to find his partner with a singleton, it would still be right to play for the drop in trumps. Lose a finesse to West and he could put his partner in with clubs and, if he (West) started with three trumps, ruff the third round of spades.

Now that you have had a fair amount of practice in the basic principles of losing tricks to the right opponents and at the right time, we can go on to more complex examples on this theme. We shall learn that it sometimes pays to lose an apparently 'unnecessary' trick in one suit in order to save two or more others elsewhere. Indeed our first example illustrates this point with two suits involved:

Hand No. 25
Dealer South
N–S vulnerable

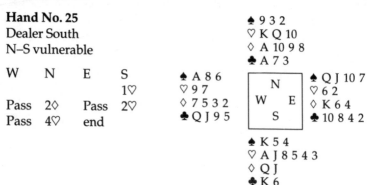

```
                                    ♠ 9 3 2
                                    ♡ K Q 10
                                    ◇ A 10 9 8
                                    ♣ A 7 3
W      N      E      S      ♠ A 8 6            ♠ Q J 10 7
                     1♡    ♡ 9 7       N      ♡ 6 2
Pass   2◇    Pass   2♡    ◇ 7 5 3 2  W    E   ◇ K 6 4
Pass   4♡    end          ♣ Q J 9 5     S    ♣ 10 8 4 2
                                    ♠ K 5 4
                                    ♡ A J 8 5 4 3
                                    ◇ Q J
                                    ♣ K 6
```

West leads the ♣Q and declarer can see six top trump tricks, two top clubs and the ♢A to total nine and can easily set up more in diamonds after the king has been knocked out. However, on the other side, the defenders are threatening three spade tricks, assuming that the ace is with West, and the ♢K, assuming that he is with East, and those four tricks will be cashed before the long diamonds can be brought in for spade discards.

Now before reading on, can you see how to make the contract with all four hands on view in the above layout?

You can see that taking the diamond finesse is a loser and indeed it is better to play the ♢A first, just in case the ♢K is singleton with East. You do not object to losing a trick to West if the finesse is right all the time. So is there another way out?

Most inexperienced declarers (and a few experienced ones!) would simply win the first club and then start thinking, unaware that they had already chucked the contract. Let us look at that club position more closely:

```
              A 7 3
            ┌─────────┐
            │    N    │
   Q J 9 5  │ W     E │  10 8 4 2
            │    S    │
            └─────────┘
              K 6
```

With hearts as trumps, it is easy to say that we can have three rounds of this club suit, winning two and losing none as the third round can be ruffed. But we have just agreed that there is no harm in losing a trick to West as he cannot profitably attack spades. There is therefore no harm in giving him an 'unnecessary' club trick provided we are given a trick in return elsewhere. Try the effect of allowing the ♣Q to hold. That leaves the two-card position:

```
              A 7
            ┌─────────┐
            │    N    │
    J 9 5   │ W     E │  10 8 4
            │    S    │
            └─────────┘
               K
```

After taking our ♣K, we can discard a loser in our hand and, at worst, we have broken even. But we can do better still. Suppose that, on the third round of clubs, we discard the ◊J. That leaves the following position in that suit:

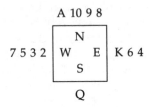

Now we are in a position to take the diamond finesse the other way – a ruffing finesse against East. Again remember that we do not mind losing a trick to West if he does, after all, have the ◊K – he cannot profitably attack spades from his side. We cash the ◊A and run the ◊10, discarding a spade if East does not cover. Either we save ourselves losing the ◊K or, if West is able to win, we are able to discard more spade losers on the other diamonds, losing, at worst, a spade and a diamond in addition to the club at the beginning.

As this is a difficult hand, let us play it out together.

(i) The ♣Q from West, allowed to hold. If West suspects what is going on, he will find the best switch to a trump, trying to attack one of the many entries that we shall need to dummy, prematurely.

(ii) A trump from West, won on dummy.

(iii) ♣K, won by South.

(iv) A trump, won by North with ♡K.

(v) ♣A, won by North, South discarding ◊J.

(vi) ◊A, won by North, South following with ◊Q; he is now out of the suit.

(vii) ◊10 from North. If East covers, South ruffs high (in case West started with a singleton). If East plays low, South discards a spade.

The play now depends on what happened on trick 7. If East covered and South ruffed, then:

(viii) South crosses to dummy with another trump, clearing the trumps (unless they were 4–0).

(ix) The ◊9 from North, South discarding a low spade.

(x) The ◊8 from North, South discarding another low spade.

South now concedes a trick to the ♠A, claiming the last two with trumps.

If East fails to cover the ◊10, South discards a spade. Now, as the cards lie above, the ◊10 holds:

(viii) The ◊9 from North. If East refuses to cover, South discards another spade, conceding a trick to the ♠A and finishing with an overtrick. If East covers, South ruffs high.

(ix) South returns to dummy in trumps.

(x) The ◊8 from North, South discarding another spade.

(xi) South concedes a trick to the ♠A, again finishing with an overtrick.

If, in fact, West has the ◊K, he will win trick 7. He still cannot profitably attack spades. If he exits in another suit, South will cross to dummy in trumps and discard two spades on the two remaining high diamonds before conceding a trick to the ♠A, making the contract exactly.

Having grasped the idea, can you do the next example in match conditions? As the idea is rather more difficult, give yourself two minutes. Start your stop-watch.

Problem 4
Hand No. 26
Dealer North
E–W vulnerable

♠ 8 4 3
♡ A Q 9 6
◊ A 2
♣ A K J 10

W	N	E	S
	1♣	Pass	1♡
Dble	4♡	end	

```
        N
   W         E
        S
```

♠ K 7 5
♡ K J 10 5 4 3
◊ Q
♣ 7 3 2

West leads the ♡8. Plan the play.

West's take-out double has shown length and values in the two unbid suits. We can see six top trump tricks, two top clubs and the ◊A to total nine, and a tenth can easily be set up in clubs after the ♣Q has been knocked out. However, if that involves losing the lead to East, a spade from his side, as long as it is high enough to beat dummy's ♠8, will ensure three tricks in that suit for the defence and our disappointment. If West holds the ♣Q, there will be no problem so the layout we have to guard against looks like this:

The deal:

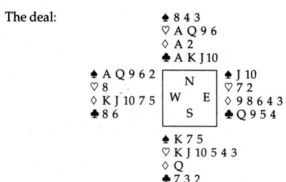

	♠ 8 4 3	
	♡ A Q 9 6	
	◊ A 2	
	♣ A K J 10	
♠ A Q 9 6 2		♠ J 10
♡ 8		♡ 7 2
◊ K J 10 7 5		◊ 9 8 6 4 3
♣ 8 6		♣ Q 9 5 4
	♠ K 7 5	
	♡ K J 10 5 4 3	
	◊ Q	
	♣ 7 3 2	

Can you see the road to success now? Playing on clubs early will involve losing the lead to East and disaster, but how about the diamond position? We can insist on two rounds, without loss if we are greedy, but if we can lose the first round to West, we shall be in a position to discard a losing club on the ◊A and take a ruffing finesse in clubs through East, caring little if West should produce the ♣Q after all.

We take two rounds of trumps, finishing in hand and play the ◊Q. If West, marked with the ◊K on his bidding, refuses to cover, we let it run and make a second diamond trick for ten in total easily. So he does cover and dummy plays low! West exits in a minor. We win in dummy and discard a club on the ◊A. Now follow top clubs and the ♣J, discarding a spade if East fails to cover. If East has the ♣Q, we will lose two spades and the diamond. If West has her, we will discard a second spade on the last club and lose a spade, a club and a diamond.

We are now going to turn to more examples of losing tricks to the correct hand in a single suit. Let us consider a typical three-card situation of the type studied in the beginners' book:

```
           A Q 7
         ┌───────┐
         │   N   │
  K 8 6  │ W   E │  J 10 5
         │   S   │
         └───────┘
           4 3 2
```

Clearly (unless North has to lead the suit twice), North-South will win two tricks and East-West one, but exactly who wins the defenders' trick may be critical in the context of a whole hand. Suppose South plays the first round from hand, successfully finessing the queen. If he continues with the ace, the defenders are in charge. If it is in their interests that West should win the third round, he will simply play low now and take his king later. On the other hand, if it is preferable that East should win the third round, West will drop his king under the ace, leaving East's jack as master.

Can South prevent this? Indeed he can by insisting on leading from weakness through strength to strength. After the first round, the two-card position remaining looks like this:

```
           A 7
         ┌───────┐
         │   N   │
   K 8   │ W   E │  J 10
         │   S   │
         └───────┘
           4 3
```

We have just seen that leading the ace from dummy puts the defenders in charge; but now let South come back to his hand via another suit and lead a low card from there and now the picture changes and declarer calls the tune. If West puts up the king, South can duck in dummy if he wishes to lose a trick to West or go up with the ace if he wishes to lose a trick to East. Alternatively, if West plays low on the second round, South will call for dummy's ace if he wishes to lose a trick to West or play low if he wishes to lose a trick to East. Can you put that idea into practice in this next example?

Problem 5
Hand No. 27
Dealer West
Both vulnerable

♠ 6 2
♡ 8 7 2
◊ A Q 9 8 2
♣ 5 4 2

W	N	E	S
1♡	Pass	Pass	Dble
Pass	2◊	Pass	3♠
Pass	4♠	end	

```
        N
   W         E
        S
```

♠ A K Q J 10 5
♡ K J
◊ 6 4 3
♣ A 10

West leads the ♣K and his partner plays an encouraging ♣7. How do you plan the play?

We have six spades and the two minor aces on top and, on the bidding, the diamond finesse is likely to be right. That totals nine so far and there is little hope for a heart trick. Meanwhile the defenders are threatening to take a club trick, a diamond and two hearts. The heart losers can only be discarded on the long diamonds and therefore we must look at that suit in more detail. To avoid a heart coming from East, the diamond trick must be lost to West and we discussed the position in the diagrams above. There is also the problem that we have no entries to dummy outside the suit itself, which means that the trick will have to be lost on the first or second round so that the third round is won in dummy. That will have to be after trumps have been drawn so that the long cards can be cashed without interference.

We look at the diamond position in that light. We have already established that we shall need a 3–2 split with the king in the West hand. But that alone is not enough. If he has three cards, we are doomed unless they are specifically K J 10. Otherwise the second trick (which we shall have to duck) will be lost to East. The chances are that we shall need to find West with a doubleton king. Now we can play the first round to the queen and then return to hand for a second round intending to let the king hold.

This is quite a mouthful already and we have hardly started. How did you play to trick one? The opening lead of the ♣K implied the possession of the ♣Q but not necessarily the ♣J. East's encouragement could well indicate that he has it. In that case, if you won the first club, West on gaining the lead with the ◊K, could lead a low club to get his partner in for the lethal heart switch. Just as it is important to lose a diamond trick to West, the same applies to clubs. Win the second round, draw trumps and play a diamond to the queen (if West plays the king on the first round, let it hold). Assuming the queen holds, return to hand by ruffing a club and play a second diamond, allowing West's king to win. After that, the rest of the suit comes in and West indeed must cash his ♡A now to avoid conceding an overtrick. We thus concede a trick in each side suit.

The deal:

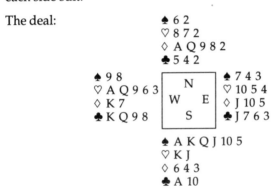

```
                    ♠ 6 2
                    ♡ 8 7 2
                    ◊ A Q 9 8 2
                    ♣ 5 4 2
    ♠ 9 8                          ♠ 7 4 3
    ♡ A Q 9 6 3      N             ♡ 10 5 4
    ◊ K 7        W       E         ◊ J 10 5
    ♣ K Q 9 8        S             ♣ J 7 6 3
                    ♠ A K Q J 10 5
                    ♡ K J
                    ◊ 6 4 3
                    ♣ A 10
```

Similar principles apply when you have to lose more than one trick in your long suit. How would you handle this example?

Problem 6
Hand No. 28
Dealer East
E–W vulnerable

			♠ J 5
			♡ Q 6 3
			◊ K Q 8 7 2
			♣ 8 4 2

W	N	E	S
		Pass	1♡
Pass	2♡	Pass	4♡
end			

```
        N
    W       E
        S
```

♠ A
♡ A K J 7 2
◊ 6 5 4 3
♣ A Q 5

West leads the ◊J. Plan the play.

We have five top trump tricks and the two black aces. Even if we have to lose two diamond tricks, we shall win three of the five rounds so that should be enough. Meanwhile, however, the defenders are threatening two tricks in each of the minors. In that light, let us look at the club position in more detail. Clearly there is no problem if the king is with East but if West has it, we are considering something like this:

```
              8 4 2
                N
    K 10 x   W     E   J 9 x
                S
              A Q 5
```

If East leads the first round (a card higher than the 8) we can at least delay trouble by rising with the ace and then only a second lead from East will ensure the two tricks. Therefore we must prevent East from getting in twice. We consider the relevance to the diamond position. Clearly from the lead, East has the ace and therefore the following layouts are possible:

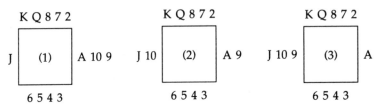

In (2), of course, the positions of the ten and nine are interchangeable. We have two approaches. Cover with an honour or allow the jack to hold.

In (1), covering is a loser. East wins and pushes a club through and will get in again for another club. Playing low is the winner. Either East plays low, in which case West is left on play and, unable to profitably attack clubs from his side, must switch. We will subsequently draw trumps, knock out East's ◊A, allowing him to switch to clubs (but *once only*) and we shall later discard a potential club loser on the fifth diamond. Note that, if East rises with the ace and gives his partner a ruff, the defenders achieve nothing. Not only is West left on play, unable to attack clubs, but he will have done nothing but ruff his partner's trick.

In (2), we gain by covering in that we lose only one diamond trick instead of two but by playing low, all we do is give up the overtrick. East can only get in once and the contract is never in any danger.

In (3), we lose by covering but again only the overtrick as East again is restricted to one shot at the clubs. By playing low we gain the overtrick.

So the critical case arises in (1) and therefore playing low is the correct play. The number of people who would call for an honour without giving the hand a second thought, even in experienced circles, is alarming.

We can juggle that diamond position around to:

K J 8 7 2

Q | N W E S | A 10 9

6 5 4 3

When the queen is led, she must be allowed to hold so that one trick is lost to each defender rather than both to East.

The deal:

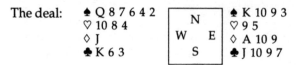

♠ Q 8 7 6 4 2
♡ 10 8 4
◊ J
♣ K 6 3

♠ K 10 9 3
♡ 9 5
◊ A 10 9
♣ J 10 9 7

In our study of no-trump contracts, we considered situations in which there were chances in two suits and learnt the principle of 'Drop first (holding the lead) then finesse.' The same applies in trump contracts. As a warm-up example, you should have no difficulty with this one –and yet, when it came up in a 'top-class' national competition, a number of well-known names went wrong!

Problem 7
Hand No. 29
Dealer West
Both vulnerable

♠ A 10 9 4 3
♡ A Q 6
◊ 10 8
♣ A J 7

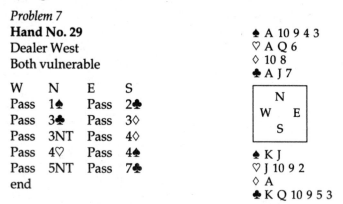

W	N	E	S
Pass	1♠	Pass	2♣
Pass	3♣	Pass	3◊
Pass	3NT	Pass	4◊
Pass	4♡	Pass	4♠
Pass	5NT	Pass	7♣
end			

♠ K J
♡ J 10 9 2
◊ A
♣ K Q 10 9 5 3

North has something of a rebid problem after South's 2♣ response. A good case can be made for 2NT, protecting the heart position but, if South has a tenace position in diamonds, it might be better to have him as declarer in the likely goal contract of 3NT. In that case, on the lead of a low heart, dummy can play low, leaving East on lead and the tenace protected. If West leads the ♡J, dummy will rise with the ♡A and then declarer will try to keep East on lead, again protecting the ♡Q.

Although 3♣, in principle, guarantees a four-card support, the other point in favour of preferring it to 2NT is that North is rich in first-round controls and a slam could well be on the cards if South is strong. In that event, the sooner clubs are agreed, the better. After 3♣ the discussion, at least for the time being, is about 3NT and, as far as North is concerned, his partner's 3◊ bid shows no more than a stopper. After 3NT, South's 4◊ bid shows first-round control with a view to a club slam. 4♡ is another cue-bid, showing first-round control, and many partnerships allow the showing of a king in partner's bid suit, hence South's 4♠ bid. North now knows that there is every prospect of his spade suit being brought in and makes a grand-slam force of 5NT, inviting his partner to bid the grand slam with any two of the three top trump honours, here, obviously, the king and queen.

We shall discuss these cue-bidding sequences in more detail later in the bidding section but the exercise now is to make an optimistic slam after the lead of the ◊K. How do you plan the play?

We have six top trump tricks, the two red aces and the ace and king of spades to total ten so far. There will be no problem if West has the ♡K among no more than three but, if he has four or more, we shall either have to ruff out the ♠Q for our thirteenth trick or ruff the fourth round of hearts in dummy, implying the likely need for a 2–2 trump split. Therefore we shall probably make the contract if the heart finesse is right; the question arises as to whether there is any hope should it be wrong. Indeed, the spade suit could be worth five tricks if the queen drops as a singleton or in a doubleton.

The best line, after winning the diamond, is to draw trumps and cash the two top spades. If the queen falls, claim the contract. If she doesn't, ruff a third round of spades high and take and repeat the heart finesse. Ruff another spade high, return to the ♡A and cash the fifth spade, discarding a losing heart if the ♡K has not appeared so far.

The deal:

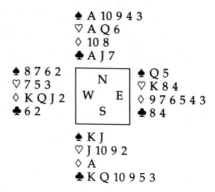

```
                        ♠ A 10 9 4 3
                        ♡ A Q 6
                        ◇ 10 8
                        ♣ A J 7
        ♠ 8 7 6 2              ┌─────────┐        ♠ Q 5
        ♡ 7 5 3               │    N    │        ♡ K 8 4
        ◇ K Q J 2            │ W     E │        ◇ 9 7 6 5 4 3
        ♣ 6 2                │    S    │        ♣ 8 4
                             └─────────┘
                        ♠ K J
                        ♡ J 10 9 2
                        ◇ A
                        ♣ K Q 10 9 5 3
```

Having grasped the idea, you can extend the principle to situations where options exist in *three* suits. Again the rule of 'drop before finesse' applies and we shall take the opportunity to improve our knowledge of how to handle suit combinations. This is a common layout (the three honours being inter-changeable):

```
              Q J 9 x
            ┌─────────┐
            │    N    │
            │ W     E │
            │    S    │
            └─────────┘
              K x x
```

One trick must be lost to the ace but there will be three tricks for us if the suit breaks 3–3 or if the ten falls in two rounds. We need to cover situations where the ten is among four and approach the suit as follows:

1 Play low towards the king and then low towards the dummy.
2 Play low towards the dummy and then low towards the king.
3 Play low towards the dummy, return to hand in another suit and play low towards the dummy again.

```
          Q J 9 4                          Q J 9 4
        ┌─────────┐                      ┌─────────┐
A 10 x x │   (1)   │ x x          x x    │   (2)   │ A 10 x x
        └─────────┘                      └─────────┘
          K x x                            K x x
```

Taking line 1:

In (1) the king will lose; the second round will hold and we shall have to take a decision as to whether to play for the drop or finesse to find the ten on the third round.

In (2) the king will win but we cannot catch the ten.

In (3) the king will win and we shall have to take a decision as in (1).

In (4) the king will lose and we cannot catch the ten.

Taking line 2:

In (1) the queen will hold; the king will lose and we shall have to take a decision as to whether to play for the drop or finesse to find the ten on the third round.

In (2) the queen will lose; the king will hold but we cannot catch the ten.

In (3) the queen will lose; the king will hold and we shall have to take a decision on the third round as in (1).

In (4) the queen will hold; the king will lose and we cannot catch the ten.

Taking line 3:

In (1) the queen and jack will both hold but we cannot catch the ten.

In (2) the queen will lose and we cannot catch the ten.

In (3) the queen will lose; the king will hold and we shall have to take a decision on the third round as to whether to finesse for or drop the ten.

In (4) the queen will hold and the ace will drop 'on air' on the second round so that we shall definitely catch the ten.

It is this last position that swings the balance in favour of line 3. In other words, adopting this line of play, we shall catch the ten on any 3–3 split or where the ace sits doubleton under the two honours. You can now combine your new knowledge with the available options in this next example.

Problem 8
Hand No. 30
Dealer South
N–S vulnerable

W	N	E	S
			1♡
Pass	2♣	Pass	2♡
Pass	5♡	Pass	6♡
end			

♠ A 4 3
♡ K 10 9
◊ A Q 2
♣ K Q 9 4

```
        N
   W         E
        S
```

♠ K 10 6
♡ A Q J 8 4 2
◊ J
♣ J 5 2

West leads a trump and all follow to two rounds. How do you continue?

We have six top trumps, at least two clubs, the ◊A and two top spades to total eleven so far, and there are a number of chances for the twelfth.

First we should try to drop the ♣10. A low club to the ♣K holds and we return to hand in trumps to try another club from hand. The ♣Q holds, neither ace nor ten having appeared. So we must now hope for a 3–3 split in the suit with a third round. No good – East shows out and West wins and sends back the ♣10 which we have to ruff. Before reading on, decide what you are going to do next.

It looks as though we shall have to depend on the diamond finesse but there is no rush. First, we cash the ace and king of spades (in that order so that we end in hand). If the queen and jack do not fall as a doubleton, only then do we try the diamond finesse, overtaking the jack with the queen.

So here there were options in *three* suits and again we tried the two drops before attempting the finesse.

The deal:

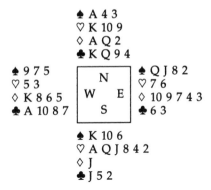

```
                    ♠ A 4 3
                    ♡ K 10 9
                    ◊ A Q 2
                    ♣ K Q 9 4
     ♠ 9 7 5                      ♠ Q J 8 2
     ♡ 5 3          N             ♡ 7 6
     ◊ K 8 6 5   W     E          ◊ 10 9 7 4 3
     ♣ A 10 8 7     S             ♣ 6 3
                    ♠ K 10 6
                    ♡ A Q J 8 4 2
                    ◊ J
                    ♣ J 5 2
```

Our line of play covered all 3–3 club splits, the possibility that the ♣10 would drop in two rounds or that the ♣A would be doubleton with West, and that the ♠ Q J would be doubleton in either hand. In any of these cases, we would still have been successful even with the diamond finesse wrong.

We shall now do some further work on options in suit combinations where the recommended line of play may vary according to what is happening in other suits. Let us try this next example together.

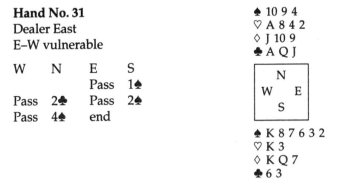

Hand No. 31
Dealer East
E–W vulnerable

```
                              ♠ 10 9 4
                              ♡ A 8 4 2
                              ◊ J 10 9
                              ♣ A Q J
W     N     E     S
            Pass  1♠              N
Pass  2♣    Pass  2♠          W       E
Pass  4♠    end                  S

                              ♠ K 8 7 6 3 2
                              ♡ K 3
                              ◊ K Q 7
                              ♣ 6 3
```

Many players, including a number of world-class authorities, would prefer a direct 2NT over 1♠ but there are a number of points against it. First, the bid, in principle, denies a four-card heart suit and South is expected to pass rather than progress to 3♡ on a poor hand with a 5422 shape.

Second, and, in my opinion, far more important, as 3NT is the likely final contract, it may well be better played from the South side. There is always a double club-stop but there are advantages in the red suits if South holds ♡ Q x or ◇ A x. I have to emphasize that I am very keen on these considerations. This attitude follows a large number of very bitter experiences of 3NT contracts failing through being played from the wrong side after neglectful bidding in this area. ·

West leads the ♡J. We shall clearly have two diamond tricks for one lost and two hearts tricks without loss to total four tricks won and one lost so far. If the club finesse holds, we shall have three tricks without loss but, if it fails, we shall have two tricks for one lost. There is nothing useful we can discard on the third round of clubs, so effectively we have six tricks outside trumps with one loss if the club finesse succeeds and five with two losses if it fails.

We consider our play in the trump suit in that light. If the club finesse fails, we cannot afford to lose more than one trump trick and therefore the only hope is that the suit breaks 2–2 with East having the ace. We shall lead a low trump from dummy, put up the king and hope for the best. If the club succeeds, however, we can afford two trump losses and must reconsider the possible trump divisions to ensure that we do not lose three tricks.

If the trumps split 2–2 with West having the ace, we shall lose exactly two tricks, irrespective of our play, so we need not worry about that. Similarly, if West has all three honours over our king there is no chance of avoiding three losses, so again we need not worry. The critical layouts are these (remembering that the queen and jack are interchangeable):

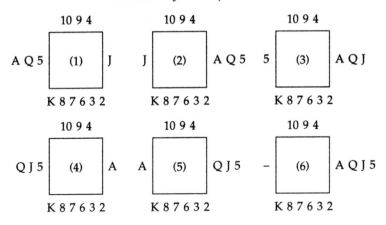

There are two possible lines of play:

1 Play a low spade from dummy, intending to rise with the king unless the ace appears from East.
2 Play a low spade from dummy, intending to cover the queen or jack but duck if the 5 appears. We intend to return to dummy and play a low card towards the king on the second round.

Line 1 succeeds in (1), (2), (3) and (4) but results in defeat in (5) and (6).

Line 2 succeeds in all cases, although it does give up the overtrick when East has exactly A x.

Line 2 should therefore be preferred. Nothing is lost if East has the ace and the length but there is a gain if West has a stiff ace.

Therefore we see that, according to the success or failure of the club finesse, two different approaches to the trumps are required. For that reason, the club finesse must be taken early and the trumps played as above according to the result.

The deal:

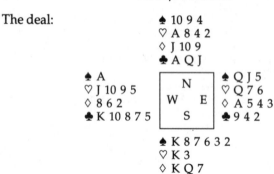

```
                    ♠ 10 9 4
                    ♡ A 8 4 2
                    ◊ J 10 9
                    ♣ A Q J
  ♠ A                              ♠ Q J 5
  ♡ J 10 9 5         N             ♡ Q 7 6
  ◊ 8 6 2        W       E         ◊ A 5 4 3
  ♣ K 10 8 7 5       S             ♣ 9 4 2
                    ♠ K 8 7 6 3 2
                    ♡ K 3
                    ◊ K Q 7
                    ♣ 6 3
```

Now – one other important point must be discussed. In which hand should we win that first round of hearts? Can you see two good reasons why we must win in hand?

First, we need to take the club finesse but – less obvious – the ♡A must be kept in dummy as we may need two entries to play spades in the position where the club finesse succeeds. Note that, against best defence, we cannot get to dummy in diamonds. East will refuse his ace unless our ◊7 is played. The keen student will recognize this situation from *The Expert Beginner*, when it came up in clubs while we played a spade slam. This habit of recognizing similar situations of this kind is the key to saving yourself a great deal of work. I have drummed this point home in my books for more advanced players. The chances of a given deal turning up twice are infinitesimally small and can be ignored for all practical purposes. But situations requiring similar handling recur continually.

The ability to recognize them and to remember and understand how to handle them is the principal asset of the expert player.

Try this next example under match conditions and see if you can do it in under two minutes. Start your stop-watch.

Problem 9
Hand No. 32
Dealer East
E–W vulnerable

♠ A K Q
♡ 7 4 2
◇ A 7 2
♣ Q J 7 6

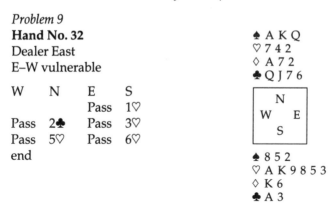

W	N	E	S
		Pass	1♡
Pass	2♣	Pass	3♡
Pass	5♡	Pass	6♡
end			

♠ 8 5 2
♡ A K 9 8 5 3
◇ K 6
♣ A 3

West leads the ◇Q. How do you plan the play?

We have three top tricks in spades, two in diamonds plus the ♣A to total six so far. This means that, if the club finesse fails, we shall need all six trump tricks and must play the two tops, hoping for a 2–2 split. If the club finesse succeeds, however, we only need five trump tricks and can afford to lose one. In that case, our prime consideration must be to avoid losing two. If there is a 2–2 or 3–1 split, the contract is not in danger. At the other extreme, if West has all the outstanding cards, there is no hope.

The critical case arises when East has the stack. Now, if we can lead trumps from dummy, observing the usual guide of 'weakness through strength to strength' we can arrange for our two top honours to catch two of East's, leaving our ♡ 9 8 solid against the remaining honour and restricting our losses to one trick.

The deal:

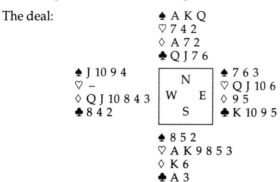

♠ A K Q
♡ 7 4 2
◇ A 7 2
♣ Q J 7 6

♠ J 10 9 4
♡ –
◇ Q J 10 8 4 3
♣ 8 4 2

♠ 7 6 3
♡ Q J 10 6
◇ 9 5
♣ K 10 9 5

♠ 8 5 2
♡ A K 9 8 5 3
◇ K 6
♣ A 3

Therefore we win the first diamond in dummy and take an immediate club finesse. If it fails, we must win the return and play hearts from the top, hoping for an even break. If, as in the diagram, the finesse is right and East decides to cover, we win and return to dummy in spades to play the ♡7, intending to run it if East plays low. (If it then loses, we have had a 3–1 or 2–2 split). Suppose East covers. We win, while West discards, confirming the position, and return to dummy in spades for a second low heart. If East plays low, we run it and there is no further problem. If he covers again, we win and play the ♡9, losing to his remaining honour, after which our ♡8 will pick up his last trump.

This was an example of a very deep finesse against outstanding honours. We have looked at a number of hands in this section where finessing played an important part. There is an old saying among bridge teachers that: 'The first thing you learn in bridge is how to take finesses; and the second is how to avoid them!' Indeed finesses very often can be avoided and this brings us to the study of endplays.

These were the types of positions we looked at in *The Expert Beginner*:

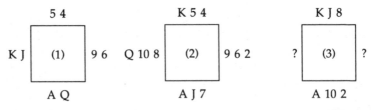

(1) Is a two-card position in which we learnt that there will be one trick each, unless West leads the suit, in which case, North-South will win both.

(2) Is a three-card position in which North-South will win two tricks and East-West one, unless West leads the suit.

(3) Is a three-card position where the queen can be caught in either hand but, if North-South have to start the suit, the declarer will have to guess whether to take a finesse against East or West. However, if East or West have to lead it, North-South will win all three tricks, irrespective of the position of the queen.

Thus we see that it can only be to our advantage if these broken holdings are played by the opponents. The object of an endplay is to make the necessary arrangements. Let us work through a simple example together.

Hand No. 33
Dealer East
Neither vulnerable

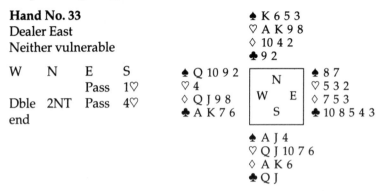

W	N	E	S
		Pass	1♡
Dble	2NT	Pass	4♡
end			

North's hand: ♠ K 6 5 3 ♡ A K 9 8 ◊ 10 4 2 ♣ 9 2

West: ♠ Q 10 9 2 ♡ 4 ◊ Q J 9 8 ♣ A K 7 6

East: ♠ 8 7 ♡ 5 3 2 ◊ 7 5 3 ♣ 10 8 5 4 3

South: ♠ A J 4 ♡ Q J 10 7 6 ◊ A K 6 ♣ Q J

After the take-out double from West, North's 2NT bid showed a good raise to 3♡.

West cashes the two top clubs and switches to the ◊Q. Even without the sight of all four hands, it is obvious to South that, with 28 points shared between his hand and his partner's, West must have the rest to justify his bidding. The two top clubs have already appeared and the ◊Q promises the jack. It is a near certainty that the spade finesse will be wrong.

That leaves us five trump tricks, two top spades and two top diamonds and we are likely to lose a diamond and a spade in addition to the two top clubs already lost. The only way out of trouble is to arrange for West to open up the spades. We win the diamond and draw trumps, West discarding two clubs. We now cash the ◊K, leaving:

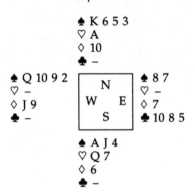

We now exit in diamonds, forcing West to win. He can now choose his road to disaster. If he plays a spade (effectively leading away from strength), we have a free finesse, saving the spade loser. If he prefers to play his diamond (or club if he has kept one), we ruff in dummy and discard the low spade from hand. This is known as a *ruff and discard*. So what effectively has happened is that we have been allowed to ruff our losing spade on dummy, saving the loser in that suit and gaining a trump winner.

Although we shall learn later that there are plenty of exceptions, the basic requirements for this type of play are that the endplayed defender should be required either to open up the awkward suit (here spades) to his cost, or play another suit, giving a ruff and discard. This second point implies that there must be at least one trump in both declarer's and dummy's hands.

Having seen the idea, try doing a couple of similar examples in match conditions in under two minutes each. Start your stopwatch.

Problem 10
Hand No. 34
Dealer South
Neither vulnerable

♠ K 6 5
♡ Q 10 9 8 6
◇ 7 3 2
♣ A K

W	N	E	S
			1♡
1♠	3♡	Pass	3♠
Pass	4♣	Pass	6♡
end			

```
      N
 W         E
      S
```

♠ A 4 3
♡ A K J 5 3
◇ A Q
♣ 8 5 3

West leads the ♠Q. Plan the play.

Problem 11
Hand No. 35
Dealer North
E–W vulnerable

♠ 5 3 2
♡ 9 8 7 6 2
◇ A Q
♣ K J 10

W	N	E	S
	Pass	Pass	1♡
1♠	3♣	Pass	3◇
Pass	4♡	end	

```
      N
 W         E
      S
```

♠ Q 7
♡ A K 5 4 3
◇ J 10 2
♣ A 5 3

Many players would prefer 3♡ over 1♠ but now South should devalue his spade holding and could well pass, relatively ignorant of his partner's hand. The 3♣ bid not only shows values in clubs on the way to 3♡ or 4♡ (or perhaps even more) but also gives South, dubious as to whether to go for game, an opportunity to ask for help in diamonds with, as we learnt in *The Expert Improver*, a *long-suit trial*.

West leads two top spades and continues with a third round, which you ruff while East follows. When you cash the ♡A, East discards the ◇3. How do you continue?

Solutions

Problem 10

We have five top trump tricks and can take a club ruff in dummy to total six. The two top spades, two top clubs and ◊A give eleven and it is clear that, on the bidding, the diamond finesse is doomed to failure.

The deal:

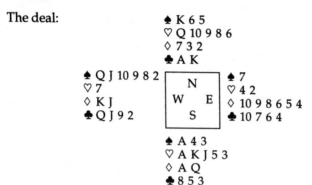

```
                    ♠ K 6 5
                    ♡ Q 10 9 8 6
                    ◊ 7 3 2
                    ♣ A K
        ♠ Q J 10 9 8 2           ♠ 7
        ♡ 7              N        ♡ 4 2
        ◊ K J         W   E      ◊ 10 9 8 6 5 4
        ♣ Q J 9 2         S      ♣ 10 7 6 4
                    ♠ A 4 3
                    ♡ A K J 5 3
                    ◊ A Q
                    ♣ 8 5 3
```

The only way out is to force West to open up that suit at a moment inconvenient for him. We win the first spade in dummy and draw trumps, West discarding a spade on the second round. Now the clubs must be eliminated so that, if West plays the suit later, he will give us a ruff and discard. We cash the two top clubs and cross back to hand with the ♠A. (That was why we preferred to win the opening lead in dummy – we would have had to use trumps otherwise – in this hand, it does not matter as we have plenty of trumps to spare; but that may not happen every time.) Now we ruff our last club in dummy, *eliminating* the suit from both hands to leave:

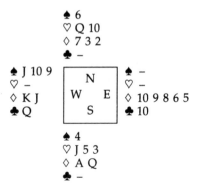

```
              ♠ 6
              ♡ Q 10
              ◊ 7 3 2
              ♣ -
♠ J 10 9                    ♠ -
♡ -          ┌─────────┐    ♡ -
◊ K J        │    N    │    ◊ 10 9 8 6 5
♣ Q          │ W     E │    ♣ 10
             │    S    │
             └─────────┘
              ♠ 4
              ♡ J 5 3
              ◊ A Q
              ♣ -
```

We now exit in spades, forcing West to win. He now has the choice of playing a diamond, to give us a free finesse, or a black card, which we would ruff in dummy, while discarding our losing ◊Q from hand. We ruff dummy's losing diamonds afterwards.

Problem 11
We have already lost two top spades and, with West's hearts solid, a trump loser is inevitable. Thus we cannot afford a diamond loser and will have to assume that the finesse is right. Even now, we have to find the ♣Q. With eight of West's cards known to be in the majors and we have credited him with the ◊K, it is short odds that the ♣Q will be with East but there is no guarantee. We can ensure the contract only if the defenders have to open up the suit.

The deal:

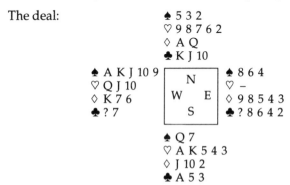

```
              ♠ 5 3 2
              ♡ 9 8 7 6 2
              ◊ A Q
              ♣ K J 10
♠ A K J 10 9                ♠ 8 6 4
♡ Q J 10     ┌─────────┐    ♡ -
◊ K 7 6      │    N    │    ◊ 9 8 5 4 3
♣ ? 7        │ W     E │    ♣ ? 8 6 4 2
             │    S    │
             └─────────┘
              ♠ Q 7
              ♡ A K 5 4 3
              ◊ J 10 2
              ♣ A 5 3
```

The ♣Q and ♣9 are as yet unplaced. After the ♡A, it looks tempting to cash the ♡K in preparation for throwing the lead to

West with the ♡Q, but that is fatal and this hand illustrates the importance of playing the entire contract out in your own mind before actually playing the cards. It is vital to eliminate diamonds completely before the throw-in. We shall therefore need to take the finesse, cash the ace and return to hand to ruff the ◊J. We can only reach our hand with the ♡K.

If we use the ♣A, the tenace position will be spoilt and now, if East has the ♣Q, we will be defeated as West can get off play in clubs. Thus we must take the diamond finesse immediately and cash the ◊A. If the ◊K does not fall, we now return to hand with the ♡K and ruff our last diamond. That leaves:

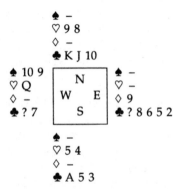

```
                    ♠ –
                    ♡ 9 8
                    ◊ –
                    ♣ K J 10
    ♠ 10 9      ┌─────────┐      ♠ –
    ♡ Q         │    N    │      ♡ –
    ◊ –         │  W   E  │      ◊ 9
    ♣ ? 7       │    S    │      ♣ ? 8 6 5 2
                └─────────┘
                    ♠ –
                    ♡ 5 4
                    ◊ –
                    ♣ A 5 3
```

We now exit in trumps, losing to West, who must either play a club, saving us the guess or play a spade, which we ruff in either hand, discarding a club loser from the other.

You should satisfy yourself that there is another way to make this contract from the above position – a perfect illustration of the use of counting a hand. The bidding and early play marked West with five spades, three hearts and, as the ◊K did not fall on the first two rounds (had he done so, the ◊J would have been established for a club discard), at least three diamonds. That accounts for eleven of his cards and he therefore cannot have more than two clubs. Instead of throwing the lead to him immediately in trumps, we could have cashed the ♣A and ♣K and *then* thrown the lead to him in trumps. Either the ♣Q falls on the two top clubs, or if she doesn't, West is left having to lead a spade, again giving us a ruff and discard.

This brings us to another use of the endplay. Not only can we avoid finesses which are anything from possible to certain losers, but we may be able to avoid top losers where no finesse is even available. This is a simple example.

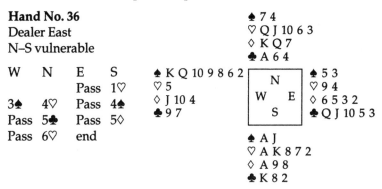

Hand No. 36
Dealer East
N–S vulnerable

W	N	E	S
		Pass	1♡
3♠	4♡	Pass	4♠
Pass	5♣	Pass	5♢
Pass	6♡	end	

West leads the ♠K and, when the dummy goes down, South is sad to see identical patterns in the two hands. However, with a long suit advertized on his left, there is a chance despite the apparent certainty of a loser in each black suit. Declarer wins the opening lead, draws trumps, West discarding a spade on the second round, and cashes the three top diamonds. Now he cashes the two top clubs, hoping to find West with, at most, a doubleton. Then he exits in spades in this position:

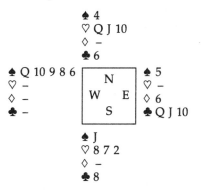

West has to win and, left with nothing but spades, has to give a ruff and discard, allowing the club loser to disappear. Note that, if

West, rather than East, had held the last diamond, there would have been no difference – it still gives a ruff and discard.

Now just to prove that you have understood the point, how would you play this hand – a slightly altered version of the above – in under two minutes? Start your stop-watch.

Problem 12

Hand No. 37

Dealer East

N–S vulnerable

♠	7 4 3		
♡	Q J 10 6		
◊	K Q 7		
♣	A 6 4		

W	N	E	S
		Pass	1♡
3♠	4♡	Pass	4♠
Pass	5♣	Pass	5◊
Pass	6♡	end	

```
      N
  W       E
      S
```

♠ A J
♡ A K 8 7 2
◊ A 9 8
♣ K 8 2

Again, West leads the ♠K and again he discards a spade on the second round of trumps. How do you play this time?

With the extra spade in dummy, the line of play suggested in Hand 36 will not work as West will be able to exit with a third round of spades. With dummy still following, there is no ruff and discard and East waits for his club trick. But – no matter! The preemptive bid marks East with a likely singleton spade and we turn our attention to him. Instead of trying to avoid the club loser, we aim to avoid the spade loser instead! We win the opening spade lead, draw trumps (the extra round necessary does not hurt us as North has four trumps), and eliminate the diamonds. Now we cash the two top clubs to leave this position:

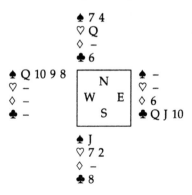

Now we exit in clubs, forcing East to win and he has the choice of giving us our ruff and discard in either minor. We discard our ♠J and ruff in dummy, claiming the last two trump tricks in hand.

Defenders' hand:

The above few examples are a mere scratch on the surface of the world of endplays and we shall learn in future studies that, where complete eliminations are impossible, we can manage on *partial* eliminations and, contrary to the above indication, it is indeed not always necessary to have trumps in both hands. But the above is a reasonable introduction to what is a very big subject. One of the principal reasons why we spent so much time discussing two-and three-card positions in a single suit in *The Expert Beginner* was to learn which suit combinations we could touch, without giving away a trick, and which we could not. Endplay studies illustrate the application.

Returning to the theme of avoiding dubious finesses, we are now going to consider a technique known as 'smoking out', which will very often save you wrong 'guesses'. Listening to the bidding will very often give you a vital clue. Let us work through this example together.

Hand No. 38
Dealer West
Neither vulnerable

♠ A J 10 6
♡ A K 8
◇ J 10 4
♣ 6 4 3

W	N	E	S
Pass	1NT	Pass	3♠
Pass	4♠	end	

```
         N
    W         E
         S
```

♠ Q 9 8 7 2
♡ Q 3
◇ 9 8 6
♣ A K Q

West cashes the three top diamonds, all following. He continues with the ♡J. How do you plan the play?

The clubs and hearts are solid so it appears to be merely a question of catching the ♠K. There doesn't seem much to discuss. The finesse offers a 50% chance of success while dropping the singleton king needs a 3–1 break (50%) with the king as singleton (¼ x 50% = 12.5%). The odds are overwhelmingly in favour of the finesse.

Or are they? One of the basic rules of both declarer play and defence is that any assumptions made must be consistent with the bidding and play to date. I said in the above paragraph that the finesse offers a 50% chance. Nonsense! The actual chance is nil! West has already produced the three top diamonds (9 points) plus the ♡J to total 10. Give him the king of spades as well and that makes 13, in which case he would surely have opened as dealer. What we are actually comparing is 12.5% against nil and now the odds are overwhelmingly in favour of the drop!

The deal:

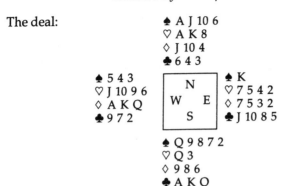

Notice that, had North been the dealer, West would have had no reason to bid after 1NT from North and 3♠ from South, even with 13 points. The above argument would not now hold and the finesse would have been the correct percentage play.

Having grasped the idea, you should have little difficulty with this next example, although, this time, a little research will be needed. See if you can do this one in under two minutes. Start your stop-watch.

Problem 13
Hand No. 39
Dealer East
Both vulnerable

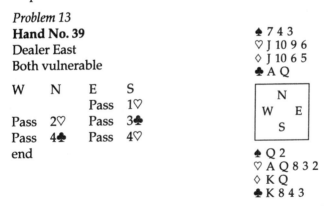

W	N	E	S
		Pass	1♡
Pass	2♡	Pass	3♣
Pass	4♣	Pass	4♡
end			

Asked for help in clubs, North has sensational support and bids 4♣ just in case South had made the long-suit trial, looking for a slam.

West leads the ♠J and East cashes the ♠K and ♠A. On the third round, you ruff, West still following. How do you continue?

East has shown up with the two top spade honours, 7 points. If he has the ◊A as well, that will give him 11, in which case, having declined to open as dealer, he will be debarred from holding the ♡K. In that event, we shall have no alternative but to play for the drop in hearts. If West has the ◊A, East can still have the ♡K, in which case the finesse will be the percentage play.

Our first duty, therefore, is to 'smoke out' the ◊A. We play our diamond honours and the ace will have to appear, otherwise the defenders will lose their trick in that suit. If East has it, we play for the drop in trumps. If West has it, we will cross to dummy in clubs and take the trump finesse.

The deal:

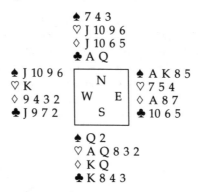

```
                    ♠ 7 4 3
                    ♡ J 10 9 6
                    ◊ J 10 6 5
                    ♣ A Q
    ♠ J 10 9 6                      ♠ A K 8 5
    ♡ K              N              ♡ 7 5 4
    ◊ 9 4 3 2    W       E          ◊ A 8 7
    ♣ J 9 7 2        S              ♣ 10 6 5
                    ♠ Q 2
                    ♡ A Q 8 3 2
                    ◊ K Q
                    ♣ K 8 4 3
```

Here the problem was how to draw trumps, but in the earlier books we emphasized that this often has to be delayed so that trumps can made separately, ruffing side suits. Beginners are commonly taught to look at their own hand (South), note the losers and see how many of them the dummy could deal with by ruffing. However, very often it pays to look for the possibility of treating the dummy as the 'master' hand and try to ruff its losers in declarer's hand.

A declarer is likely to consider a 'reverse dummy' when there are three good trumps in the dummy and there is a 4–3 fit in a side suit, where it will be inconvenient to look after the long card in the likely event of a 4–2 or more unbalanced split. This is a typical example:

Hand No. 40
Dealer South
E–W vulnerable

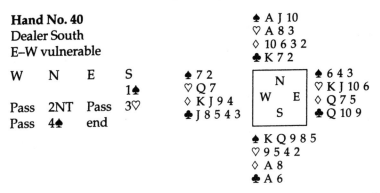

W	N	E	S
			1♠
Pass	2NT	Pass	3♡
Pass	4♠	end	

♠ A J 10
♡ A 8 3
◊ 10 6 3 2
♣ K 7 2

♠ 7 2
♡ Q 7
◊ K J 9 4
♣ J 8 5 4 3

♠ 6 4 3
♡ K J 10 6
◊ Q 7 5
♣ Q 10 9

♠ K Q 9 8 5
♡ 9 5 4 2
◊ A 8
♣ A 6

We have five trump tricks, two clubs and the two red aces to total nine on top. It will pay to play this hand out twice according to the opening lead. Say West leads a club. Now we can arrange to ruff the fourth losing heart in dummy. We win and play the ace and another heart, losing. Say they now switch to a trump. We win and play a third round of hearts. If they prove to split 3–3, the fourth heart is high and there is nothing further to discuss. As it is, the third heart loses to East as West shows out and East plays a second trump. We win in hand and ruff the fourth heart high in dummy to make our tenth trick.

However, let us try again but from West's point of view. The bidding suggests that North-South's hearts are 4–3 or, less likely, 4–2 and therefore ruffs on dummy are threatened. He therefore leads a trump. Now the defenders are a move ahead. If we pursue the above line of play we will be defeated. Each time the defenders gain the lead in hearts, they will persist with trumps, removing dummy's holding in time and the ruff will not materialize. We will now lose three heart tricks and the inevitable diamond. The solution is to reverse the dummy and try to ruff minor-suit losers in hand. We win the trump lead and set up the ruffs in hand by playing the ace and another diamond. The defenders are likely to play a second trump which we win in dummy and ruff a diamond. The ace and king of clubs are followed by the last club, ruffed in hand and, on returning to dummy with the ♡A, we ruff the last diamond in hand. We have thus taken three minor-suit ruffs in hand and there is still a high trump in dummy to cash. These, added to the two top trump tricks taken early on plus the four top tricks in side suits, total ten.

Having grasped the idea, you should have no difficulty with this next example and should be able to do it in under ninety seconds.

Problem 14
Hand No. 41
Dealer North
Both vulnerable

♠ K J 9
♡ 6 2
◇ A J 7 5
♣ A K J 7

W	N	E	S
	1♣	Pass	1♠
Pass	2◇	Pass	2♡
Pass	3♠	Pass	4♠
end			

```
      N
   W     E
      S
```

♠ A Q 10 6 4
♡ K 9 5 4
◇ 2
♣ 8 5 4

We could have a fairly lengthy discussion about the bidding of this hand, notably regarding North's first rebid. Give it to a panel of experts and there will be several who would rebid 2NT without a second thought, describing the hand as 17–18 points, balanced, with the poor heart holding being partially mitigated by the fact that, if 3NT is the final contract, the bigger hand, at least, will be closed. Others would prefer a direct 3♠ (for which many would demand a four-card trump support). This would allow for 3NT to be played by partner and I think it is instructive that cases where 3NT is preferred to 4♠ are likely to arise when partner has only four spades and therefore, by implication of his 1♠ bid, three or fewer hearts. Now it is likely to be crucial to have partner as declarer. My choice, as above, is for a forcing reverse with 2◇. True, this promises five clubs but, as I have emphasized many times in the earlier books, it seldom does a great deal of harm to lie about the length of a minor and, particularly in this case, it is most unlikely to do much harm when there is the intention to support spades anyway and the four-card club suit is very strong and will not be disastrous if played in a 4–3 fit.

So you see three schools of thought on the subject and there is no correct bid. The important thing is to be able to justify the bid you do choose. After 2◊, note South's use of the fourth-suit-forcing 2♡. He has the hearts well stopped for no-trumps but this gives partner a chance to clarify his hand further, while keeping options for game in spades or no-trumps open.

West leads the ◊K. How do you plan the play? Start your stopwatch.

We have five top trump tricks and three in the minors to total eight and, in the absence of a trump lead, we cannot be denied one heart ruff. Therefore, we see that, if the ♡A is well placed with East, ten tricks will present no problem. If it isn't, the defenders are bound to switch to trumps each time they gain the lead in hearts, restricting us to one ruff in dummy and leaving us banking on the club finesse. Admittedly, we will be unlucky to fail with ♡A and ♣Q badly placed but can we improve our chances?

The solution lies in reversing the dummy. Win the opening lead and ruff a diamond in hand. Return to dummy with the ♣A and ruff another diamond. Return to dummy again with the ♣K and (if the ◊Q has not already fallen to set up our ◊J), ruff the last diamond. Now exit with a club. Assuming that the ♣Q has not already fallen, this trick will be lost but now nothing can prevent us from ruffing dummy's fourth club in hand. That gives us four ruffs in hand and, with three top trump tricks waiting in dummy, we have seven trump tricks in all. Add the three top minor-suit winners and we have ten tricks altogether.

The deal:

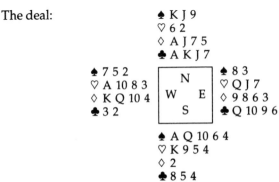

```
                    ♠ K J 9
                    ♡ 6 2
                    ◊ A J 7 5
                    ♣ A K J 7
    ♠ 7 5 2          ┌───────┐      ♠ 8 3
    ♡ A 10 8 3       │   N   │      ♡ Q J 7
    ◊ K Q 10 4    W  │       │  E   ◊ 9 8 6 3
    ♣ 3 2            │   S   │      ♣ Q 10 9 6
                    └───────┘
                    ♠ A Q 10 6 4
                    ♡ K 9 5 4
                    ◊ 2
                    ♣ 8 5 4
```

We are going to conclude with a nine-question test covering the points learnt in this section. You should be able to do each in about a minute, completing the whole test in comfortably under ten minutes. Start your stop-watch.

Problem 15
Hand No. 42
Dealer North
E–W vulnerable

♠ 7 5 2
♡ K Q 9
♢ Q 9 7 5
♣ K J 2

W	N	E	S
	Pass	Pass	1♢
Pass	3♢	Pass	3♡
Pass	4♣	Pass	6♢
end			

```
      N
  W       E
      S
```

♠ A 8
♡ A J 7 4
♢ A J 10 8 6
♣ A 7

After North's first response, South could well settle for an immediate 3NT but, when North shows no values in spades (he would have bid 3♠ with a half-stop or 3NT with a full stop), South knows that there is only one loser in that suit and now a slam may be on. North's bid of 4♣ showed club values (more informative than a simple 4♢).

West leads the ♠K. Plan the play.

Problem 16
Hand No. 43
Dealer South
N–S vulnerable

♠ A 8 7 5
♡ A 3
♢ 9 7 4
♣ A K 7 2

W	N	E	S
			1♠
Pass	2♣	Pass	2NT
Pass	3♠	Pass	4♢
Pass	4♡	Pass	4♠
Pass	5♣	Pass	5♡
Pass	6♠	end	

```
      N
  W       E
      S
```

♠ K Q J 10 6
♡ K 8 7
♢ A Q 10
♣ 5 4

North's 3♠ bid is forcing; and therefore it costs nothing for South to cue-bid his ◊A below game. More cue-bidding followed.

West leads the ♡J. When you draw trumps, they prove to split 2–2. Plan the play.

Problem 17
Hand No. 44
Dealer East
Both vulnerable

W	N	E	S
		Pass	1♡
Pass	2◊	Pass	3◊
Pass	3♡	Pass	4♡
end			

♠ 9 7 5
♡ A J 4
◊ J 9 6 5 3
♣ A J

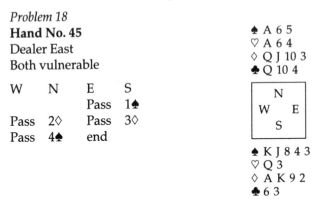

♠ A J 10
♡ K Q 10 6 5
◊ A 7 4 2
♣ 7

West leads the ◊10. Plan the play.

Problem 18
Hand No. 45
Dealer East
Both vulnerable

W	N	E	S
		Pass	1♠
Pass	2◊	Pass	3◊
Pass	4♠	end	

♠ A 6 5
♡ A 6 4
◊ Q J 10 3
♣ Q 10 4

♠ K J 8 4 3
♡ Q 3
◊ A K 9 2
♣ 6 3

West leads the ♣9. You put on dummy's ♣10 but East produces the ♣J and cashes the ♣K. He continues with the ♣A, which you ruff, West still following. How do you continue?

Problem 19
Hand No. 46
Dealer North
E–W vulnerable

♠ 6 5 3
♡ 9 7 6 5
◇ A K 9 3
♣ K 2

W	N	E	S
	Pass	Pass	4♡
end			

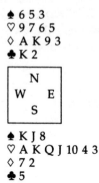

♠ K J 8
♡ A K Q J 10 4 3
◇ 7 2
♣ 5

West leads the ♣Q and you ruff the second round of the suit. All follow to the ace of trumps. How do you continue?

Problem 20
Hand No. 47
Dealer North
N–S vulnerable

♠ A 10 9 8
♡ A 7
◇ 7 4 2
♣ Q 7 6 5

W	N	E	S
	Pass	Pass	2NT
Pass	3♣	Pass	3♠
Pass	5♠	Pass	6♠
end			

♠ K Q J 4
♡ K 9 6
◇ A K Q 8
♣ K 2

West leads the ♡Q. Plan the play.

Problem 21
Hand No. 48
Dealer West
Neither vulnerable

♠ Q J 10
♡ A K J
♢ 8 7 4
♣ 8 7 6 4

W	N	E	S
Pass	Pass	Pass	1♢
Pass	2NT	Pass	4♢
Pass	4♡	Pass	6♢
end			

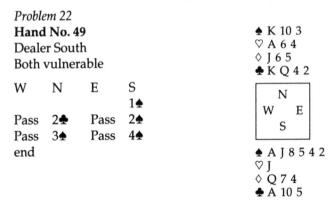

♠ A 4
♡ Q 10 8
♢ A Q 10 6 5 3
♣ A K

After North had shown 11–12 points, South's jump to 4♢ (going past 3NT) is forcing and sets the suit as trumps, asking his partner to cue-bid, if possible, with a view to a slam.

West leads the ♣Q. Plan the play.

Problem 22
Hand No. 49
Dealer South
Both vulnerable

♠ K 10 3
♡ A 6 4
♢ J 6 5
♣ K Q 4 2

W	N	E	S
			1♠
Pass	2♣	Pass	2♠
Pass	3♠	Pass	4♠
end			

♠ A J 8 5 4 2
♡ J
♢ Q 7 4
♣ A 10 5

West leads the ♡K. Plan the play.

Problem 23
Hand No. 50
Dealer West
Both vulnerable

♠ 9 8 5 4
♡ 8 6 4 2
◇ A K 9
♣ 6 2

W	N	E	S
3♣	Pass	Pass	4♣
Pass	4♡	Pass	4♠
Pass	5♠	Pass	6♠
end			

```
        N
    W       E
        S
```

♠ A K Q J 10 3
♡ A Q
◇ Q 8 2
♣ A Q

West leads the ◇5. Plan the play.

Solutions

Problem 15

It seems to be a question of catching the king of trumps but there is also the possibility of a successful club finesse, in which case we could discard our spade loser and still get home. How do we combine the chances? We cannot take the diamond finesse immediately because, if it loses, we shall lose a spade trick and the contract immediately, possibly with the club finesse right all the time. Similarly, if we try the club finesse first, we could lose that way with the trump finesse right.

The guide of 'drop first, then finesse' gives us the best chance of two bites at the cherry. We have a greater chance of dropping a singleton ◇K (¼ x 50% = 12.5%) than a doubleton ♣Q (⅓ x 17.1% = 5.7%) and it should also be appreciated that playing for the club drop first is a non-starter anyway. If the ♣Q did indeed drop in two rounds, we probably could not cash the third round for a spade discard without being ruffed!

The correct line, therefore, is to win the opening lead and lay down the ◇A. If the ◇K fails to appear, cash the ♣A and try the finesse, hoping for an early spade discard.

The deal:

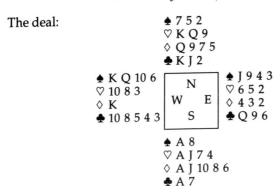

```
                    ♠ 7 5 2
                    ♡ K Q 9
                    ◊ Q 9 7 5
                    ♣ K J 2
  ♠ K Q 10 6                      ♠ J 9 4 3
  ♡ 10 8 3         N              ♡ 6 5 2
  ◊ K           W     E           ◊ 4 3 2
  ♣ 10 8 5 4 3      S             ♣ Q 9 6
                    ♠ A 8
                    ♡ A J 7 4
                    ◊ A J 10 8 6
                    ♣ A 7
```

Problem 16

We have five top spade tricks and can take a heart ruff in the short-trump hand to make six. Add the two top hearts, two top clubs and the ◊A gives eleven, so it seems a question of avoiding two diamond losers. One line of play is simply to take two diamond finesses through East, giving us a 75% chance. However, once the trumps have broken, we can make this contract for certain. By drawing trumps and eliminating the clubs and hearts, we can endplay West should he be unkind enough to turn up with both outstanding diamond honours.

    This hand shows the importance of planning the *whole hand* before playing a card to the first trick. In which hand should we win the first heart? We need to finish the elimination in dummy so that we can start diamonds from there, so we should keep as many entries in that hand as possible. We win the lead in hand and draw trumps. Now follow the ace and king of clubs and a third round, ruffed in hand. We then cross back to the ♡A and play the last club, again ruffing in hand. Finally, we return to dummy with a heart ruff to leave a position like this:

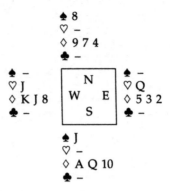

Now we play a low diamond from dummy and put either the ten or queen on. If this loses to West, he will have the choice of either returning the suit round to our tenace, thereby giving us a free finesse, or playing his heart, giving a ruff and discard.

The deal:

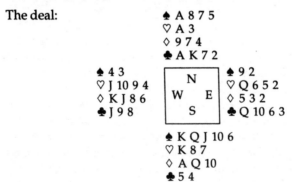

Notice that, had we won the first heart on dummy and then drawn trumps, we would have been in difficulties. We now finish the elimination in the wrong hand. The observant student will rush to point out that, even in that case, we can still make the contract by exiting with the ◇Q or ◇10 from hand, West still being obliged to win and to be left endplayed. However, exiting with the ◇10 is fatal if the diamond position turns out to be:

```
            9 7 4
          ┌───────┐
          │   N   │
   K x x  │ W   E │  J x x
          │   S   │
          └───────┘
           A Q 10
```

and exiting with the queen fails if the diamond position turns out to be:

```
            9 7 4
          ┌───────┐
          │   N   │
   J x x  │ W   E │  K x x
          │   S   │
          └───────┘
           A Q 10
```

Playing from dummy, leading from weakness towards strength, is always safe and the play should be arranged accordingly.

Problem 17

We have five top trump tricks and three or four diamonds, depending on the split. The two black aces brings our total to ten. However, enemy plans may result in two tricks lost in diamonds, assuming a 3–1 split, and two in spades should West have both outstanding honours. We therefore realize that the contract is not in danger if the diamonds break evenly; at worst, we could lose a diamond and two spades and, in reality, we shall be in time to discard one of our spades on dummy's fifth diamond to finish with an overtrick. We must therefore consider the 3–1 split (likely, as West has led a suit bid and supported against him) and the possibility of his holding both spade honours. We can set out the two three-card positions typical of the types studied in *The Expert Beginner*.

```
       ◊ J 9 6                        ♠ 9 7 5
     ┌───────┐                      ┌───────┐
     │   N   │                      │   N   │
◊ 10 │ W   E │ ◊ K Q 8     ♠ K Q x  │ W   E │ ♠ x x x
     │   S   │                      │   S   │
     └───────┘                      └───────┘
      ◊ A 7 4                        ♠ A J 10
```

In diamonds, we are bound to lose two tricks and win one but we
see that we have some choice regarding which defender wins the
two tricks. We shall see, when considering the spades, that this
could be vital. In the right-hand diagram, we shall lose two tricks
and win one, *unless* West leads the suit. In that event, we could win
two tricks and lose only one. It was mentioned above that, if we
can establish the long diamonds in time, we can discard a spade
loser on the fifth round, ensuring that we will never lose more than
one trick in that suit. We therefore realize that the dangerous
situation arises if East is permitted to lead the suit twice before the
diamonds are established and cashed. So we reconsider the
diamond position. If we cover the ten with the jack, East will play
an honour and now both tricks will be lost to East. He can then
play spades, from his weakness through our strength to his partner's strength, and now we lose four tricks before we can win ten.

The solution is to ensure that we lose a diamond trick to *West* by
playing low in both hands on the first trick, allowing the ◊10 to
hold. West now cannot profitably attack spades and will probably
switch to clubs. We win in dummy, draw trumps and play the ace
and another diamond. We win the spade return and play the rest
of the diamonds, discarding a spade loser, conceding one spade
trick at the end.

The deal:

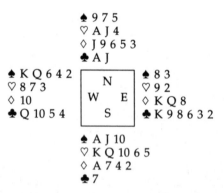

```
              ♠ 9 7 5
              ♡ A J 4
              ◊ J 9 6 5 3
              ♣ A J
♠ K Q 6 4 2    ┌─────────┐    ♠ 8 3
♡ 8 7 3        │    N    │    ♡ 9 2
◊ 10           │  W   E  │    ◊ K Q 8
♣ Q 10 5 4     │    S    │    ♣ K 9 8 6 3 2
              └─────────┘
              ♠ A J 10
              ♡ K Q 10 6 5
              ◊ A 7 4 2
              ♣ 7
```

It seems so automatic to cover that ◊10 with the ◊J when we hold
the ◊9. Notice that, once dummy has played low, East cannot
afford to put up an honour. If he does, the J 9 will be solid against
his K 8 and we will only lose one diamond trick.

Problem 18

Barring the unlikely possibility of the ♡K being a singleton, there is an inevitable heart loser, so the fate of this contract seems to hang on finding the ♠Q. The percentage play, considering the suit in isolation, is to cash the ♠A, covering the possibility of a singleton ♠Q with West, and then take the finesse against East. However, before committing ourselves to that line, we can do a little research, which could prove very revealing. East has already shown up with 8 points in clubs and, if he has the ♡K as well, that would give him 11. He passed as dealer and is therefore debarred from holding the ♠Q. In that event, we should assume that she is with West and prefer to play the ace and king, hoping for the drop.

The deal:

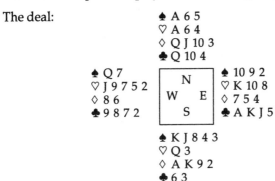

```
                    ♠ A 6 5
                    ♡ A 6 4
                    ◇ Q J 10 3
                    ♣ Q 10 4
    ♠ Q 7                          ♠ 10 9 2
    ♡ J 9 7 5 2        N           ♡ K 10 8
    ◇ 8 6          W       E       ◇ 7 5 4
    ♣ 9 8 7 2         S           ♣ A K J 5
                    ♠ K J 8 4 3
                    ♡ Q 3
                    ◇ A K 9 2
                    ♣ 6 3
```

We therefore smoke out the ♡K by playing the ace and another heart. If West has the ♡K, we take the percentage line in trumps, finessing against East. If East has the ♡K, we play for the drop.

Problem 19

We have seven top trump tricks and two top diamonds to total nine and it seems to be question of avoiding three spade losers. The three-card position is the converse of that in Problem 16:

```
        x x x                         x x x
         N                             N
K J x  W   E  x x x         A Q 10  W   E  x x x
         S                             S
       A Q 10                         K J 8
```

On the left, we saw that we can arrange to reduce the two losers to one by drawing trumps, eliminating the side-suits and playing a low card towards the queen or ten. West is forced to win and must either return the suit, giving us a free finesse, or lead another suit, conceding a ruff and discard.

On the right, the position is similar, except that we are trying to reduce our losses from three to two. When we play a low card to the jack or king, West again has to win and must give us free finesse, by leading away from his strength, or a ruff and discard.

On this occasion, however, extra care is required to arrange the elimination, bearing in mind that, for reasons explained in the solution to Problem 16, we must finish in dummy so that we can start the spades from there. We need to ruff both diamonds so, after drawing trumps, we will cash the two top diamonds and ruff a third round. We return to dummy and ruff a fourth round, returning to dummy once more to start the spades. These entries can only be attained in trumps, which means that the two low trumps in our hand must be held until needed.

We therefore ruff the second club *high*. After the ace of trumps and two top diamonds, we ruff the third diamond *high* and return to dummy by overtaking the ♡3 with the ♡7. Now we ruff the fourth diamond *high* and return to dummy again by overtaking our ♡4 with the ♡9. That leaves a position like this:

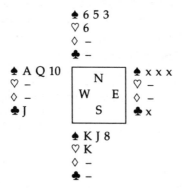

```
              ♠ 6 5 3
              ♡ 6
              ◊ –
              ♣ –
  ♠ A Q 10    ┌─────────┐   ♠ x x x
  ♡ –         │    N    │   ♡ –
  ◊ –         │  W   E  │   ◊ –
  ♣ J         │    S    │   ♣ x
              └─────────┘
              ♠ K J 8
              ♡ K
              ◊ –
              ♣ –
```

Now a spade to the jack or king forces West to win and lead away from his strength in the suit or give a ruff and discard with the club.

The deal:

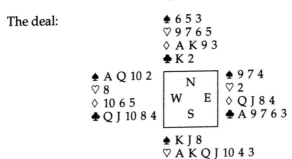

```
              ♠ 6 5 3
              ♡ 9 7 6 5
              ◊ A K 9 3
              ♣ K 2
♠ A Q 10 2                    ♠ 9 7 4
♡ 8            N              ♡ 2
◊ 10 6 5    W     E           ◊ Q J 8 4
♣ Q J 10 8 4     S            ♣ A 9 7 6 3
              ♠ K J 8
              ♡ A K Q J 10 4 3
              ◊ 7 2
              ♣ 5
```

Quite a mouthful, but the story is not over by a long way! Let us look at those spades again.

```
        6 5 3
          N
A Q 10  W     E   x x x
          S
        K J 8
```

We have just seen that, if we can force West to lead a round, we shall save a trick. But if East can lead the suit, we are in trouble. With that in mind, how did you play to trick one when the ♣Q was led? It is obvious that the ♣A is with East, so it is clear that we shall lose one trick and win none, irrespective of our play. In the context of the club suit alone, that is quite correct. But, when considering the whole hand, the choice is critical. Suppose we cover with the ♣K. East wins and now, if he switches to spades, say we try the ♠J, West can win and switch to any other suit cheaply; probably he will try to cash another club. The spades are now reduced to the two-card position:

```
        x x
          N
A 10    W     E   x x
          S
        K 8
```

West cannot be forced to lead them and we lose two more tricks. But now try the effect of playing low at trick one and the defence is sunk. If East allows the ♣Q to hold, West cannot profitably attack spades from his side and we can reduce to the three-card position above. On the other hand, if East overtakes with the ♣A to switch to spades, he sets up dummy's ♣K as our tenth trick, on which we shall discard a losing spade.

In my books for advanced players, I tend to differ from other authors in that, whereas the usual format is to take readers up to the critical point in play and then ask for a continuation, I occasionally stop well short of, or go way past, the moment of truth. This is much nearer to reality in that no player, in any class of bridge, is allowed a timely tap on the shoulder!

Problem 20

We have four top trump tricks, two top hearts, three top diamonds and at least one club, after knocking out the ♣A, to total ten so far. A heart ruff on dummy will give one more. The twelfth could come from a fourth diamond if the suit breaks evenly; but, if it doesn't, we could have problems. We could try to ruff the fourth losing diamond on dummy but that implies that three top rounds would have to be played first. That could not be done safely before trumps are drawn, which would take a minimum of three rounds. That would leave only one trump in dummy, ruling out the possibility of ruffing both the diamond *and* the heart.

One possible solution is to play just two rounds of trumps and then start on diamonds, still being safe if they break 3–3 but giving us the chance that, if there is a 4–2 split, the hand with the long diamonds also has the outstanding trump. However, there is a better line, the 4–3 diamond fit giving the clue. Try reversing the dummy, aiming to ruff two clubs in our hand instead of the two red-suit ruffs in dummy.

With the scarcity of entries to dummy, it is probably best to preserve the ♡A and win the opening lead in hand. Suppose the deal looks like this:

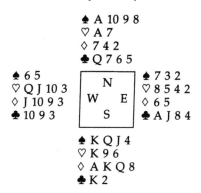

```
              ♠ A 10 9 8
              ♡ A 7
              ◊ 7 4 2
              ♣ Q 7 6 5
  ♠ 6 5                        ♠ 7 3 2
  ♡ Q J 10 3      N           ♡ 8 5 4 2
  ◊ J 10 9 3    W   E         ◊ 6 5
  ♣ 10 9 3        S           ♣ A J 8 4
              ♠ K Q J 4
              ♡ K 9 6
              ◊ A K Q 8
              ♣ K 2
```

We play the ♣K at trick two and East, confident that we have at least another club (having opened 2NT) can make matters awkward by playing low. He wins the second round and plays a heart, won on dummy. A club, ruffed with an honour, is followed by the ♠4 to the ♠8 and another club ruff. Now we overtake our last trump with the ♠A and draw trumps, surviving even if they break 4–1. Play the hand over for yourself, winning the first heart in dummy, and you will see that the entry situation leads to defeat if the trumps are indeed 4–1.

Problem 21

Outside the trump suit, six tricks are available on top and the spade finesse may provide a seventh. If it succeeds, we shall need five trump tricks; if not, we must hope for all six. We look at the trump suit in that light. To take all the tricks, the best line is to finesse the ◊Q, succeeding if East holds a doubleton king or exactly ◊ K x x. However, if we need only five tricks, our first priority is to avoid losing two. Should West turn up with both outstanding honours among a trebleton or more, there is no hope. But we can ensure the contract against any other distribution by cashing the ace first and then leading from dummy towards the queen and ten. This protects against a singleton honour in West's hand or a doubleton K J while still preserving the contract if East has both honours at the expense of the possible overtrick. Note that, if we preferred to finesse the ten first and it lost to the jack, we would sit wondering whether to play for the second finesse or drop of the king if East followed low on the second round.

Similarly if we finesse the queen first, losing to the king, we would be in a similar dilemma regarding how to catch the jack on the second round.

So we see that the best method of handling the trump suit depends on the position of the ♠K and our first duty is to smoke him out. We win the first club in hand and cross to dummy in hearts to run the ♠Q. If it loses, we will win the presumed club return, cross again to dummy in hearts and play a trump to the queen, hoping for the best. If the spade finesse succeeds, we cash the ◊A. If an honour drops, there is no further problem. If both defenders play low, we shall return to dummy in hearts to play a low diamond towards our tenace, losing only if East now discards. Finally, if West shows out on the ◊A, we still have two more entries to dummy in hearts to play diamonds through East's ◊ K J x for the double finesse, conceding one trick only.

The deal:

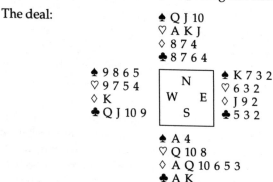

```
                 ♠ Q J 10
                 ♡ A K J
                 ◊ 8 7 4
                 ♣ 8 7 6 4
   ♠ 9 8 6 5                    ♠ K 7 3 2
   ♡ 9 7 5 4         N          ♡ 6 3 2
   ◊ K            W     E       ◊ J 9 2
   ♣ Q J 10 9        S          ♣ 5 3 2
                 ♠ A 4
                 ♡ Q 10 8
                 ◊ A Q 10 6 5 3
                 ♣ A K
```

Problem 22

There is the ♡A plus three club tricks on top and a possible fourth if the ♣J falls in three rounds. In addition, there are five or six trumps, according to whether the queen can be caught. Therefore the contract is only in danger if three diamond tricks and the ♠Q are lost. Let us first look at the diamond position in detail. There will be no danger if the ace and king are in the same hand. A low card played towards either honour followed by another low card towards the other will ensure one trick. However, if the honours are split, as here:

```
              J 6 5
          ┌─────────┐
          │    N    │
  K 10 x  │  W   E  │  A 9 x
          │    S    │
          └─────────┘
              Q 7 4
```

then, as we learnt in the beginners' book, we shall lose three tricks if we have to start the suit ourselves but only two if either opponent has to lead it.

We also note that, in the club suit, we shall be certain of four tricks, irrespective of the split or position of the jack, if West leads it.

In the trump suit, in positions where the queen is missing and there are options to play for the drop or the finesse (in one or both directions), it is usually wise to ask whether any benefit can be gained if the trick is lost to a specific opponent. As we have just seen when considering both minors, this hand is a case in point. If a trick is lost to West, and he can be forced to open up either minor, he will have to give us a trick. We therefore win the first heart and start an immediate elimination of the suit by ruffing a heart in hand. We then cross to dummy with the ♣K (this does not disturb the tenace position) and ruff the last heart to complete the elimination. Now the ♠K is followed by another spade towards the ace-jack. If East plays low, we put in the jack. If it holds, the contract is not in danger. If it loses, West must lead a minor, to our advantage, or a heart, giving a ruff and discard. If East shows out on the second spade, we win and still have the chance that the clubs are 3–3 or that the two diamond honours are together.

The deal:

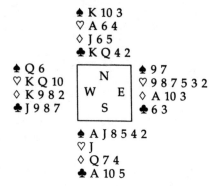

```
                    ♠ K 10 3
                    ♡ A 6 4
                    ◇ J 6 5
                    ♣ K Q 4 2
    ♠ Q 6           ┌─────────┐      ♠ 9 7
    ♡ K Q 10        │    N    │      ♡ 9 8 7 5 3 2
    ◇ K 9 8 2       │  W   E  │      ◇ A 10 3
    ♣ J 9 8 7       │    S    │      ♣ 6 3
                    └─────────┘
                    ♠ A J 8 5 4 2
                    ♡ J
                    ◇ Q 7 4
                    ♣ A 10 5
```

Problem 23

We have eleven top tricks and chances of finesses in clubs and
hearts. On the bidding, the club is a sure loser and the question
arises as to whether anything can be done if West holds the ♡K as
well.

The deal:

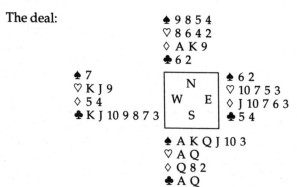

```
                    ♠ 9 8 5 4
                    ♡ 8 6 4 2
                    ◇ A K 9
                    ♣ 6 2
    ♠ 7             ┌─────────┐      ♠ 6 2
    ♡ K J 9         │    N    │      ♡ 10 7 5 3
    ◇ 5 4           │  W   E  │      ◇ J 10 7 6 3
    ♣ K J 10 9 8 7 3│    S    │      ♣ 5 4
                    └─────────┘
                    ♠ A K Q J 10 3
                    ♡ A Q
                    ◇ Q 8 2
                    ♣ A Q
```

The heart loser can be saved if West can be forced to lead the suit.
On winning the opening lead, we draw trumps and cash the other
two top diamonds, leaving this position:

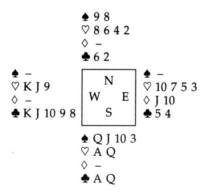

<pre>
            ♠ 9 8
            ♡ 8 6 4 2
            ◊ –
            ♣ 6 2
♠ –   ♠ –
♡ K J 9   N   ♡ 10 7 5 3
◊ –   W   E   ◊ J 10
♣ K J 10 9 8   S   ♣ 5 4
            ♠ Q J 10 3
            ♡ A Q
            ◊ –
            ♣ A Q
</pre>

Now, by playing the ace and queen of clubs, we eliminate the suit and throw the lead to West at the same time. He must then either lead away from his hearts or concede a ruff and discard by persisting with clubs.

That concludes the section on declarer play and the importance of playing and replaying these hands over and over again, including the variations, cannot be emphasized too often. Complete familiarity with the positions arising will save you incalculable strain at the table later on.

Defence against No-trump Contracts

In this section, we shall look at some of the stratagems studied in the declarer section from the other point of view and learn one or two counter strokes. We shall then introduce some new plays which, because of their view of enemy cards, tend to be confined to defenders. Finally, we shall spend some time on discarding because, at least in my experience, it is in this respect the countless contracts and overtricks are thrown at declarer.

As we have already learnt, a declarer often aims to make his no-trump contract by establishing a long suit. We shall start with a few disruptive tactics. We learnt in the earlier books that it often pays to hold up a control until the hand opposite the long suit runs out. These are obvious examples in situations where North has no side-suit entries:

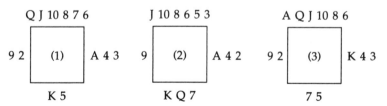

These tend to crop up when the suit is a minor after South has opened 2NT and been raised to 3NT or similar auctions. South has five winners and one loser in each case but, with only a doubleton in his hand, must lose the first round if he is to enjoy the rest of the suit. It is up to the defenders to ensure that he is 'disappointed'.

In (1), West plays the nine on the first round, signalling an even number (unless it is a singleton), here obviously a doubleton, and East holds up his ace to the second round, after which dummy is dead.

In (2), East does not know whether the nine is a singleton or doubleton. He obviously refuses the first round and when West shows out on the second, he knows he must refuse that as well to ensure that the suit is shut out.

In (3), again West's nine may be the start of a peter and East allows North's queen to hold. The chances are that South will return to hand in another suit and repeat the finesse, restricting himself to one trick in the suit.

In the following diagrams, the situation may be less clear:

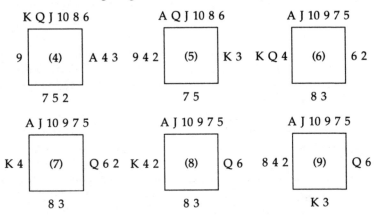

In (4), South plays a low card to the king. The nine may be a singleton or the start of a peter to show a doubleton. In either case, East must hold up for at least one round. When a second round is played from dummy, East has to make a decision before he sees his partner follow or discard. If he holds up again, he will certainly cut out the suit but he allows two tricks, which may be enough for the contract. One might be insufficient.

In (5), South plays low to the queen and East is faced with a dilemma. If he wins, he allows declarer five tricks in the suit. To give his side a chance of cutting it out, he must take his life in his hands and duck, smoothly and without hesitation. South is likely to return to hand and repeat the finesse, playing for (over):

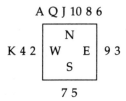

A Q J 10 8 6

K 4 2   N / W   E / S   9 3

7 5

and finish up with one trick instead of six!

In the next three examples, we consider the position where declarer is missing both king and queen. These are solid against the ace, whether they are in the same hand or not, and thus the defenders can always ensure cutting out the suit (where South has a doubleton only) by refusing the first round. However, there is a great deal of scope for deception and stealing, which could be important if it is a question of one or two tricks in the suit.

In (6), West must play low to ensure that the suit is cut out. South makes two tricks and no more. If West were to play an honour, South could duck and bring the whole suit in by finessing the second time.

In (7), again the defenders can hold South to two tricks by playing low from both hands when South plays low to the jack. However, West can do better still by rising with the king on the first round. South is now sunk completely. If he ducks, playing for the position in (6), he will finesse the second time and finish with no tricks in the suit at all! If he wins, he will take one trick only. Note the same applies if the king and queen are exchanged.

In (8), again the defenders can hold declarer to two tricks by ducking in both hands. If West puts up the king, South may bring the suit in for five tricks by ducking the first round and rising with the ace the second time on the basis that, with K Q x, West could have made sure of cutting out the suit by ducking the first round.

However in (9), we see the corollary. If South needs six tricks in the suit, he has little alternative but to cash the king and finesse against West, hoping for a 3–2 split. But, if he only needs five, he might try the effect of a low card to the jack on the first round. East may well be right to duck, thinking that his partner has K x x. Now South overtakes his king for six tricks if either defender started with a doubleton queen. There are endless variations on this theme and scope for bluff and double bluff. We can extend to weaker suits where the defenders have two or more stops and there is one or more entry to dummy. The basic principle, however, is that the defenders should try to hold up their stops to exhaust the short hand and force declarer to use an outside entry.

However, a word of warning must be added! The above discussion applies to the long suit in isolation. The consideration of a whole hand may demand different tactics. Holding up involves surrendering a trick which may be unnecessary. The best way to learn is by bitter experience and I should like you to do the following examples against the stop-watch, aiming for ninety seconds each to complete the test in under eight minutes. In each case, you should state how you intend to play to the long suit, how your play affects the number of tricks declarer will win and lose in that suit and the relevance to the whole hand. Start your stop-watch.

Problem 1
Hand No. 51
Dealer East
N–S vulnerable

♠ 8 4
♡ 7 3
◇ 7 5 4
♣ K Q J 10 8 7

W	N	E	S
		Pass	2NT
Pass	3NT	end	

♠ J 10 5
♡ J 10 9 8 5
◇ Q 8
♣ A 3 2

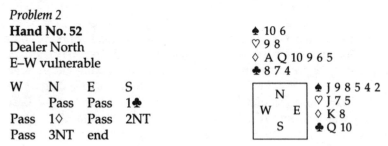

You lead the ♡J to ♡3, ♡2 and ♡A. South leads the ♣9 to the ♣2, ♣7 and ♣6. He continues with the ♣5. How do you defend?

Problem 2
Hand No. 52
Dealer North
E–W vulnerable

♠ 10 6
♡ 9 8
◇ A Q 10 9 6 5
♣ 8 7 4

W	N	E	S
	Pass	Pass	1♣
Pass	1◇	Pass	2NT
Pass	3NT	end	

♠ J 9 8 5 4 2
♡ J 7 5
◇ K 8
♣ Q 10

West leads the ♡6 to the ♡9, ♡J and ♡K. South continues with the ◊J, on which partner plays the ◊2 and dummy the ◊5. How do you defend and would it make any difference if partner played the ◊7?

Problem 3
Hand No. 53
Dealer West
Both vulnerable

♠ 9 6 3
♡ Q 5 4
◊ A J 10 9 7
♣ 8 2

W	N	E	S
Pass	Pass	Pass	1♣
Pass	1◊	Pass	3NT
end			

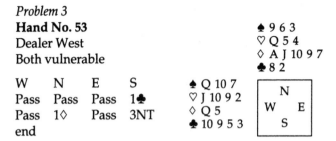

♠ Q 10 7
♡ J 10 9 2
◊ Q 5
♣ 10 9 5 3

You lead the ♡J to the ♡4, ♡7 and ♡A. South now plays the ◊8. How do you defend?

Problem 4
Hand No. 54
Dealer South
Both vulnerable

♠ 9 6 3
♡ Q 5 4
◊ A J 10 9 7 2
♣ 8

W	N	E	S
			1♣
Pass	1◊	Pass	2NT
Pass	3NT	end	

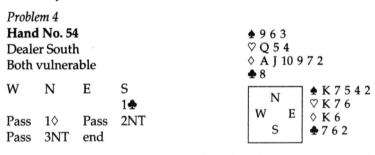

♠ K 7 5 4 2
♡ K 7 6
◊ K 6
♣ 7 6 2

Partner leads the ♡J and dummy plays low. You encourage with the ♡7 and South's ♡A wins. The ◊8 runs to the ◊4 and ◊2. How do you defend?

Problem 5
Hand No. 55
Dealer East
Both vulnerable

♠ A 7 4
♡ 8 2
◊ A J 10 9 8 2
♣ 8 3

W	N	E	S
		Pass	1♣
Pass	1◊	Pass	2NT
Pass	3NT	end	

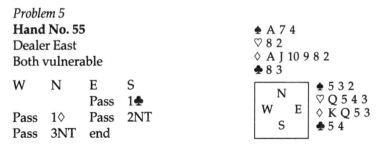

♠ 5 3 2
♡ Q 5 4 3
◊ K Q 5 3
♣ 5 4

Partner leads the ♠J. South's king wins and he plays the ◊6 to the ◊7 and ◊8. How do you defend?

Solutions

Problem 1

Partner's ♣6 may be a singleton or the beginning of a peter to show a doubleton. In the first case, we shall have to hold up a second time to exhaust South's trebleton. Otherwise we can win now. We must therefore weigh up the cost of going wrong. If we win and South has a third club, the whole suit will come in and South, with 20-plus points, will surely make the contract easily. If we hold up again and South turns up with a doubleton, we will have lost an unnecessary trick but South may well not have seven outside top tricks in his own hand. It is no certainty but the odds favour holding up again.

The deal:

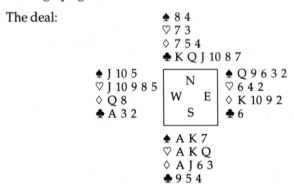

```
                    ♠ 8 4
                    ♡ 7 3
                    ◊ 7 5 4
                    ♣ K Q J 10 8 7
    ♠ J 10 5            N        ♠ Q 9 6 3 2
    ♡ J 10 9 8 5                 ♡ 6 4 2
    ◊ Q 8       W         E      ◊ K 10 9 2
    ♣ A 3 2          S          ♣ 6
                    ♠ A K 7
                    ♡ A K Q
                    ◊ A J 6 3
                    ♣ 9 5 4
```

South is now held to eight tricks. Note that he needed the ♣A to drop in two rounds to make the contract and that, with his predominance of quick, as opposed to slow tricks, 5♣ cannot be beaten.

Problem 2

North has punted 3NT on the 'all or nothing' theory – that either all his diamonds will come in or not. There therefore seems an even stronger case for ducking (smoothly and without hesitation!) here than in the last case. However, there are a number of other considerations which swing the balance the opposite way. First, let us consider that lead. 11 – 6 = 5 and we can see four cards higher than the six between our hand and dummy. Therefore South's king is the only high heart in his hand and the suit is now ready to cash. West is likely to have five; if he only has four, that would leave South with four, which he might well have bid rather than commit himself to no-trumps.

I have to admit that there are a number of players, including many in the top grade, who are in the habit of suppressing poorish four-card majors in this kind of position with the express purpose of misleading opponents in this respect. I can only say that I have, on many occasions, scored good results through their missing 4–4 major-suit fits. In my experience, this style of bidding loses in the long term.

Second, our club holding is a dream for declarer. Partner's ◊2 indicates a trebleton, leaving South with two and therefore, assuming he has not suppressed a four-card major, he must have at least five clubs. Partner is marked with the ace-queen of hearts for 6 points and we can see 13. Therefore if we give partner a spade honour, we are considering a position like this:

The deal:

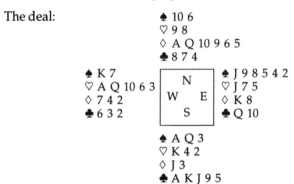

```
                    ♠ 10 6
                    ♡ 9 8
                    ◊ A Q 10 9 6 5
                    ♣ 8 7 4
   ♠ K 7                              ♠ J 9 8 5 4 2
   ♡ A Q 10 6 3        N              ♡ J 7 5
   ◊ 7 4 2         W       E          ◊ K 8
   ♣ 6 3 2             S              ♣ Q 10
                    ♠ A Q 3
                    ♡ K 4 2
                    ◊ J 3
                    ♣ A K J 9 5
```

South has already taken a heart trick and is now good for five clubs, a spade and the ◊A to total eight. Ducking the diamond therefore gives him a ninth trick as it costs him nothing to try the top clubs (drop before finesse) before committing himself to a second diamond finesse. We must therefore win the diamond and return a heart.

If West indicates an even number of diamonds, then South is marked with a trebleton and ducking can never gain – all the more must we win. Note that partner cannot have four diamonds – that would leave South with a singleton and, in that case, he would have overtaken the ◊J with the ◊Q, giving himself the best chance – that West started with a doubleton king.

I urge you to get into the habit of picking up these *negative* inferences – noting what was *not* bid and what was *not* played. Bearing in mind that, particularly against weak opposition, you will have to be prepared to look silly occasionally, these are a mine of information in respect of placing unseen cards.

Problem 3

Partner has encouraged the heart lead and is likely to have the ♡K. In that case, dummy has no side-suit entry to the diamonds and it is clear that, unless partner has the ◊K, the defence has no hope. Giving partner that card, therefore, there are two possible lines. Play low now (expecting partner to do likewise) or put up the queen. We can see that the queen is better because now South is held to one trick in the suit and if he tries to bring it in by ducking, intending to finesse the second time, he will not make any at all. If we duck all round, South takes two tricks in the suit and that may well be enough if his clubs are solid.

The deal:

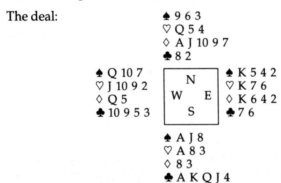

```
                    ♠ 9 6 3
                    ♡ Q 5 4
                    ◊ A J 10 9 7
                    ♣ 8 2
  ♠ Q 10 7                        ♠ K 5 4 2
  ♡ J 10 9 2        N            ♡ K 7 6
  ◊ Q 5         W       E         ◊ K 6 4 2
  ♣ 10 9 5 3        S            ♣ 7 6
                    ♠ A J 8
                    ♡ A 8 3
                    ◊ 8 3
                    ♣ A K Q J 4
```

South can now settle for one or two off, according to his level of greed.

Problem 4

This illustrates the converse of the earlier problem when we had to consider whether or not to hold up the ◊K over a long suit on dummy.

First, the heart suit, although lying favourably for us, is not ready to cash. Second, the club position is not necessarily favourable for declarer. It is therefore far more likely that he will need to bring the diamond suit in for five tricks to make the contract. If South has the ◊Q, there is nothing we can do. But it looks as though partner has her and she is probably in a trebleton. As we just learnt, with a doubleton, he should play her on the first round.

The deal:

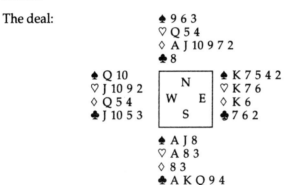

```
                    ♠ 9 6 3
                    ♡ Q 5 4
                    ◊ A J 10 9 7 2
                    ♣ 8
    ♠ Q 10                          ♠ K 7 5 4 2
    ♡ J 10 9 2          N           ♡ K 7 6
    ◊ Q 5 4        W       E        ◊ K 6
    ♣ J 10 5 3         S            ♣ 7 6 2
                    ♠ A J 8
                    ♡ A 8 3
                    ◊ 8 3
                    ♣ A K Q 9 4
```

This time, we must duck and allow South two tricks in the suit but he is still one short for the contract.

Problem 5

Here the ♠A constitutes an extra entry to dummy but we have two certain stops. The principle of trying to exhaust the short diamond hand (South) still applies. If we win now and South has a second diamond, he will be able to reach dummy and continue the suit to knock out our second stop without using the ♠A. But if we duck, the suit is dead and South can take one more trick only.

The deal:

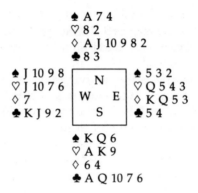

```
            ♠ A 7 4
            ♡ 8 2
            ◇ A J 10 9 8 2
            ♣ 8 3
♠ J 10 9 8          N        ♠ 5 3 2
♡ J 10 7 6                   ♡ Q 5 4 3
◇ 7          W         E     ◇ K Q 5 3
♣ K J 9 2          S         ♣ 5 4
            ♠ K Q 6
            ♡ A K 9
            ◇ 6 4
            ♣ A Q 10 7 6
```

The hand is not over yet as South must now switch to clubs, threatening to take two tricks in that suit in addition to two diamonds and five tops in the majors. However, with West having three stops in the suit, the defence can get to five tricks first if West switches to hearts on winning his first club trick.

Of course, if East is able to remove the ♠A prematurely, he can afford to win the first diamond. This would apply if West had led the ♠Q and had weaker clubs. Now ducking the first diamond would allow declarer one diamond trick too many and a successful switch to clubs in time to make the contract.

We can now combine our study of establishing and spoiling long suits with that pertaining to losing tricks into the correct hand. Many players would go wrong in a situation like this through automatic play to general rules.

Hand No. 56
Dealer South
Both vulnerable

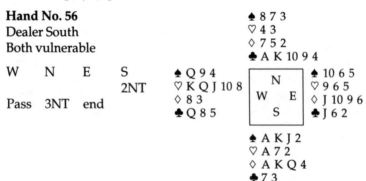

```
                              ♠ 8 7 3
                              ♡ 4 3
                              ◇ 7 5 2
                              ♣ A K 10 9 4

W    N    E    S      ♠ Q 9 4        N       ♠ 10 6 5
               2NT    ♡ K Q J 10 8           ♡ 9 6 5
                      ◇ 8 3      W      E     ◇ J 10 9 6
Pass 3NT  end         ♣ Q 8 5        S       ♣ J 6 2

                              ♠ A K J 2
                              ♡ A 7 2
                              ◇ A K Q 4
                              ♣ 7 3
```

West leads the ♡K and persists with the suit, South holding up to the third round to exhaust East. There are chances in spades and diamonds but, if South can lose a club trick to East, he can bring the suit in on dummy. He plays a low club and now the spot-light turns on West. If he plays low, South puts on the ten, losing to East, and the contract is made with an overtrick. But now try the effect of West's putting in the ♣Q. Now South is sunk. If he ducks, West cashes the rest of the hearts for five tricks. If he wins in dummy, he can never bring in the long clubs. He is now forced to try the other suits and is disappointed with diamonds failing to break and the spade queen protected in the same hand as the long hearts.

In situations where it is not possible to prevent declarer setting up his long suit, it may be feasible for the defenders to establish enough tricks to defeat the contract first, even where they have failed to find the best opening lead. There are a number of card combinations in which defenders have an advantage over declarer in that they can see the lie of half the enemy forces and are therefore able to play with more accuracy than declarer. Let us look at a few examples.

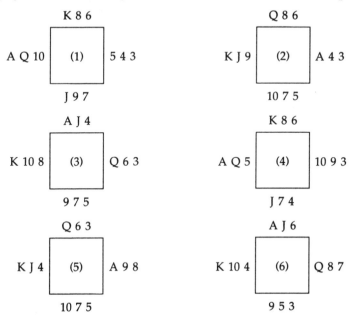

In each case, I have shown a three-card position; usually the defenders will have the thirteenth card. In (1), (2) and (3), West, on lead, has a form of double tenace and his play to net the maximum number of tricks is the *middle* card. In (1), the queen forces North's king and West is then hoping that his partner will soon win a trick in another suit to push a second round through South's jack to his A 10 tenace for two tricks. In (2), West leads the jack; if North fails to cover, three tricks are automatic. If he does cover, East wins and another round through South's ten assures two more tricks. In (3), West leads the ten. If North plays low or wins with the ace, two tricks are easy. If he covers with the jack, East's queen wins and a second round through South's nine to the K 8 assures a second trick in the suit.

In (4), (5) and (6) West is weaker in that his third card is low and he must now hope that his partner has a solid holding so that, again, a finesse against South can be organized. Again he leads the second highest card in each case for the maximum gain. Satisfy yourself that, in all six of the above positions, the lead of the highest or lowest card gives South a chance to rescue a trick or at least delay the ability of the defenders to win their full quota, being unable to continue the attack from the correct side. For example, in (1), if West starts with the ace, he cannot continue without allowing South two tricks and, if he starts with the ten, he surrenders two tricks immediately.

Having seen the idea, I should like you to do the following examples in match conditions, aiming to break the one-minute barrier for each to complete the test in under three minutes. Start your stop-watch.

Problem 6
Hand No. 57
Dealer East
N–S vulnerable

♠ 9 5 4
♡ A 4
◇ Q 9 8
♣ A Q J 10 7

			♠ Q 10 6 2
	N		♡ K 10 3 2
W		E	◇ 10 4 2
	S		♣ K 5

W	N	E	S
		Pass	1◇
Pass	2♣	Pass	2NT
Pass	3NT	end	

West leads the ♡5 and dummy plays low. How do you defend?

Problem 7
Hand No. 58
Dealer North
Neither vulnerable

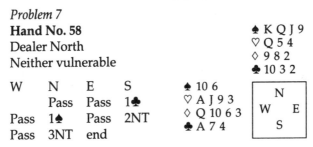

♠ K Q J 9
♡ Q 5 4
◇ 9 8 2
♣ 10 3 2

W	N	E	S
	Pass	Pass	1♣
Pass	1♠	Pass	2NT
Pass	3NT	end	

♠ 10 6
♡ A J 9 3
◇ Q 10 6 3
♣ A 7 4

You lead the ◇3 to the ◇2, ◇7 and ◇J. South leads the ♣8. How do you defend?

Problem 8
Hand No. 59
Dealer East
E–W vulnerable

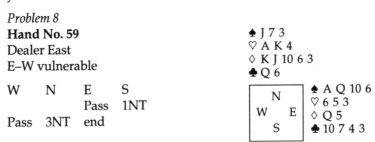

♠ J 7 3
♡ A K 4
◇ K J 10 6 3
♣ Q 6

W	N	E	S
		Pass	1NT
Pass	3NT	end	

♠ A Q 10 6
♡ 6 5 3
◇ Q 5
♣ 10 7 4 3

West leads the ♡J, won by South's ♡Q. He now runs the ◇9 round to your ◇Q. How do you continue?

Solutions

Problem 6

There are two possible approaches to this hand. One is to win and carry on hearts, removing the ace from the dummy. Then pluck up the courage to refuse the first club finesse and hope that South started with only a doubleton (partner should play a high card on the first round to indicate an even number, in this case four). Sadly, this is a non-starter as the ◇Q, which we cannot beat, will always serve as an entry to dummy if needed.

We shall therefore have to accept that the club suit cannot be stopped and that the race is on – we must take five tricks first.

There are 13 points in the dummy and 8 in our hand. Giving 15 to South for his bid leaves partner with 4. His lead of the ♡5 clearly comes from a four-card suit as the ♡4, ♡3, ♡2 are all visible. If we were to continue hearts, the best we could hope for is three tricks in it plus the ♣K – not enough to defeat the contract. We therefore look elsewhere. There is obviously no hope in diamonds, with South having bid them and the ◊Q well placed in dummy, so it has to be spades. Partner will have to have either ace or king and we need three tricks. If he has the jack as well, there is no problem. The critical case arises where South has the jack and now we shall need to find partner with the eight and seven to organize a finesse against the nine.

The deal:

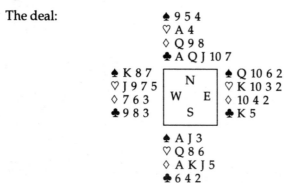

```
                    ♠ 9 5 4
                    ♡ A 4
                    ◊ Q 9 8
                    ♣ A Q J 10 7
    ♠ K 8 7                      ♠ Q 10 6 2
    ♡ J 9 7 5        N           ♡ K 10 3 2
    ◊ 7 6 3      W       E       ◊ 10 4 2
    ♣ 9 8 3          S           ♣ K 5
                    ♠ A J 3
                    ♡ Q 8 6
                    ◊ A K J 5
                    ♣ 6 4 2
```

The middle-card rule applies and we switch to the ♣10. Nothing now can prevent our taking three spade tricks, a heart and a club. South could, of course, have made the contract by winning trick one with the ♡A but would have looked silly if West had started with five or six hearts to the king.

Problem 7

We have found a disastrous lead and South clearly has ◊ A K J. We have 11 points and, with 8 on dummy, and South likely to have 17 or 18, we can hope for little more than a king from partner. That gives South the ♠A and therefore four spade tricks and three diamonds already. The lead of the ♣8 is suspicious to say the least. It is too much to hope that South is being generous enough to allow partner a cheap trick in the suit. Either East has the ♣K or nothing in the suit at all. If indeed East has the king, South will easily take at least one trick in clubs and one in hearts to make the contract in comfort. We must therefore credit South with all the club honours and partner with the ♡K and now there is a chance.

The deal:

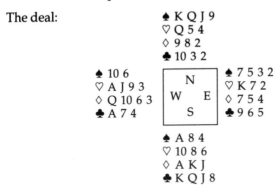

```
              ♠ K Q J 9
              ♡ Q 5 4
              ◊ 9 8 2
              ♣ 10 3 2
♠ 10 6                        ♠ 7 5 3 2
♡ A J 9 3          N          ♡ K 7 2
◊ Q 10 6 3     W      E       ◊ 7 5 4
♣ A 7 4            S          ♣ 9 6 5
              ♠ A 8 4
              ♡ 10 8 6
              ◊ A K J
              ♣ K Q J 8
```

Our five tricks must come from the ♣A and four hearts and the middle-card rule applies again – we must start with the ♡J and South has no answer.

Problem 8

South is marked with about 13 points and, with 14 in dummy and 8 in our hand, we can expect about 5 with partner. He has already shown the ♡J. Had South the ◊A, he would surely have cashed it, (to cover a possible singleton queen in our hand) before trying the finesse.

The deal:

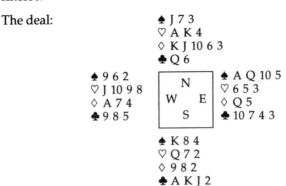

```
              ♠ J 7 3
              ♡ A K 4
              ◊ K J 10 6 3
              ♣ Q 6
♠ 9 6 2                       ♠ A Q 10 5
♡ J 10 9 8         N          ♡ 6 5 3
◊ A 7 4        W      E       ◊ Q 5
♣ 9 8 5            S          ♣ 10 7 4 3
              ♠ K 8 4
              ♡ Q 7 2
              ◊ 9 8 2
              ♣ A K J 2
```

South has four club tricks and three hearts and therefore, if he can bring the diamonds in, he will make the contract comfortably. The race is therefore on and, with no hope in hearts, we must turn our attention to spades. Again the middle-card rule applies and we start with the ♠Q. If South wins, West will be on play after the second round of diamonds and we take three more spade tricks. If South ducks, we play a low spade to preserve communication with partner so that again we can take two more spade tricks when he gets in with the ◊A.

Even if South can bring in a long suit, that need not be the end of the story as he may not have enough tricks. However, we shall inevitably have to discard as the long suit is cashed and we now turn to problems in this area. Careful discarding is particularly important when defending against high-level contracts and therefore mistakes will be very heavily penalised. Sadly, the higher the contract, the weaker the defenders' hands will be and therefore the easier it is to lose interest in the proceedings. To drive the point home, I gave an example hand in *The Expert Improver* where the East player, having started with no more than a couple of tens, had to discard with great care to avoid giving away vital information about his partner's holding.

To be successful in this area, the most important consideration is to decide how many rounds of each suit you expect to be played. If it is clear that you cannot prevent that number, then you should consider keeping as many cards in the suit, *even if they are not necessarily winners*. This is an obvious example:

A Q 10 7

```
          N
8 6 4 | W   E | J 9 5
          S
```

K 3 2

There is not much hope for West in this situation but it would often be a mistake to discard from his holding. Contrast the two situations: declarer plays the ace, followed by the king and then the three. If West discards now, South has no option but to go up with dummy's queen, confident that the jack will fall. But if West has kept all three cards intact and can follow suit, South has a chance to go wrong and (particularly if he has asked himself why you have been so keen to hold on to the suit!) might finesse the ten, playing for this layout:

```
        A Q 10 7
        ┌─────────┐
        │    N    │
J 8 6 4 │ W     E │ 9 5
        │    S    │
        └─────────┘
         K 3 2
```

Probability and statistics fanatics will refrain from rushing to point out that, unless there is evidence of a skew distribution, the drop is a slightly better percentage play and therefore the discard may well not cost. While this is true, there may be other factors, for example South may be keen to keep West off play. In any case, the following situation crops up regularly:

```
        A K J 8
        ┌─────────┐
        │    N    │
9 3 2   │ W     E │ Q 4
        │    S    │
        └─────────┘
        10 7 6 5
```

Say South runs a long suit and West needs to find two discards. It is already very suspicious if West discards one of the above suit. He will give the impression of someone with nothing to guard and now South is likely to prefer the drop to the finesse. If West discards twice, South cannot go wrong. He will cash the ace, return to hand in another suit and then play a second round of this suit. When West shows out, all will be revealed. If West wisely keeps his trebleton intact, South is likely to prefer the percentage play of the finesse.

The other source of continual discarding errors is the impression that a card cannot possibly be a winner because it is not high enough:

A K 7 5 2

South is running another suit and many players would give little chance of the jack making a trick, pessimistically placing the queen with South. But the position could easily be:

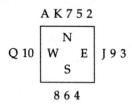

A K 7 5 2

8 6 4

West's queen falls, but the jack is promoted. For these reasons, the importance of anticipating the source of enemy tricks cannot be over-emphasized as the key to correct discarding. Proficiency in this aspect of defence is a crucial factor in making you a formidable opponent.

I should like you to try the following examples under match conditions but, as you must work out every card, the time limit for this new subject will be relaxed and you have two minutes for each question and therefore eight minutes for the whole test. For full credit, you must give a good reason why you have chosen a particular discard.

Problem 9
Hand No. 60
Dealer North
N–S vulnerable

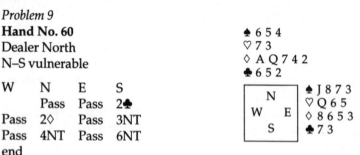

W	N	E	S
	Pass	Pass	2♣
Pass	2◊	Pass	3NT
Pass	4NT	Pass	6NT
end			

West leads the ♡J which holds, South following with the ♡2. West

continues with the ♡4, South taking your ♡Q with his ♡A. He now
cashes the four top clubs, partner following with the ♣4, ♣10, ♣9
and ♣8 in that order. You can easily spare your last heart on the
third round but, as dummy discards a low diamond on the fourth,
you are down to your four spades and four diamonds. What do
you discard now?

Problem 10
Hand No. 61
Dealer North
Both vulnerable

```
                              ♠ 6 4 3
                              ♡ K J 10 6
                              ◊ K Q 9
                              ♣ Q 8 2
              ♠ K Q J 10 7 2 ┌─────────┐
              ♡ 8 3 2        │    N    │
              ◊ 7 6          │ W     E │
              ♣ A J          │    S    │
                             └─────────┘
```

W	N	E	S
	Pass	Pass	1◊
1♠	2♠	Pass	3NT
end			

North's unassuming cue-bid after passing shows a near-opening
hand, offering possible game contracts of 4♡ (if his partner can bid
the suit), 3NT (if partner can stop the spades) or possibly 5◊. Note
that, as he has limited his hand by the original pass, the cue-bid
only forces the partnership as far as 3◊ (suit agreement) – not
necessarily to game. This particularly applies as the opening bid
was in third position and therefore could be light.

You lead the ♠K to the ♠3, partner's ♠9 and South's ♠5. On your
♠Q, East discards the ♣3 and South wins as there is little point in
holding up again. Having started with ◊ A J 5 4 3, he reels off five
rounds of the suit on which you will have to find three discards.
What are they and would it make any difference if your heart
holding were changed to ♡ Q 3 2?

Problem 11
Hand No. 62
Dealer South
N–S vulnerable

```
              ♠ Q 8 2
              ♡ A K Q 6
              ◊ 6 4 2
              ♣ K Q J
        ┌─────────┐ ♠ K 4 3
        │    N    │ ♡ 8 7 4 2
        │ W     E │ ◊ 9 7
        │    S    │ ♣ 10 9 8 4
        └─────────┘
```

W	N	E	S
			1◊
Pass	1♡	Pass	3NT
Pass	7NT	end	

West leads the ♠J to the ♠2, ♠4 and ♣A. South follows with three rounds of clubs, all following, and five rounds of diamonds (having started with ◊ A K Q J 3), partner discarding the ♠7 and ♠9 on the last two rounds and dummy the ♠8 and ♣Q. What are your three discards on the long diamonds and, with dummy keeping its four hearts, which four cards do you keep?

Problem 12
Hand No. 63
Dealer East
N–S vulnerable

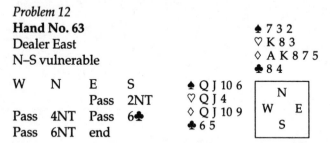

			♠ 7 3 2
			♡ K 8 3
			◊ A K 8 7 5
			♣ 8 4

W	N	E	S		
		Pass	2NT	♠ Q J 10 6
Pass	4NT	Pass	6♣	♡ Q J 4
Pass	6NT	end		◊ Q J 10 9
				♣ 6 5

You lead the ♠Q to the ♠2, ♠4 and ♠A. South, who started with ♣ A K Q J 9, reels of five rounds of the suit. It is a nightmare come true. You will have to find three discards – what are they?

Solutions

Problem 9
South's 3NT bid showed about 25–27 points and, as he accepted the slam invitation (remember that 4NT is quantitative, rather than Blackwood – no suit had been agreed and in any case, the weak hand should not be taking charge of the auction), he should be at the top of that range. He has already shown the top four clubs (10) and (by inference) the top two hearts (7). That leaves 9 or 10 unaccounted for. First consider the ◊K. If West has it, South will be able to take the finesse and must have the three top spades for his bid. That would give him three spade tricks, two diamonds, two hearts and four clubs to total eleven. If South has a fourth spade, we must keep our spades intact and discard a diamond now and another diamond on the last top heart. But that is no good; South must have at least two diamonds and now the whole diamond suit will come in.

As I mentioned many times in *The Expert Improver*, when a

finessable card is missing, it is usually wise to credit it to declarer as there is unlikely to be much hope otherwise. Therefore we give South the ◊K and thus he needs only the ace and king of spades. That gives him four club tricks, two spades, two hearts and three diamonds to total eleven and, provided he has only two diamond cards in his hand, we can break the contract by keeping our diamonds and discarding a spade, intending to discard another spade on the ♡K.

The deal:

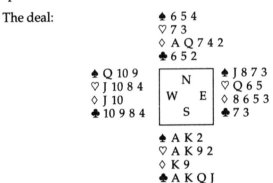

```
                 ♠ 6 5 4
                 ♡ 7 3
                 ◊ A Q 7 4 2
                 ♣ 6 5 2
  ♠ Q 10 9                        ♠ J 8 7 3
  ♡ J 10 8 4          N           ♡ Q 6 5
  ◊ J 10          W       E       ◊ 8 6 5 3
  ♣ 10 9 8 4          S           ♣ 7 3
                 ♠ A K 2
                 ♡ A K 9 2
                 ◊ K 9
                 ♣ A K Q J
```

You should have noted several points about this hand. First, did you notice how partner followed to the clubs? After the ♣4, all his clubs were solid so that he could play them in any order to give you information. In this position, playing *high* cards first, he indicated interest in *higher-ranking* suits, according to the McKenney principle. So West was trying to indicate that he had the spades covered, i.e. that it was safe for us to abandon the suit. (We were able to work it out anyway!)

Second, you also should have remarked on South's refusal of the first trick. We are nowhere near the study of squeeze-play (forcing an opponent to discard potential winners as here in diamonds and spades) but you will learn that losing a trick early like this is usually an advisable tactic in order to advance the play and thereby reduce the opponents' cards as much as possible. The fewer cards one has, the more difficult it is to discard without giving something away. In this case, by losing the first (or second) round of hearts, South could insist on three rounds of the suit being played, whereas, had he insisted on winning both times, he would be restricted to two and our discarding problem would have been that much easier.

Third, you should also have noticed that 6♣ (a heart ruff on dummy providing the extra trick) and 6◊ (made by simply giving up a diamond) are both unbeatable and both North and South were at fault in the bidding. It costs nothing for North to show his suit over 3NT but, even if he doesn't, South, rich in top controls and therefore better suited to a trump contract, could have tried 6♣ over 4NT. North could always remove it with a doubleton club. In either case, the partnership could always end in 6NT.

Problem 10

South has shown the ♠A and ◊ A J and must clearly have the ♡A for his bid; if he hasn't, he will be heavily defeated. So that gives him one trick in spades, five in diamonds and at least two in hearts to total eight so far. This implies that, if the defence is to have any chance at all, partner will have to hold the ♡Q and we can now see the point of the hand.

The deal:

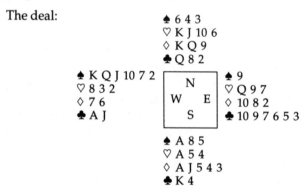

$$
\begin{array}{c}
\spadesuit\ 6\ 4\ 3 \\
\heartsuit\ K\ J\ 10\ 6 \\
\diamondsuit\ K\ Q\ 9 \\
\clubsuit\ Q\ 8\ 2
\end{array}
$$

$$
\begin{array}{ll}
\spadesuit\ K\ Q\ J\ 10\ 7\ 2 & \spadesuit\ 9 \\
\heartsuit\ 8\ 3\ 2 & \heartsuit\ Q\ 9\ 7 \\
\diamondsuit\ 7\ 6 & \diamondsuit\ 10\ 8\ 2 \\
\clubsuit\ A\ J & \clubsuit\ 10\ 9\ 7\ 6\ 5\ 3
\end{array}
$$

$$
\begin{array}{c}
\spadesuit\ A\ 8\ 5 \\
\heartsuit\ A\ 5\ 4 \\
\diamondsuit\ A\ J\ 5\ 4\ 3 \\
\clubsuit\ K\ 4
\end{array}
$$

The number of people who would discard those three 'useless' hearts without giving the matter another thought is alarming. But we can see that this is the certain way to give declarer the contract. He will simply play a low card to the ♡K and, when we show out, all will be revealed. The one card we do not need is the ♣J so that should be the first discard. The other two are less clear. We cannot discard two spades as that would leave us with only three tricks in the suit and now South does not need to guess the heart position –

he simply knocks out our ♣A and takes a club trick. It will look very suspicious to discard two hearts. We are marked with six spades and the ♣A on the bidding and early play; we have also shown two diamonds. To discard two hearts would leave us with only a singleton and again declarer will play low to the ♡K and when we show a low card, again the finesse against East is marked.

The correct discards are therefore the ♣J, one spade and one heart, keeping enough spades to defeat the contract without giving too much away about the heart position. Does it make any difference if we have the ♡Q instead of the ♡8? Not in the slightest! This is still our best chance.

Problem 11
This is a very easy problem but the number of people who would go wrong in this situation is staggering. There are three points to guide you:

1 Partner led the ♠J, promising the ♠10 which he still holds as master in that suit. There is therefore no need for us to hold on to the ♠K.
2 It is obvious that the last four tricks will be played in hearts and thus we must keep our four hearts.
3 Our highest heart is bigger than dummy's lowest and therefore, as long as South does not have the ♡J, we will make the last trick. Admittedly, this leaves South with the four top diamonds and the two black aces for 18 points only, but with the fifth diamond in a solid suit, he is easily worth the 19 points promised by his 3NT bid.

If indeed South does have the ♡J, he is solid for the contract, irrespective of our discard.

The deal:

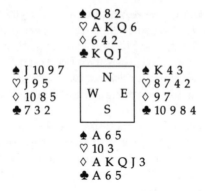

```
                    ♠ Q 8 2
                    ♡ A K Q 6
                    ◊ 6 4 2
                    ♣ K Q J
   ♠ J 10 9 7                      ♠ K 4 3
   ♡ J 9 5          N              ♡ 8 7 4 2
   ◊ 10 8 5      W     E           ◊ 9 7
   ♣ 7 3 2          S              ♣ 10 9 8 4
                    ♠ A 6 5
                    ♡ 10 3
                    ◊ A K Q J 3
                    ♣ A 6 5
```

North was slightly optimistic in the bidding in that his three club honours were in a trebleton and therefore not pulling their full weight, but it will be instructive for you to replay the hand, exchanging the positions of the East and West hands. Now a spade lead gives a free finesse and the contract and is therefore ruled out. However, even with a different lead, after the ♠A, five rounds of diamonds and three of clubs, our hand has to commit itself to a discard of the ♠K or a heart *before* dummy; whatever we discard, dummy discards from the other suit and now the contract will be made.

Problem 12
With 9 points in our hand and 10 in dummy, it is clear that South must have the rest, leaving partner with none. However, that does not mean that his hand will be useless in defence. We can see that South, in addition to his five clubs, has the two tops in each of the other suits to total 11.

The first point is that we have a double stop in diamonds and must keep it intact. If we discard one, South will simply give up a trick in the suit and dummy's ace and king will pick up the rest, leaving the road clear for a long card to score the twelfth trick. We can afford to discard one spade but the other two discards will have to be hearts and we must hope that partner has the ten and nine.

The deal:

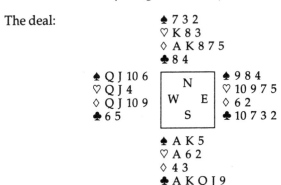

```
              ♠ 7 3 2
              ♡ K 8 3
              ◇ A K 8 7 5
              ♣ 8 4
♠ Q J 10 6         N        ♠ 9 8 4
♡ Q J 4                     ♡ 10 9 7 5
◇ Q J 10 9    W       E     ◇ 6 2
♣ 6 5             S         ♣ 10 7 3 2
              ♠ A K 5
              ♡ A 6 2
              ◇ 4 3
              ♣ A K Q J 9
```

We are going to conclude with seven miscellaneous questions covering the topics studied in this section. Having seen the idea, you should be able to do each in under ninety seconds to complete the test in under ten minutes. In each example, you should state how you think declarer is trying to make the contract and how you propose to stop him. You should also, as far as possible, be able to write down how you think the twenty-six unseen cards are distributed between partner and declarer and demonstrate that your answers are consistent with the bidding and play to date. Start your stop-watch.

Problem 13

Hand No. 64

Dealer East

E–W vulnerable

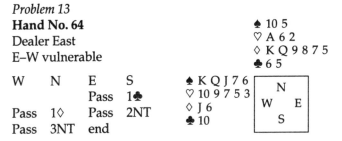

W	N	E	S
		Pass	1♣
Pass	1◇	Pass	2NT
Pass	3NT	end	

```
♠ 10 5
♡ A 6 2
◇ K Q 9 8 7 5
♣ 6 5
♠ K Q J 7 6      N
♡ 10 9 7 5 3
◇ J 6         W       E
♣ 10             S
```

You lead top spades and South takes the third round, partner following with the ♠2, ♠3 and ♠9. Now South leads the ◇4. How do you defend?

Problem 14

Hand No. 65

Dealer East

Both vulnerable

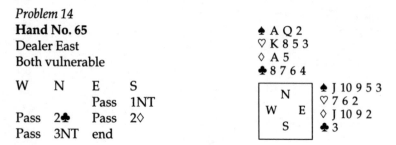

W	N	E	S
		Pass	1NT
Pass	2♣	Pass	2◊
Pass	3NT	end	

West cashes the four top clubs, South following while you discard your three hearts. West continues with the ♡Q, which South wins with the ♡A while you can afford to discard a low spade. South now leads a second round of hearts to West's ♡9 and dummy's ♡K. You are down to four spades and four diamonds and something has to go! What do you discard this time?

Problem 15

Hand No. 66

Dealer South

Neither vulnerable

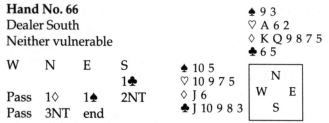

W	N	E	S
			1♣
Pass	1◊	1♠	2NT
Pass	3NT	end	

You lead the ♠10 and it holds, East encouraging with the ♠8 and South playing the ♠4. On the second round, East puts in the ♠J and South's ace wins. He continues with the ◊4. How do you defend?

Problem 16

Hand No. 67

Dealer South

Neither vulnerable

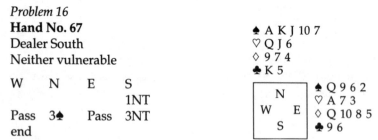

W	N	E	S
			1NT
Pass	3♠	Pass	3NT
end			

West leads the ♡10 to dummy's ♡J. How do you defend?

Problem 17
Hand No. 68
Dealer East
Both vulnerable

♠ Q 7 3
♡ A 6 4
◊ K J 9 8 7 5
♣ 7

W	N	E	S
		Pass	1♣
Pass	1◊	Pass	1♡
Pass	1♠	Pass	1NT
Pass	3◊	Pass	3NT
end			

♠ J 10 4
♡ 7 2
◊ Q 6
♣ Q 10 9 5 4 3

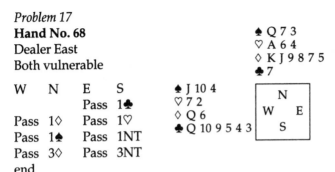

You lead the ♠J to the ♣3, ♠9 and ♠K. South continues with the ◊4.
How do you defend?

Problem 18
Hand No. 69
Dealer South
N–S vulnerable

♠ A Q 8 7 2
♡ 6 5 4
◊ 4 2
♣ A Q 7

W	N	E	S
			2NT
Pass	3♣	Pass	3NT
Pass	6NT	end	

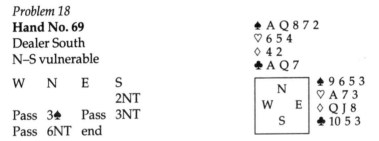

♠ 9 6 5 3
♡ A 7 3
◊ Q J 8
♣ 10 5 3

West leads the ♡10 to your ♡A and South's ♡J. You return the suit
to South's ♡K. He cashes the ♡Q and four rounds of clubs, having
started with ♣ K J 6 4. On the last round, you are down to your
spades and diamonds. What do you discard?

Problem 19
Hand No. 70
Dealer South
Both vulnerable

♠ 6
♡ A 6 4
◊ K J 9 8 7 5
♣ 7 4 3

W	N	E	S
			1♣
Pass	1◊	Pass	3NT
end			

♠ K 10 9 8 4
♡ 7 2
◊ Q 6
♣ Q 10 9 6

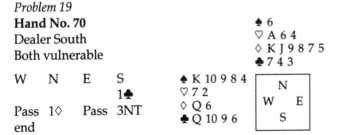

You lead the ♠10 to the ♣6, ♠2 and ♠Q. South continues with the
◊4. How do you defend?

Solutions

Problem 13

We have no entry to our established spades but we see that South could be in similar difficulties in respect of the diamonds. It is clear that, unless partner has ◊ A 10 x, the defence has no hope of preventing the suit being established and therefore will not be able to defeat the contract. The diamond position is a classic example of the kind of set up discussed in *The Expert Beginner*:

```
            K Q 9 8 7 5
              ┌─────┐
              │  N  │
        J 6   │ W E │  A 10 x
              │  S  │
              └─────┘
               x x
```

Clearly, the defenders will win two tricks but *which* defender wins them, and in what order the tricks are won is important. Suppose we play an innocent 'second-hand-low'. Dummy will also play low and partner's ten will win. Now with the ♡A kept intact on dummy, declarer can play a second round, again losing to East, and later enter dummy with the ♡A to enjoy the rest of the suit, making the contract for the loss of two spades and two diamonds. But now try the effect of putting up the ◊J and the picture changes decisively. If South ducks, we cash our spades and another diamond to put the contract two off. So he must rise with one of dummy's honours and now partner ducks! The two stoppers remain intact and now, while South can still set up the suit, he lacks the extra entry needed to cash it.

The deal:

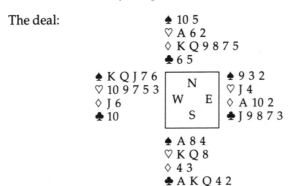

```
                    ♠ 10 5
                    ♡ A 6 2
                    ◇ K Q 9 8 7 5
                    ♣ 6 5
  ♠ K Q J 7 6    ┌──────────┐    ♠ 9 3 2
  ♡ 10 9 7 5 3   │    N     │    ♡ J 4
  ◇ J 6          │ W      E │    ◇ A 10 2
  ♣ 10           │    S     │    ♣ J 9 8 7 3
                 └──────────┘
                    ♠ A 8 4
                    ♡ K Q 8
                    ◇ 4 3
                    ♣ A K Q 4 2
```

Forced to turn to clubs, he is held to eight tricks when they break 5–1.

Problem 14

With West having shown 10 points in clubs and, by implication, 3 in hearts, South must have the rest of the high cards and is therefore assured of three tricks each in spades and diamonds plus the two top hearts. The clue to our discard lies in the bidding. South denied a four-card major and therefore cannot have more than three spades. He may, however, have four diamonds. The safe discard is therefore a spade.

The deal:

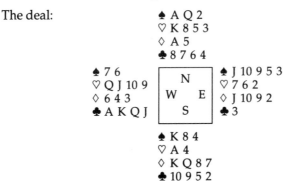

```
                    ♠ A Q 2
                    ♡ K 8 5 3
                    ◇ A 5
                    ♣ 8 7 6 4
  ♠ 7 6         ┌──────────┐    ♠ J 10 9 5 3
  ♡ Q J 10 9    │    N     │    ♡ 7 6 2
  ◇ 6 4 3       │ W      E │    ◇ J 10 9 2
  ♣ A K Q J     │    S     │    ♣ 3
                └──────────┘
                    ♠ K 8 4
                    ♡ A 4
                    ◇ K Q 8 7
                    ♣ 10 9 5 2
```

Problem 15

The diamond position will need to be identical to that in Problem 13, but the rest of the hand has changed in that partner has the defenders' long suit and we need him to win both diamond tricks.

To put up the jack this time would be fatal – exactly what South wants. He will duck and thereby lose the trick to the hand exhausted of spades. He will now have time to set up and cash the diamonds before we can enjoy our spades. But now try the effect of playing low and South is sunk. If he goes up with an honour from dummy, partner ducks and the diamonds are dead for lack of entries. If he ducks, partner's ◇10 wins and East can knock out declarer's last spade stop while he still has the ◇A. The sophisticated student with an eye to advanced play will notice that, in the case where South plays an honour from dummy and partner mistakenly wins, we can still defeat the contract by *discarding the ◇J* on the third round of spades, ensuring that East will win any future diamond trick. Effectively we are transposing:

In diagram (1), South can insist on losing a trick to the harmless West hand by playing the low card from his hand and allowing the jack to hold. In (2), however, he cannot keep East off play.

The deal:

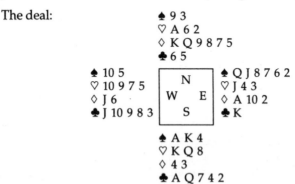

Problem 16

The first question to ask is 'Who has the ♡K?' The ♡10 would be a legitimate lead from 10 9 8 x or K 10 9 x or longer suits. The way to tackle this problem is to consider the consequences of each assumption. South's bid of 3NT over 3♠ gives the vital clue. He is likely to have a doubleton spade or (less likely but possible) a flat 3343 or 3334 hand. In either case, he must have at least three hearts, leaving partner with, at most, four. If they include the ♡K, we can work out that we will take three heart tricks and the ♠Q but no more. With 8 points in our hand, 14 in dummy and at least 12 with South, partner is left with a maximum of 6. However the other three points are comprised, there is no way that we shall be able to set up and cash five tricks if we continue hearts. You should satisfy yourself of this by trying out various deals consistent with the bidding.

There is a chance, however, if we assume that partner has the ◊K or ◊A. Now we can take three diamond tricks in addition to the ♡A and ♠Q, provided we abandon hearts and switch to diamonds at once.

The deal:

```
                    ♠ A K J 10 7
                    ♡ Q J 6
                    ◊ 9 7 4
                    ♣ K 5
  ♠ 8 3                              ♠ Q 9 6 2
  ♡ 10 9 8 2         ┌─────────┐     ♡ A 7 3
  ◊ K 6 3            │    N    │     ◊ Q 10 8 5
  ♣ Q 10 7 2         │  W   E  │     ♣ 9 6
                     │    S    │
                     └─────────┘
                    ♠ 5 4
                    ♡ K 5 4
                    ◊ A J 2
                    ♣ A J 8 4 3
```

In order to pin the jack, the middle card from the East holding, i.e. the ten, is correct and now South has no answer.

Problem 17

As in Problems 13 and 15, it is clear that South will make the contract in some comfort if the diamond suit can be brought in. This implies that the defenders will need a double stop, i.e. partner holding ◊ A 10 x. Partner's encouragement of the opening lead marks him with the ♠A – just as well – if the ♠Q were an entry to dummy, there would be no hope of preventing the diamonds being established and cashed.

The deal:

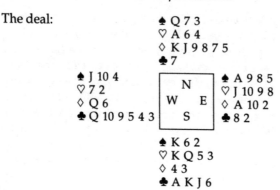

Now, if we play second-hand-low, South will be successful if he puts in the nine, forcing partner to win this first round. East cannot profitably attack spades from his side and South will have time to play a second round of diamonds to knock out the ace and use the ♡A as entry to cash them. However, if we put in the ◊Q now, South is sunk. If he goes up with the ◊K, partner will hold up and the diamonds are dead. If he plays low, we can cash three immediate spade tricks and still have the ◊A to come for our fifth trick.

Problem 18

We have 7 points and the opponents are in a slam which leaves little, if anything, for partner. South has already won two tricks in hearts and four in clubs to total six so far. He will obviously have the two top diamonds – eight – and therefore we can see that, if the spade suit comes in, there will be enough tricks. Our only hope is that partner has the jack and ten so that our nine will be a stopper:

The deal:

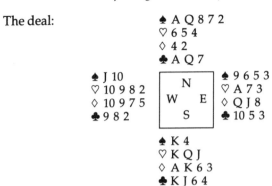

♠ A Q 8 7 2
♡ 6 5 4
◇ 4 2
♣ A Q 7

♠ J 10
♡ 10 9 8 2
◇ 10 9 7 5
♣ 9 8 2

♠ 9 6 5 3
♡ A 7 3
◇ Q J 8
♣ 10 5 3

♠ K 4
♡ K Q J
◇ A K 6 3
♣ K J 6 4

At all costs, we must keep our spade holding intact and discard a diamond, hoping that partner has the ◇10 and can control the third round.

Problem 19

The diamond position (unchanged from Problem 17) should be familiar by now. Again, partner will have to be credited with A 10 x if the defence is to have any chance. In that case, with only one side entry to dummy, South will have to lose the first round if he is to bring the suit in. With partner having discouraged the spades, South must be credited with A Q J and the next round will have to come from partner's side of the table. For that reason, we must play to this trick so that, if South ducks completely, partner can win and push a spade through. If we were to play the ◇Q, South could ensure the contract by allowing her to hold, after which he will have time to knock out the ◇A while his spade stopper remains intact.

The deal:

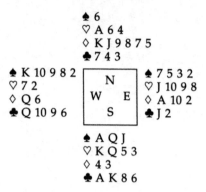

```
                        ♠ 6
                        ♡ A 6 4
                        ◊ K J 9 8 7 5
                        ♣ 7 4 3
        ♠ K 10 9 8 2                    ♠ 7 5 3 2
        ♡ 7 2            N              ♡ J 10 9 8
        ◊ Q 6       W        E          ◊ A 10 2
        ♣ Q 10 9 6        S             ♣ J 2
                        ♠ A Q J
                        ♡ K Q 5 3
                        ◊ 4 3
                        ♣ A K 8 6
```

As if it needed repeating, you are encouraged to replay all the hands, noting the variations, until you understand each one. Then you can go on to the complications of the trump suit in the next section.

SECTION 4:

Defence against Trump Contracts

We are going to start this section with the subject of 'losing tricks to the right hand' (which is obviously closely connected to the study of endplays) as seen from the defenders' point of view; and, in connection with it, we shall learn a little more about defensive signalling. In this area, problems very often arise when West has a fairly strong hand and East is very weak. If West has tenace positions over declarer, he will need to put his partner on lead – difficult if East has very poor cards. Let us start with a common example in which defenders continually allow declarer to make a contract to which he has no right.

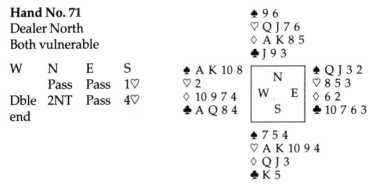

Hand No. 71
Dealer North
Both vulnerable

	♠ 9 6
	♡ Q J 7 6
	◇ A K 8 5
	♣ J 9 3

W	N	E	S
	Pass	Pass	1♡
Dble	2NT	Pass	4♡
end			

♠ A K 10 8   ♠ Q J 3 2
♡ 2   ♡ 8 5 3
◇ 10 9 7 4   ◇ 6 2
♣ A Q 8 4   ♣ 10 7 6 3

♠ 7 5 4
♡ A K 10 9 4
◇ Q J 3
♣ K 5

West cashes his two top spades and exits passively in one of the red suits. South draws trumps, discards a losing club on the fourth round of diamonds, ruffs his losing spade in dummy and concedes one club trick for the contract. And yet, the defenders had four tricks for the taking – two spades and two clubs. The problem was to how to get East in to push a club through. East was at fault – which spade did he play on the first trick?

The three would hardly look encouraging. The correct card was the queen!

In an earlier book, I explained the principle of 'going as near to the card played as possible' to show a solid holding and this is a case in point.

It costs nothing for East to part with his queen as he knows only two rounds of spades are going to stand up anyway. The important point to realize is that, particularly if the club position is broken as above, *he* must win the second spade trick. By playing his queen under his partner's ace, he promises the jack (and denies the king). Now West can safely lead a low spade at trick two, won by East, and now two club tricks defeat the contract. Let us juggle the spade around to illustrate similar positions:

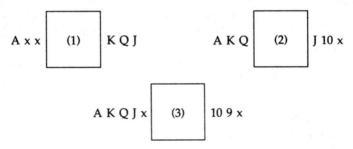

In (1), the king played under the ace promises the queen. In (2), I recommend the lead of the queen from ace-king-queen. East drops the jack to promise the ten. In (3), I recommend the lead of the jack from A K Q J. Now East drops the ten to promise the nine. The principle applies when discarding. Suppose that West leads a suit; South wins and starts drawing trumps, East discarding early. A particularly important example arises when East holds something like Q J 10 x x in a side-suit. The discard of the queen, promising the lower honours but denying the king, may be a vital guide to West's defence:

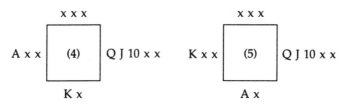

In (4), West is warned that touching the suit will cost a trick and will probably avoid leading it, holding the tenace position over South. In (5), he is happy to attack it, effectively leading from K Q J.

Having seen the idea, I should like you to do the next three examples in match conditions. You should be able to do each in well under forty-five seconds, completing the test in less than two minutes. Start your stop-watch.

Problem 1

Hand No. 72
Dealer South
E–W vulnerable

♠ 9 8 2
♡ Q J 10 4
◊ 4 3
♣ Q J 3 2

W	N	E	S
			1♡
Pass	2♡	Pass	4♡
end			

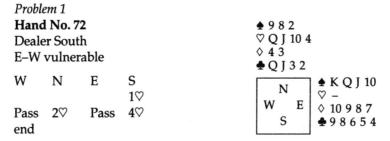

♠ K Q J 10
♡ –
◊ 10 9 8 7
♣ 9 8 6 5 4

West leads the ♣10 to the ♣2, ♣4 and ♣A. South plays the ♡2, won by partner's ♡K. What do you discard?

Problem 2

Hand No. 73
Dealer South
Neither vulnerable

♠ 9 8 2
♡ Q J 10 4
◊ K 10 3
♣ Q 9 3

W	N	E	S
			1♡
Pass	2♡	Pass	4♡
end			

♠ A 7 5 4
♡ A K 3
◊ J 6 5 4
♣ 10 7

You lead the ♣10 to the ♣3, ♣4 and ♣A. South plays the ♡2 and you win with the ♡A, partner discarding the ♠Q. How do you continue and plan the defence of the rest of the hand?

Problem 3
Hand No. 74
Dealer North
E–W vulnerable

♠ 9 8 3
♡ Q J 10 4
◊ A K Q J 10
♣ Q

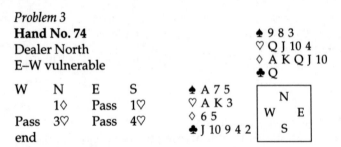

W	N	E	S
	1◊	Pass	1♡
Pass	3♡	Pass	4♡
end			

♠ A 7 5
♡ A K 3
◊ 6 5
♣ J 10 9 4 2

You lead the ♣J to the ♣Q, ♣K and ♣A. South plays the ♡2 to your ♡K, partner discarding the ♠Q. How do you continue?

Solutions

Problem 1
Clearly we will want partner to switch to spades. The ♠10 would certainly be an encouraging card but it is best, especially as the spades are rock solid, to make the position clear to partner by discarding the ♠K! This cannot cost as only three rounds of spades will be played and there is no need to keep all four of our spades.

The deal:

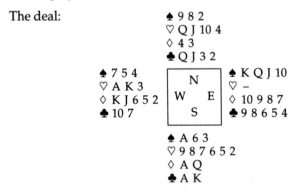

♠ 9 8 2
♡ Q J 10 4
◊ 4 3
♣ Q J 3 2

♠ 7 5 4
♡ A K 3
◊ K J 6 5 2
♣ 10 7

♠ K Q J 10
♡ –
◊ 10 9 8 7
♣ 9 8 6 5 4

♠ A 6 3
♡ 9 8 7 6 5 2
◊ A Q
♣ A K

Many players would overcall with 2◊ on the West hand but there are three good arguments against it. First, the vulnerability is adverse and a heavy defeat would be very costly. Second, the suit is neither long nor strong enough. Third (a point often missed and underestimated in importance), the outside honours are in the opponents' bid suit, hearts, and therefore will not be working for long-suit tricks. The hand is thus better suited to defence and an overcall, particularly two-over-one, is best avoided.

Note that, unless West switches to spades immediately, South will have time to draw trumps and enjoy two discards on the clubs, finishing with four trump tricks, four clubs and the other two aces.

Problem 2
Partner has indicated ♠ Q J 10 and South is marked with the ♠K. To play spades now would cost a trick and passive defence is called for. Partner has discouraged clubs and it is clear that South has the honours in that suit so it is safe to play a second club. When regaining the lead in trumps, it is best to get off play with a third round of trumps and avoid touching diamonds.

The deal:

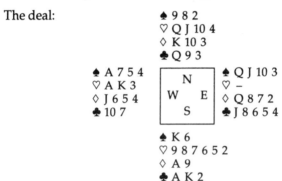

```
                    ♠ 9 8 2
                    ♡ Q J 10 4
                    ◊ K 10 3
                    ♣ Q 9 3
     ♠ A 7 5 4        ┌─────────┐      ♠ Q J 10 3
     ♡ A K 3          │    N    │      ♡ -
     ◊ J 6 5 4        │ W     E │      ◊ Q 8 7 2
     ♣ 10 7           │    S    │      ♣ J 8 6 5 4
                      └─────────┘
                    ♠ K 6
                    ♡ 9 8 7 6 5 2
                    ◊ A 9
                    ♣ A K 2
```

In the above layout, we would get away with the ◊J, but a low diamond would give South an extra trick and the contract. It is therefore best not touched at all. South should be left to take his nine tricks and we should wait for our two spades.

Problem 3
This looks like a repeat of Problem 2, but that only applies in the context of the spade suit considered in isolation. The rest of the hand shows a dramatic change in that, if we defend passively, South is going to discard his losers on those solid diamonds. For that reason, spades must be attacked at once, *even if it means giving an unnecessary trick in that suit*. South cannot enjoy those diamonds until trumps are drawn and we are in time to take two spade tricks

(for one lost) in addition to the two top trumps.

The deal:

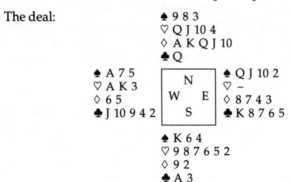

```
                        ♠ 9 8 3
                        ♡ Q J 10 4
                        ◊ A K Q J 10
                        ♣ Q
        ♠ A 7 5                          ♠ Q J 10 2
        ♡ A K 3              N           ♡ –
        ◊ 6 5           W        E       ◊ 8 7 4 3
        ♣ J 10 9 4 2         S           ♣ K 8 7 6 5
                        ♠ K 6 4
                        ♡ 9 8 7 6 5 2
                        ◊ 9 2
                        ♣ A 3
```

These two hands illustrate the hopelessness of religiously adhering to partner's signals rather than *using the information given*. I stressed this point in my defensive signalling book *Signal Success in Bridge*. In the earlier books in this series, I recommended that readers study the early chapters of that book and I now suggest that you continue towards the more difficult signals, always remembering that signals are there to *give information* rather than to *command* or *forbid* partner to lead a particular suit.

We can now extend our study towards the avoidance of being endplayed. In *The Expert Beginner*, I showed a hand in which the diamond position looked like this:

```
                    A K Q 10
                        N
            x       W        E       J x x x
                        S

                    x x x x
```

West's failure to follow to the second round revealed the position and we learnt that the loser could only be avoided if East could be forced to lead the third round. Fortunately, the heart position in this hand looked like this (with one having been discarded early):

A x x

```
      N
x x x W   E  Q J 10
      S
```

K x x

and I explained that, after eliminating the black suits, South would cash the ♡A and ♡K and then play a third round. East would be forced to win and lead away from his ◊J. I also explained that, had any of the three heart honours been in the West hand:

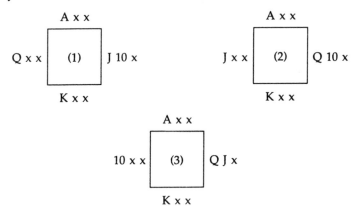

A x x

Q x x | (1) | J 10 x

K x x

A x x

J x x | (2) | Q 10 x

K x x

A x x

10 x x | (3) | Q J x

K x x

the defenders could have arranged for West, rather than East, to win the third round, saving East from having to lead away from his diamonds. In (1), West wins automatically. In (2), East must throw his queen on the first or second round. In (3), East must throw both his queen and jack on the first two rounds to leave West's ten as master.

That hand was a no-trump contract. In a trump contract, the element of ruff and discard may come into play if South is able to keep trumps in both his hand and dummy. Let us look at an example.

Hand No. 75
Dealer North
Both vulnerable

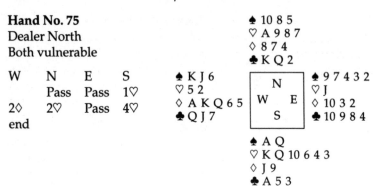

W	N	E	S
	Pass	Pass	1♡
2◊	2♡	Pass	4♡
end			

North:
♠ 10 8 5
♡ A 9 8 7
◊ 8 7 4
♣ K Q 2

West:
♠ K J 6
♡ 5 2
◊ A K Q 6 5
♣ Q J 7

East:
♠ 9 7 4 3 2
♡ J
◊ 10 3 2
♣ 10 9 8 4

South:
♠ A Q
♡ K Q 10 6 4 3
◊ J 9
♣ A 5 3

West leads top diamonds, South ruffing the third round. He draws trumps in two rounds and plays the ♣A, ♣K and a third round. If West wins, South will make the contract. West must now either give South a free finesse in spades or play a diamond, allowing South to ruff in dummy while discarding his potentially losing ♣Q. West should have anticipated the danger. He has 16 points and his partner has shown the ♡J. Thus the opponents are likely to have the rest of the points to justify being in game. He must avoid winning a club trick by playing his honours on the first two rounds. Now East wins the third round and pushes a spade through South's tenace to defeat the contract.

How could East have helped? A discard of the ♣10 on the second round of trumps, promising the ♣9 while denying the ♣J, would have clarified the position to his partner.

You should now be able to do the next two examples in match conditions in under a minute. Start your stop-watch.

Problem 4
Hand No. 76
Dealer East
E–W vulnerable

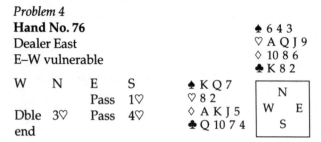

W	N	E	S
	Pass	Pass	1♡
Dble	3♡	Pass	4♡
end			

North:
♠ 6 4 3
♡ A Q J 9
◊ 10 8 6
♣ K 8 2

West:
♠ K Q 7
♡ 8 2
◊ A K J 5
♣ Q 10 7 4

With a strong holding in all three side suits, it seems that, if South is going to make this contract, it will be by ruffing, so you make the correct lead of a trump, which declarer takes in dummy, partner following with the ♡3. The ◊6 follows to the ◊2, ◊Q and your ◊K. Your second trump is again won in dummy, partner discarding the ♠J, and South now ruffs a diamond. Returning to dummy in trumps, while you discard the ♣4 and partner the ◊3, declarer ruffs dummy's last diamond. Now follow the ♠A and the ♠8. How do you defend?

Problem 5
Hand No. 77
Dealer West
Both vulnerable

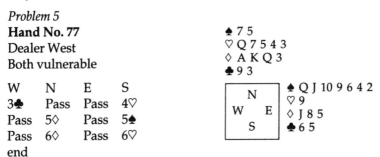

		♠ 7 5
		♡ Q 7 5 4 3
		◊ A K Q 3
		♣ 9 3

W	N	E	S
3♣	Pass	Pass	4♡
Pass	5◊	Pass	5♠
Pass	6◊	Pass	6♡
end			

```
          N        ♠ Q J 10 9 6 4 2
      W       E    ♡ 9
          S        ◊ J 8 5
                   ♣ 6 5
```

North's 5◊ bid is a cue-bid, agreeing hearts rather than an attempt to play in 5◊. There is no point in arguing with partner when you have not promised any hearts, particularly when the alternative contract involves raising the level of bidding.

West leads the ◊10, won in dummy. Declarer cashes the two top hearts, partner following. What do you discard on the second round and what would you have discarded had your hand been: ♠J 10 9 8 6 4 2   ♡9   ◊J 8 5   ♣Q 5?

Solutions

Problem 4
The play so far has marked South with six trumps and one diamond and, with partner having shown the ♠J, South is likely to have the rest of the points; at least he will need the ace and jack of clubs to have any chance at all. To defeat the contract, we shall need two tricks in spades and one in clubs, implying that South's shape will need to be 3613.

The deal:

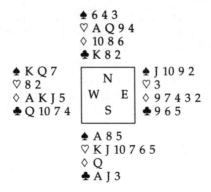

```
              ♠ 6 4 3
              ♡ A Q 9 4
              ◊ 10 8 6
              ♣ K 8 2
♠ K Q 7                        ♠ J 10 9 2
♡ 8 2            N             ♡ 3
◊ A K J 5    W     E           ◊ 9 7 4 3 2
♣ Q 10 7 4       S             ♣ 9 6 5
              ♠ A 8 5
              ♡ K J 10 7 6 5
              ◊ Q
              ♣ A J 3
```

The ♣Q is well placed in our hand but we must avoid opening up the suit, otherwise we will give South a free finesse. Equally, we must avoid leading a fourth round of diamonds as this will give him a ruff and discard. Let us look at the two three-card positions in the black suits:

```
        ♠ 6 4 3                         ♣ K 8 2
          N                               N
♠ K Q 7  W   E  ♠ 10 9 x      ♣ Q 10 7  W   E  ♣ x x x
          S                               S
        ♠ A x x                         ♣ A J x
```

In spades, declarer will win one trick and the defenders two, but we have control over who wins the defenders' tricks. If we play low on the ♠A, we will have to win both tricks and be left on play, forced to open up the clubs or give a ruff and discard as explained above. But partner's discard of the ♠J has promised the ♠10. We can therefore safely throw an honour under the ♠A and win the second round with our other honour. We now play our ♠7 to give the lead to partner. He exits with a club and declarer is now unable to avoid the club loser.

You are strongly urged to play this hand out, card by card, to satisfy yourself that you understand the importance of the order of play and that it is not good enough to throw an honour under the ♠A and then play low on the second round, allowing partner to win that trick. He will exit in clubs and our ♣10 will force dummy's

♣K. But now a third round of spades will leave us on play and we will be forced to give a ruff and discard or lead a club in this two-card position:

```
              ♣ 8 2
            ┌───────┐
            │   N   │
  ♣ Q 7     │ W   E │    ♣ x x
            │   S   │
            └───────┘
              ♣ A J
```

Again South is given a free finesse.

Problem 5

The first point to note is that partner failed to lead a club at the beginning. The implication is that he has a broken holding – typically A Q or K J. With our hand and dummy devoid of honours, South must have the high cards partner is missing. We can now see the danger. South has five obvious tricks in trumps and four in diamonds and the contract could well depend on whether he can force partner to open up the clubs to our cost.

The club suit is best attacked from our side and the only hope of our getting in lies in spades. The discard of the ♠Q tells partner that we have the ♠J so that he knows what to do in this situation:

The deal:

```
                   ♠ 7 5
                   ♡ Q 7 5 4 3
                   ◇ A K Q 3
                   ♣ 9 3
  ♠ K 3                          ♠ Q J 10 9 6 4 2 (J 10 9 8 6 4 2)
  ♡ 8 2           ┌───────┐      ♡ 9
  ◇ 10 9          │   N   │      ◇ J 8 5
  ♣ K J 10 8 7 4 2│ W   E │      ♣ 6 5 (Q 5)
                  │   S   │
                  └───────┘
                   ♠ A 8 (A Q)
                   ♡ A K J 10 6
                   ◇ 7 6 4 2
                   ♣ A Q (A 6)
```

After drawing trumps, South will cash his four diamonds and then play the ♠A and another spade. If partner wins this trick, he will be left with nothing but clubs and be forced to give South a free finesse and the contract. He must therefore throw his ♠K under the ♠A to ensure that we win the second round, after which a club from *our* side defeats the contract.

With the second hand shown (cards in brackets), we deny the ♠Q by discarding the ♠J. Now partner knows that he cannot afford to decline the spade trick and must hope that we have a club honour so that he can safely attack clubs from his side.

We are now going on to further study in respect of defenders' communications. These types of three-card positions crop up frequently:

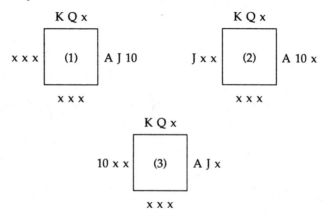

There are no problems if South, North or West leads the first round. North will be obliged to play an honour (or concede two tricks immediately). East's ace wins, after which, in all three diagrams, the ten and jack are solid against dummy's remaining honour and it will be one trick each. What many players do not realize, however, is that the defenders can ensure two tricks in the suit even with East on lead, provided that he starts with a low card and West (or North or South) leads the second round in the remaining two-card positions:

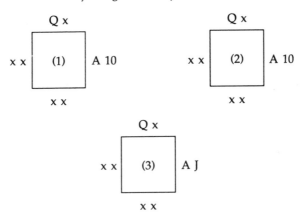

In (1), East started with the jack (promising the ten) and in (2) and (3) with the low card.

These positions are relatively easy to spot when the king and queen are visible on dummy but, of course, it could be that West has the ace and the king and queen are in the closed hand. Provided East has an entry the same play still applies. See if you can do the following examples in under a minute each. Start your stop-watch.

Problem 6
Hand No. 78
Dealer West
N–S vulnerable

♠ J 9 6
♡ 4 2
◇ A Q J 10 3
♣ K Q 4

W	N	E	S
Pass	1NT	Pass	4♠
end			

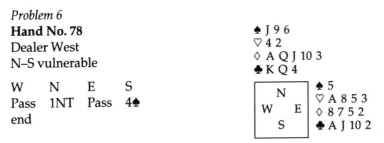

♠ 5
♡ A 8 5 3
◇ 8 7 5 2
♣ A J 10 2

West leads the ♡J and South drops the ♡Q under your ♡A. How do you continue?

Problem 7
Hand No. 79
Dealer East
E–W vulnerable

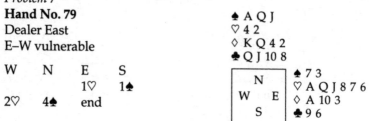

♠ A Q J
♡ 4 2
◇ K Q 4 2
♣ Q J 10 8

W	N	E	S
		1♡	1♠
2♡	4♠	end	

♠ 7 3
♡ A Q J 8 7 6
◇ A 10 3
♣ 9 6

West leads the ♡10 to your ♡A, South dropping the ♡K. How do you continue?

Problem 8
Hand No. 80
Dealer East
Both vulnerable

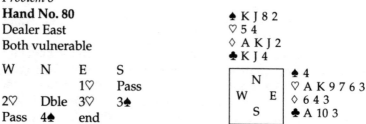

♠ K J 8 2
♡ 5 4
◇ A K J 2
♣ K J 4

W	N	E	S
		1♡	Pass
2♡	Dble	3♡	3♠
Pass	4♠	end	

♠ 4
♡ A K 9 7 6 3
◇ 6 4 3
♣ A 10 3

West leads the ♡J and South drops the ♡Q under your ♡K. How do you continue?

Problem 9
Hand No. 81
Dealer West
Both vulnerable

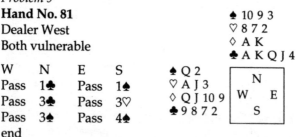

♠ 10 9 3
♡ 8 7 2
◇ A K
♣ A K Q J 4

W	N	E	S
Pass	1♣	Pass	1♠
Pass	3♣	Pass	3♡
Pass	3♠	Pass	4♠
end			

♠ Q 2
♡ A J 3
◇ Q J 10 9
♣ 9 8 7 2

Note how North has avoided bidding no-trumps. He does not want the lead coming round to those weak major suit holdings.

You lead the ◇Q to dummy's ◇K. South runs the ♠10 round to your ♠Q. How do you continue?

Solutions

Problem 6

There is clearly no further joy in hearts and the diamond position is catastrophic. With the ◊K dead in partner's hand, that card is best credited to South and our only hope is that partner has a trump trick and that South cannot profitably enjoy discards on the diamonds before trumps are drawn.

The deal:

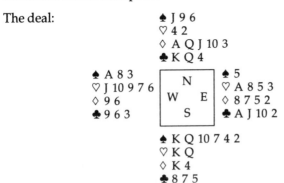

```
                        ♠ J 9 6
                        ♡ 4 2
                        ◊ A Q J 10 3
                        ♣ K Q 4
    ♠ A 8 3                          ♠ 5
    ♡ J 10 9 7 6      N              ♡ A 8 5 3
    ◊ 9 6          W     E           ◊ 8 7 5 2
    ♣ 9 6 3           S              ♣ A J 10 2
                        ♠ K Q 10 7 4 2
                        ♡ K Q
                        ◊ K 4
                        ♣ 8 7 5
```

On those assumptions, we have a trick in hearts and one in trumps and therefore must hope for two in clubs. They must be attacked at once and we start with the ♣J, promising the ♣10. When partner gets in with the ♠A, a second round of clubs ensures two more tricks.

Problem 7

This time, there is no hope for a trump trick as the ♠K must surely be with South and would be hopelessly placed in partner's hand anyway. Partner's points to justify his 2♡ bid can only be in clubs, so we can see three tricks (one club, one diamond, one heart) and the fourth can only come from a second diamond trick. Partner must thus be credited with the ◊J and we must switch to the ◊3 now so that partner is ready to push the second round through dummy when in with the ♣K.

The deal:

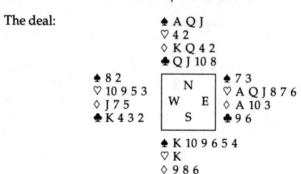

```
            ♠ A Q J
            ♡ 4 2
            ◇ K Q 4 2
            ♣ Q J 10 8
♠ 8 2                       ♠ 7 3
♡ 10 9 5 3                  ♡ A Q J 8 7 6
◇ J 7 5                     ◇ A 10 3
♣ K 4 3 2                   ♣ 9 6
            ♠ K 10 9 6 5 4
            ♡ K
            ◇ 9 8 6
            ♣ A 7 5
```

Problem 8

The diamond position is clearly hopeless and the ◇Q is best credited to South. Therefore the only hope lies in a trump trick and two clubs. This is a slight variation on the above theme in that the ♣Q and ♣J have exchanged places:

The deal:

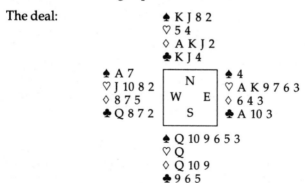

```
            ♠ K J 8 2
            ♡ 5 4
            ◇ A K J 2
            ♣ K J 4
♠ A 7                       ♠ 4
♡ J 10 8 2                  ♡ A K 9 7 6 3
◇ 8 7 5                     ◇ 6 4 3
♣ Q 8 7 2                   ♣ A 10 3
            ♠ Q 10 9 6 5 3
            ♡ Q
            ◇ Q 10 9
            ♣ 9 6 5
```

The line of defence, however, is unchanged. We simply switch to the ♣3 and partner's ♣Q will force dummy's ♣K. When partner takes his trump ace, a second club through dummy's jack will ensure two more tricks.

Problem 9

With the solid clubs waiting to be cashed, desperate measures are called for and it is clear that our tricks can only come from the majors. Partner will therefore have to be credited with the ♠A (any other honour can be finessed against). We must thus set up two heart tricks. There will be no problem if partner has a heart honour but South is likely to have both – the critical case is here:

The deal:

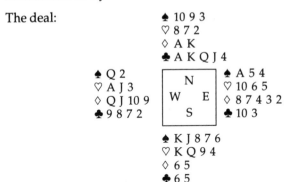

```
              ♠ 10 9 3
              ♡ 8 7 2
              ◇ A K
              ♣ A K Q J 4
  ♠ Q 2                        ♠ A 5 4
  ♡ A J 3          N           ♡ 10 6 5
  ◇ Q J 10 9   W     E         ◇ 8 7 4 3 2
  ♣ 9 8 7 2        S           ♣ 10 3
              ♠ K J 8 7 6
              ♡ K Q 9 4
              ◇ 6 5
              ♣ 6 5
```

We must switch to the ♡3 and partner's ♡10 will knock out an honour from South. On regaining the lead in trumps, East can push through a heart for two more tricks.

In each of these examples, our ace had to be withheld until the second round. The same applies when we are trying to organize a ruff in a suit where the ace is facing a doubleton.

```
        ┌─────┐                      ┌─────┐
  x x   │ (1) │  A x x x    A x x x  │ (2) │   x x
        └─────┘                      └─────┘
```

The fact that a trick has to be lost before the ruff can be enjoyed implies that the declarer is unable to draw trumps immediately, i.e. that the defenders are able to win an early trump trick. In cases where the hand with the ace, (East in (1), West in (2)), has the trump trick or a quick outside entry, the defenders may win the first or second round. But where that hand has no outside entry, the first round needs to be ducked. Let us look at a few examples.

Hand No. 82
Dealer North
Both vulnerable

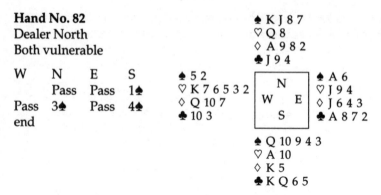

West leads the ♣10. With the ace of trumps in his hand, East can afford to rise with the ♣A on the first round and return the suit, giving himself the chance that the lead is a singleton. Actually, South wins and starts drawing trumps. East wins the first round and leads a third club for his partner to ruff. West exits in diamonds and the defenders then wait for their setting heart trick.

But now let us make a slight alteration, exchanging the positions of the ♠A and ♠5:

Hand No. 83
Dealer North
Both vulnerable

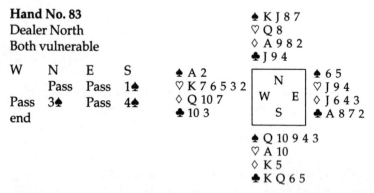

Again West leads the ♣10. This time, if East wins and returns the suit, the contract cannot be defeated. When West gets in with the ♠A, he will have no means of reaching his partner's hand to obtain the club ruff. For that reason, East must play low on the opening lead (actually encouraging with the ♣8). Now, when West takes his ♠A, a second round of clubs puts his partner on lead and the club ruff followed by a diamond exit defeats the contract.

There are at least two obvious problems in practice. First, how does East distinguish between a singleton (when he must win immediately) and a doubleton (when he may have to hold up for one round) in his partner's hand? Second, in cases where he suspects a doubleton, how can he be sure that his partner has trump control? Where there is no trump control, it may be necessary to win and switch to another suit, looking for tricks there.

When we get to more advanced play, we shall learn that there is a signalling system which sometimes helps but very often, there is no sure way. However, the bidding and sight of dummy will often provide good guides. Also, when the suit is not led (as often happens where East has the doubleton and West the ace to three or more), the actual opening lead may give useful information.

I should like you to try the following four examples against the stop-watch, aiming for under seventy-five seconds each to complete the test in under five minutes. Start your stopwatch.

Problem 10
Hand No. 84
Dealer West
Neither vulnerable

♠ K J 10 4
♡ 10 2
◇ A Q 7
♣ K J 5 4

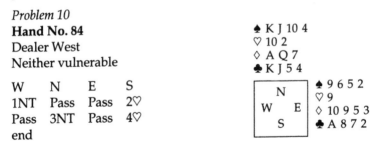

♠ 9 6 5 2
♡ 9
◇ 10 9 5 3
♣ A 8 7 2

W	N	E	S
1NT	Pass	Pass	2♡
Pass	3NT	Pass	4♡
end			

West leads the ♣9 to dummy's ♣K. How do you defend?

Problem 11
Hand No. 85
Dealer South
Both vulnerable

♠ Q J 10 4
♡ A 8 4
◇ K Q 10 5
♣ 10 4

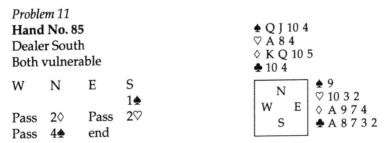

♠ 9
♡ 10 3 2
◇ A 9 7 4
♣ A 8 7 3 2

W	N	E	S
			1♠
Pass	2◇	Pass	2♡
Pass	4♠	end	

West leads the ♣Q to the ♣4, ♣A and South's ♣K. How do you continue?

Problem 12
Hand No. 86
Dealer South
Both vulnerable

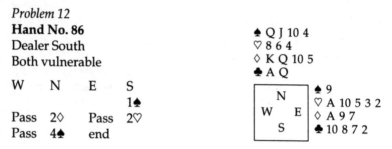

W	N	E	S
			1♠
Pass	2◇	Pass	2♡
Pass	4♠	end	

West leads the ♡9 and dummy plays the ♡4. How do you defend? Would it make any difference if you held ♠9 ♡ A 10 5 3 2 ◇ 9 7 2 ♣ K 8 7 2?

Problem 13
Hand No. 87
Dealer East
E–W vulnerable

♠ 8 6 5 4 2
♡ K Q 10 8
◇ Q
♣ K J 9

♠ 7
♡ A 9 7 3
◇ A K 10 7 5
♣ 10 6 5

W	N	E	S
		Pass	1NT
Pass	2♣	Pass	2♠
Pass	4♠	end	

You lead the ◇A to the ◇Q, ◇6 and ◇2. How do you continue?

Solutions

Problem 10
The first question to ask is 'Who has got the ♣Q?' If it is West, he has led the ♣9 – from what? From Q 9 doubleton, he would lead the queen; from Q 10 9, he would lead the ten and from Q 9 x or a longer suit, he would lead a low card. Clearly, therefore, South has the ♣Q and partner has led from a singleton or doubleton. (With three, he would lead the middle card and from 10 9 x, he would lead the ten). The singleton is ruled out by the 1NT opening bid. Therefore it must be a doubleton. We have no entry to our hand and must hope for partner to hold an early trump trick. We

therefore play an encouraging ♣8 to this trick and hope to give him a ruff on the third round.

The deal:

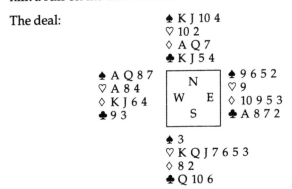

```
                    ♠ K J 10 4
                    ♡ 10 2
                    ◊ A Q 7
                    ♣ K J 5 4
   ♠ A Q 8 7                        ♠ 9 6 5 2
   ♡ A 8 4          N               ♡ 9
   ◊ K J 6 4      W   E             ◊ 10 9 5 3
   ♣ 9 3            S               ♣ A 8 7 2
                    ♠ 3
                    ♡ K Q J 7 6 5 3
                    ◊ 8 2
                    ♣ Q 10 6
```

Note the excellent play by South. He knew very well what was going on and tried to give us the maximum temptation to take the ace at the wrong moment.

Problem 11

There will clearly be no further joy in clubs and, with South having bid hearts, any tricks there can hardly run away. In any case, to play the suit can only help declarer to find missing honours in partner's hand. The diamond position is also grim and, irrespective of the position of the ◊J, we cannot hope for more than one trick. We can see 8 points in our hand and 12 in dummy and partner has already indicated the queen and jack in clubs. That accounts for 23 so far and with South having opened the bidding, partner is unlikely to have more than another trick in high cards.

So where is the fourth trick to come from? The only hope is a ruff and that would have to be in diamonds. This implies that partner will have to have a singleton (in which case we must cash the ace and take the ruff immediately) or a doubleton (in which case we must preserve communications by playing a low diamond now, hoping that partner has the ace or king of trumps and can get in before his trumps are eliminated).

Now before reading on, can you give two good reasons for preferring to assume the doubleton rather than the singleton? First, with a singleton, partner is likely to have led it in preference to the less dynamic club. Second, a singleton diamond in partner's hand implies four in the declarer's, and he has already indicated five spades, four hearts and one club, leaving, at most three diamonds. We therefore switch to a low diamond.

The deal:

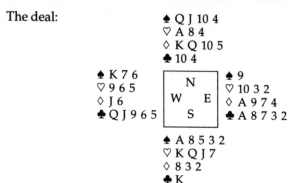

```
              ♠ Q J 10 4
              ♡ A 8 4
              ◊ K Q 10 5
              ♣ 10 4
  ♠ K 7 6                      ♠ 9
  ♡ 9 6 5        N            ♡ 10 3 2
  ◊ J 6       W     E          ◊ A 9 7 4
  ♣ Q J 9 6 5     S           ♣ A 8 7 3 2
              ♠ A 8 5 3 2
              ♡ K Q J 7
              ◊ 8 3 2
              ♣ K
```

Nothing now can prevent a third-round ruff which, along with the two minor aces and the king of trumps, will defeat the contract.

Problem 12

Here South has bid hearts and promised a four-card suit, leaving partner with a singleton; he would have little reason to lead round to a bid suit otherwise. It is safe to go up with the ace and return the suit for a ruff and this holds even without the bid as we have an entry in the ◊A. When partner ruffs, we shall want him to switch to diamonds (the *higher-ranking* of the two minor suits) so we return a *high* heart, the ten. With the ♣K and no ◊A, we would return the ♡2, indicating the desire for the *lower-ranking* suit. That would give us a club trick if South proved to have something like: ♠ A 8 5 3 2 ♡ K Q J 7 ◊ A ♣ x x x as he has no quick way to reach dummy to discard losing clubs on its high diamonds.

The deal:

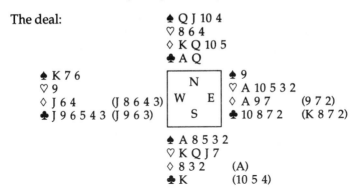

```
                        ♠ Q J 10 4
                        ♡ 8 6 4
                        ◇ K Q 10 5
                        ♣ A Q
  ♠ K 7 6                               ♠ 9
  ♡ 9                                   ♡ A 10 5 3 2
  ◇ J 6 4      (J 8 6 4 3)    W   E     ◇ A 9 7       (9 7 2)
  ♣ J 9 6 5 4 3 (J 9 6 3)               ♣ 10 8 7 2    (K 8 7 2)
                        ♠ A 8 5 3 2
                        ♡ K Q J 7
                        ◇ 8 3 2        (A)
                        ♣ K            (10 5 4)
```

Problem 13

There may be club tricks available but they are unlikely to run away. If partner has ♣ A Q, South's losers can only be discarded on hearts, which means that we will have a second chance to lead clubs when in with the ♡A. The critical position arises when South has strong clubs and partner has a trump trick – which would almost certainly have to be the ♠A as any lower honour would be badly placed under South. In that case, the only hope is a heart ruff. We now have to decide whether to play partner for a singleton heart, i.e. ace and another; or a doubleton, i.e. lead a low heart now and expect partner to return the suit when in with the ♠A. The bidding gives the vital clue. A singleton heart in partner's hand implies four with South and that was denied by the 2♠ bid.

The deal:

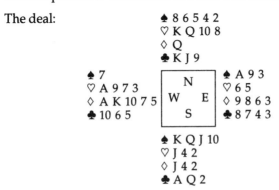

```
                        ♠ 8 6 5 4 2
                        ♡ K Q 10 8
                        ◇ Q
                        ♣ K J 9
  ♠ 7                                   ♠ A 9 3
  ♡ A 9 7 3                             ♡ 6 5
  ◇ A K 10 7 5   W   E                  ◇ 9 8 6 3
  ♣ 10 6 5                              ♣ 8 7 4 3
                        ♠ K Q J 10
                        ♡ J 4 2
                        ◇ J 4 2
                        ♣ A Q 2
```

We must therefore switch to a low heart.

The organization of ruffs is an excellent lead in to the study of trump promotion. Very often, trumps which are not high enough to make tricks in their own right can be promoted if higher trumps belonging to declarer can be diverted for use as ruffers. Let us look at some simple examples.

These kinds of trump layouts occur daily and there seems little hope for East-West. In (1), South's ace and king will swallow up the defenders' trumps and that will be the end of the story. Similarly, in (2), the ace, king and queen will swallow defenders' trumps and again there seems little more to discuss. However, the defence's right to the opening lead can easily swing the pendulum the other way. Taking (1) as example, suppose this is the complete deal:

Hand No. 88
Dealer North
Neither vulnerable

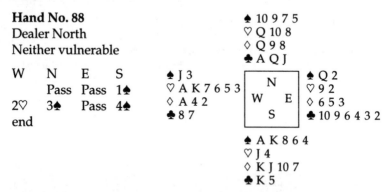

W	N	E	S
	Pass	Pass	1♠
2♡	3♠	Pass	4♠
end			

West cashes the two top hearts and, on seeing his partner peter to show the doubleton, leads a third round. East ruffs with the queen of spades and South has no answer. If he overruffs, he leaves the following effective two-card position in trumps:

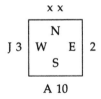

Now the jack of trumps cannot be caught. The ◊A has still to be cashed and the contract is defeated. We can juggle the trump suit around to show other positions in which the defenders can produce a trick out of nothing by playing their trumps to separate tricks.

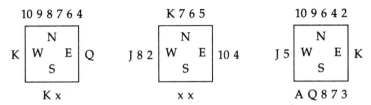

In each case, East ruffs the third round with his *highest* (if he has more than one) trump to promote his partner's high card. Note that it is not good enough to ruff with a low trump and that he should ruff high even if West's side-suit card (here in hearts) is higher than dummy's. Indeed it is good play in this kind of situation (say we exchange the positions of the ♡Q and ♡7):

```
               10 8 7
              ┌────────┐
              │   N    │
A K Q 6 5 3   │ W    E │  9 2
              │   S    │
              └────────┘
                J 4
```

for West to lead a *low* heart on the third round to force his partner to do the right thing.

The play of a high trump by East to force South to overruff and thus promote a card in the West hand is called an *uppercut*. If we turn the position of the heart suit round, we can see that the defenders can force a trump trick out of nothing with even fewer resources than above.

Hand No. 89
Dealer North
Neither vulnerable

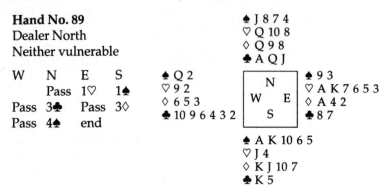

| ♠ J 8 7 4 |
| ♡ Q 10 8 |
| ◊ Q 9 8 |
| ♣ A Q J |

| ♠ Q 2 |
| ♡ 9 2 |
| ◊ 6 5 3 |
| ♣ 10 9 6 4 3 2 |

| ♠ 9 3 |
| ♡ A K 7 6 5 3 |
| ◊ A 4 2 |
| ♣ 8 7 |

| ♠ A K 10 6 5 |
| ♡ J 4 |
| ◊ K J 10 7 |
| ♣ K 5 |

W	N	E	S
	Pass	1♡	1♠
Pass	3♣	Pass	3◊
Pass	4♠	end	

West leads the ♡9 and East cashes the two tops and leads a third round. Again South has no answer. If he ruffs high, West simply discards and his ♠Q cannot be caught. If he ruffs low or discards, West must make a trump trick. Note that, this time (again exchanging the positions of the ♡Q and ♡7), there is no need for East to be clever by playing a low heart on the third round.

Again we can juggle the trump suit around and see more positions in which the defenders can promote a trick:

```
      J 8 7 6 4            10 8 6 5              9 7 5 3
      ┌───────┐           ┌───────┐            ┌───────┐
      │   N   │           │   N   │            │   N   │
   K  │ W   E │ 5    J 4 2 │ W   E │ 7  10 8 6 4│ W   E │  —
      │   S   │           │   S   │            │   S   │
      └───────┘           └───────┘            └───────┘
     A Q 10 9 3 2          A K Q 9 3           A K Q J 2
```

In each case, South must either ruff high to promote West's honour or allow West a trick by ruffing. This play is known as a *trump promotion*.

We can extend the idea to positions in which the defenders are already entitled to one trick and can increase their tally to two by an uppercut by East or, in West's case, *refusing to overruff*.

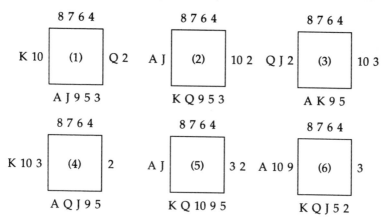

In (1), (2) and (3), West has the long side-suit and East the shortage, as in Hand 88. In each case, East puts on his high trump, forcing South to overruff and thereby promote West's trumps.

In (4), (5) and (6), East has the long side-suit and West the shortage, as in Hand 89. On the third round from East, if South ruffs low, he allows West a cheap trick; so he must ruff high. West refuses to overruff and his lower trumps are promoted.

Having seen the idea, I should like you to do the following four examples in match conditions. You should be aiming to beat thirty seconds per example to complete the test in under two minutes. Start your stop-watch.

Problem 14
Hand No. 90
Dealer North
N–S vulnerable

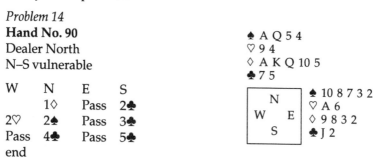

♠ A Q 5 4
♡ 9 4
♢ A K Q 10 5
♣ 7 5

W	N	E	S
	1♢	Pass	2♣
2♡	2♠	Pass	3♣
Pass	4♣	Pass	5♣
end			

♠ 10 8 7 3 2
♡ A 6
♢ 9 8 3 2
♣ J 2

West leads the ♡K to dummy's ♡4. How do you defend?

Problem 15
Hand No. 91
Dealer West
Neither vulnerable

♠ A K Q J 5
♡ 4 2
◇ K 5 2
♣ 9 6 4

W	N	E	S
Pass	1♠	2♣	2♡
Pass	2◇	Pass	4♡
end			

♠ 10 3 2
♡ Q 8 7 5
◇ Q J 9 4
♣ 8 3

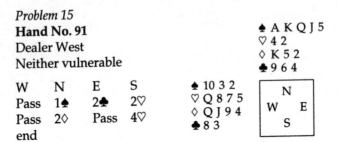

You lead the ♣8. Partner's ♣10 wins and he follows with the ♣A and ♣K. South follows to the first two but ruffs the third round with the ♡J. How do you defend?

Problem 16
Hand No. 92
Dealer East

♠ 8 3 2
♡ A Q
◇ A K 10 4
♣ 8 7 3 2

W	N	E	S
		Pass	1♠
2♣	2◇	Pass	2♡
Pass	4♠	end	

♠ A 4
♡ 7 5 4 3 2
◇ 9 8 7 5
♣ J 4

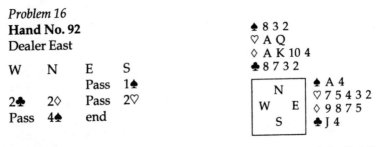

West leads the ♣A followed by the ♣K. You peter while South drops the ♣6 and ♣Q. Now West plays the ♣5 to dummy's ♣8. How do you defend?

Problem 17
Hand No. 93
Dealer West
E–W vulnerable

♠ 8 7
♡ K 7 5 4
◇ A Q 6 3
♣ Q 6 3

W	N	E	S
Pass	Pass	Pass	1♠
Pass	2NT	Pass	4♠
end			

♠ A 6 4
♡ J 8 6 3 2
◇ 10 8 5
♣ 7 5

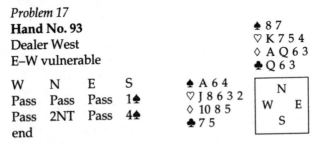

You lead the ♣7 to the ♣3, ♣J and ♣2. Partner cashes the ♣A, all following, and then plays the ♣K which South ruffs with the ♠K. How do you defend?

Solutions

Problem 14

We will clearly make two heart tricks but it is hard to see where the necessary third is coming from. The positions in both spades and diamonds could hardly be better for declarer and thus the only hope lies in trumps. If partner has Q x x or better, there will be no problem but, in the more likely cases where he has Q x or 10 x x, we shall need to use our ♣J to force out one of South's high honours before trumps are touched. This will have to be done on the third round of hearts. We must therefore overtake partner's ♡K and return the suit so that he is on lead for that third round. Irrespective of which heart he plays, we shall put on the ♣J and hopefully promote a trump trick for him.

The deal:

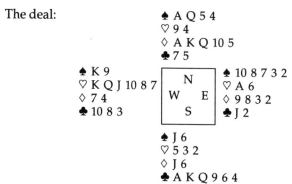

```
                    ♠ A Q 5 4
                    ♡ 9 4
                    ◊ A K Q 10 5
                    ♣ 7 5
   ♠ K 9              ┌──────┐      ♠ 10 8 7 3 2
   ♡ K Q J 10 8 7     │  N   │      ♡ A 6
   ◊ 7 4            W │      │ E    ◊ 9 8 3 2
   ♣ 10 8 3           │  S   │      ♣ J 2
                      └──────┘
                    ♠ J 6
                    ♡ 5 3 2
                    ◊ J 6
                    ♣ A K Q 9 6 4
```

Problem 15

If South has ♡ A K J 10 9 x, he will still be able to pick up our trumps but there is no law insisting that his trumps have to be so strong. Partner need only hold a stiff ♡9 and, by refusing to overruff, we have promoted our ♡8 to a winner for the setting trick. We therefore discard a losing spade now and wait patiently.

The deal:

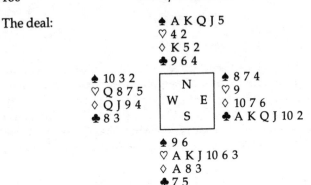

Note that, even if South's trumps are A K J 10 9 x or better, nothing has been lost – our natural trump trick will never run away.

Problem 16

Partner, despite clearly holding the ♣10 and ♣9, has gone out of his way to play a lower card than dummy. Clearly he is crying out for us to ruff and that can only be because he wants a trump promotion. He will probably have Q x, J x x or the like and the honour will be promoted if our ♠A is removed from the scene before a round of trumps has been played. We must therefore play it now.

The deal:

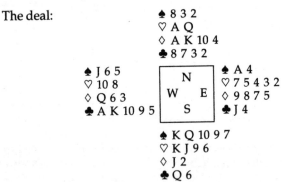

Partner's ♠J will take the setting trick. If we fail to play the ♠A, declarer will cross to dummy twice (once in each red suit) to lead trumps from there. Our ace will now beat air and partner's jack will be caught. Effectively, we have transposed from one three-card position to another:

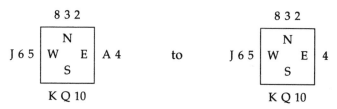

In each of these, North-South takes two tricks to East-West's one but, in the second case, we have already taken the extra trick by ruffing.

Problem 17

There doesn't seem much hope of a trump promotion this time but look at the deal:

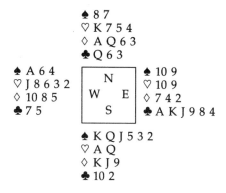

In any event, there is nothing to be gained by overruffing and by discarding (effectively letting the ♠K 'beat air') our lowly ♠6 comes into play. We had to assume that partner had two cards to beat dummy's 8 7 but no more was needed.

We are going to conclude this section with a seven-question miscellaneous test covering the subjects studied. You should be aiming to get under ninety seconds per example to finish in under ten minutes. As usual, give a full analysis, demonstrating consistency with the bidding and early play, and reproducing the full deal as accurately as possible. Start your stop-watch.

Problem 18
Hand No. 94
Dealer South
Neither vulnerable

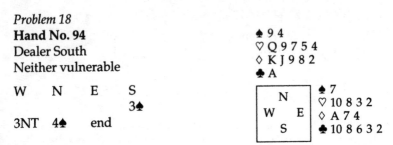

W	N	E	S
			3♣
3NT	4♣	end	

West leads the ♡A, all following. He switches to the ◊6 and dummy's ◊K is played. How do you defend?

Problem 19
Hand No. 95
Dealer North
E–W vulnerable

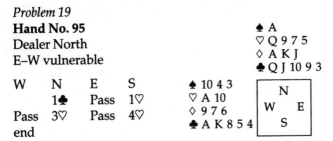

W	N	E	S
	1♣	Pass	1♡
Pass	3♡	Pass	4♡
end			

You lead the ♣A to the ♣3, partner's ♣2 and South's ♣6. How do you continue?

Problem 20
Hand No. 96
Dealer North
E–W vulnerable

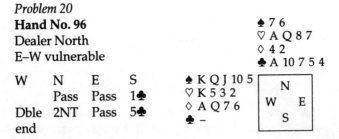

W	N	E	S
	Pass	Pass	1♣
Dble	2NT	Pass	5♣
end			

North's 2NT bid promised a good raise to 3♣. You lead the ♠K to the ♠6, ♠9 and ♠A. South cashes the ♣K, partner following with the ♣2, and plays a low heart to the ♡Q, which wins. On the ♡A, partner drops the ♡10 and declarer follows. South ruffs a heart, partner playing the ♡J, and returns to dummy in trumps, overtaking the ♣9 with the ♣10 while partner discards the ◊3, and ruffs dummy's last heart, bringing down your ♡K. Now South plays the ♠2. How do you defend?

Problem 21
Hand No. 97
Dealer North
Both vulnerable

♠ J 10 7 6 5 3
♡ 10 5 3
◊ 8 6
♣ A K

W	N	E	S
	Pass	Pass	1♠
Pass	3♠	Pass	4♠
end			

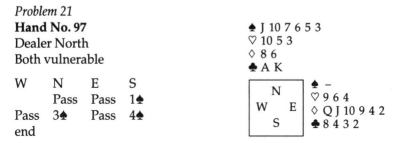

N
W E
S

♠ –
♡ 9 6 4
◊ Q J 10 9 4 2
♣ 8 4 3 2

Partner leads the ♣J to dummy's ace. The ♠J is led from dummy. What do you discard?

Problem 22
Hand No. 98
Dealer East
N–S vulnerable

♠ K 10 6
♡ 9 7
◊ A J 9 8 2
♣ K J 3

W	N	E	S
		Pass	1♠
Pass	2◊	Pass	2♠
Pass	4♠	end	

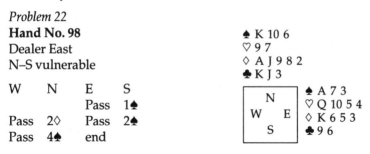

N
W E
S

♠ A 7 3
♡ Q 10 5 4
◊ K 6 5 3
♣ 9 6

West leads the ◊10 and dummy plays low. How do you defend?

Problem 23
Hand No. 99
Dealer West
E–W vulnerable

♠ 6 4 3
♡ 10 8 7 3 2
◊ Q J 9
♣ A K

W	N	E	S
Pass	Pass	Pass	1♡
Pass	3♡	Pass	4♡
end			

♠ Q J 10 5
♡ J 6
◊ 8 5 3
♣ Q 8 5 4

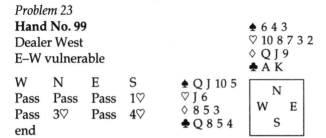

N
W E
S

You lead the ♠Q. Partner overtakes with the ♠K, cashes the ♠A and leads a third round to your ♠10, South following throughout. How do you continue?

Problem 24
Hand No. 100
Dealer West
E–W vulnerable

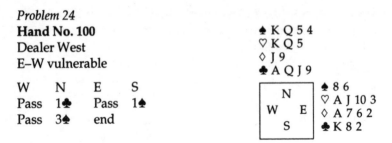

W	N	E	S
Pass	1♣	Pass	1♠
Pass	3♠	end	

West leads the ◇K to dummy's ◇9. How do you defend?

Solutions

Problem 18
First, which card should we play at trick one? Partner has obviously led from ace-king and, with the encouragement/discouragement situation clear (we cannot have any worthwhile high cards in the suit), we are expected to give count. The ♡3 is very unclear (South should still play the ♡6 from a holding of ♡ 6 2) so it is best to play the ♡8. With a preemptive bid in the South hand, partner should realize that this is far more likely to come from a four-card suit than a doubleton. Partner knows that we must be very short of spades after that auction and, with a doubleton heart, we would be left with considerable length in one or both minors and might well have competed over 4♠.

Notice the train of thought. The inferences that can be picked up by considering what has not happened are as frequent as those from what has happened. Getting into the habit of picking them up is invaluable even if they are of little help on a particular hand.

Now, when partner leads the ◇6 and dummy plays the ◇K, we have to ask ourselves what is happening. Has partner led away from the ◇Q and South (very reasonably on the bidding) mis-guessed, or is there another explanation? Indeed, if partner has the ◇Q, he has no reason to touch the suit as the position will not run away. South will have to play it himself. Partner should either be drawing trumps, to prevent club ruffs, or attacking clubs, trying to remove dummy's entries to the diamonds. No, partner has led diamonds for another reason. His 3NT bid indicates a spade stop and therefore trump control and he is angling for a ruff. It is most unlikely that partner (after that bid) has a singleton diamond (which would leave South with four alongside his seven-card spade suit) – a doubleton is far more probable. Lacking an outside entry, we must hold up our ace and be ready to use it as entry to give a ruff when partner takes the ♠A.

The deal:

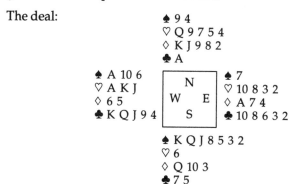

```
                    ♠ 9 4
                    ♡ Q 9 7 5 4
                    ◇ K J 9 8 2
                    ♣ A
    ♠ A 10 6                        ♠ 7
    ♡ A K J         N               ♡ 10 8 3 2
    ◇ 6 5       W       E           ◇ A 7 4
    ♣ K Q J 9 4     S               ♣ 10 8 6 3 2
                    ♠ K Q J 8 5 3 2
                    ♡ 6
                    ◇ Q 10 3
                    ♣ 7 5
```

Note again, the excellent play by South – giving you maximum temptation to take the ◇A at the wrong moment.

Problem 19

Let us first consider the clubs. It will be obvious to partner that we have led from ace-king – we would have no reason to lead an unsupported ace of a suit bid over us. Thus the relevant information is count and the ♣2 must indicate an odd number – here obviously a singleton. We can thus see three top tricks in clubs and hearts but where is the fourth to come from? Even giving partner the ◇Q, a trick in that suit is most unlikely. South could have the chance to discard the ◇J on the ♠K if he has it or he might be able to discard a losing diamond in his hand on a club honour in dummy, once our ace has been knocked out.

A far better chance lies in the trump suit. South must have the ♡K if he is to have any chance at all but, if partner has the jack and eight, we have a chance. We learnt earlier that we can cause havoc by forcing declarer to use his high trumps as ruffers and saw examples where one such strike is lethal. Sometimes we have to swing the axe twice.

The deal:

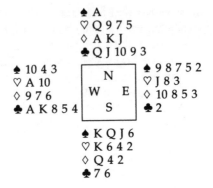

```
              ♠ A
              ♡ Q 9 7 5
              ◊ A K J
              ♣ Q J 10 9 3
♠ 10 4 3                        ♠ 9 8 7 5 2
♡ A 10                          ♡ J 8 3
◊ 9 7 6                         ◊ 10 8 5 3
♣ A K 8 5 4                     ♣ 2
              ♠ K Q J 6
              ♡ K 6 4 2
              ◊ Q 4 2
              ♣ 7 6
```

We cash our ♣K and lead a third round. Partner ruffs with the ♡8 to force South to overruff with the ♡K. That leaves, effectively, the following two-card position in trumps:

```
              Q 9
       A 10  [N W E S]  J 3
              6 4
```

With South on lead, all seems to be well; he can lead a low card towards dummy and it appears to be one trick each. But we will rise with the ♡A and lead yet another club. Dummy has to follow and East's ♡J takes the setting trick. Note that it would *not* help declarer even if dummy had run out of clubs by this stage. He would simply have the option of ruffing with the ♡Q but that would leave the ♡J as master.

Problem 20

Partner's ♠9 at trick one and his later discard of the ◊3, warning us that he cannot help in that suit, has told us exactly what to do. If we win this trick, what comes next? A diamond gives a free trick to South's king and a spade is likely to give a ruff and discard. Let us count the hand to confirm this. Partner showed out on the second trump, leaving South seven and he, himself, ruffed the third round of hearts. That accounts for nine of his cards and the ♠A, and the low spade just led makes eleven. If he is 3217, he will be able to ruff a spade on dummy, conceding a spade and a diamond, leaving us with no hope. The critical case arises when he is 2227:

The deal:

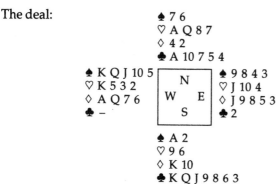

♠ 7 6
♡ A Q 8 7
◇ 4 2
♣ A 10 7 5 4

♠ K Q J 10 5   ♠ 9 8 4 3
♡ K 5 3 2   ♡ J 10 4
◇ A Q 7 6   ◇ J 9 8 5 3
♣ —   ♣ 2

♠ A 2
♡ 9 6
◇ K 10
♣ K Q J 9 8 6 3

Now all hangs on who wins this spade trick and we can thank partner for his foresight at trick one. With his very weak hand, he showed the one possibility to get on lead, anticipating that there might be a tenace position in diamonds. We therefore play low to this trick, allowing partner's ♠8 to win, after which a diamond from his side defeats the contract.

Note, therefore, that we must not discard the ♠5 on the trumps or, for that matter, a heart (which would allow dummy's fourth heart to be set up). Only high spades or low diamonds are safe.

3NT played by South is unbeatable on this hand but could not be bid after North's 2NT. Played by North, a diamond lead from East would be lethal.

Problem 21

It is likely that partner will win an early trump trick and, in that case, he will be sitting there, wondering what to do. From his side, it may not be clear whether active (attacking one of the red suits) or passive (merely getting off play in clubs or trumps) defence will be appropriate. In truth, we do not know either and it is our duty to give partner vital information. Here the diamond position may well be critical. It is likely that the two high honours are split between South and West. In that case, West should avoid leading the suit if he has the ace but it may be vital for him to lead it if he has the king.

The deal:

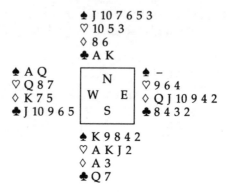

```
              ♠ J 10 7 6 5 3
              ♡ 10 5 3
              ◊ 8 6
              ♣ A K
♠ A Q                        ♠ -
♡ Q 8 7          N           ♡ 9 6 4
◊ K 7 5      W     E         ◊ Q J 10 9 4 2
♣ J 10 9 6 5     S           ♣ 8 4 3 2
              ♠ K 9 8 4 2
              ♡ A K J 2
              ◊ A 3
              ♣ Q 7
```

Here is the case in point. Suppose West thinks that, merely by waiting, he will take two trump tricks, a heart and a diamond. To avoid an endplay, he will cash his second trump and get off play with clubs – fatal. South wins, gives up the ♡Q and discards a diamond on the fourth round of hearts.

Our discard should be the ◊Q and now partner can play the ◊K (effectively king from king-queen). Later we shall win the second round and get off play in hearts (from the safe side) and wait for our setting trick in that suit.

Problem 22

It is possible that the lead is a singleton but, with partner known to be short in spades, this is unlikely. Even if it is a singleton, the ruff will not necessarily run away. It would only be lost if he has a singleton spade as well but that implies eleven cards in clubs and hearts, in which case he could surely have managed a take-out double or unusual 2NT over 2♠ at favourable vulnerability. There are alternative lines of defence in trying to set up heart tricks or aiming for a club ruff. If South has the ♡A or ♡ K J and guesses well, only one trick will be available in that suit and, if partner has a tenace over declarer, again it can wait until we take our ♠A.

What *cannot* wait is the club ruff, crediting partner with the ♣A. We must therefore win the first diamond and switch to the ♣9 and see which card partner plays. If he encourages, we shall credit him with the ♣A and rise with the ♠A on the first round to continue clubs for the ruff. If he discourages, then a heart switch is probably a better chance than the diamond ruff.

The deal:

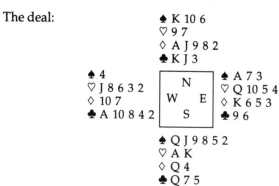

Problem 23

We have three tricks to date and the fourth can only come from diamonds or trumps. If partner has the ◊A, declarer has no chance. If partner has ◊ K 10 and declarer has three cards in the suit, the contract will be defeated if we simply exit passively in clubs or trumps. It would be fatal to give a ruff and discard by leading a fourth round of spades. However, partner might have a trump honour and now that very spade is the *only* way to defeat the contract. Partner will ruff with his honour, forcing an overruff and now our ♡J cannot be caught.

So which is it to be? Or do you think it is a pure guess? In fact, opposite a competent partner, there is no guess – the spade, angling for the uppercut, must be right.

The deal:

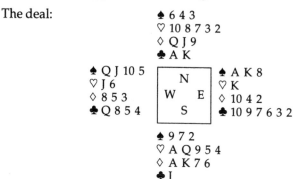

Now before reading on, can you say why? The clue lies in the way partner played the spades. He overtook and returned the suit because he knew that his ♡K was dead under the ace and that the only hope was that it might be used to promote a trick in your hand. For that reason, he had to arrange that we were on lead after the third round. If his hand had been:

♠ A K 8   ♡ 4   ◊ K 10 4 2   ♣ 10 9 7 6 3,

he would have realized that passive defence was likely be successful and allowed our ♠Q to hold the first trick. After winning two more rounds, *he* would have been on lead and quietly exited in trumps or clubs, giving us no chance to go wrong.

This is our first, and very tiny scratch on the surface of defensive cooperation under what I describe in *Signal Success in Bridge* as 'The Captain's Privilege'. The defender who *knows how to conduct the defence* takes charge of proceedings, guiding his relatively ignorant partner.

Problem 24

We have two diamond tricks, the ♡A and the ♣K, but where is the fifth to come from? Obviously, if declarer can establish those clubs, he will make the contract in comfort as he clearly has both outstanding trump honours. The only hope is an extra heart trick. We can clearly see that, but there is no guarantee that partner is so well informed. This is another situation in which we should take charge. We overtake partner's ◊K and return the ♡J. Later, when we get in with the ♣K, we will return a diamond to put partner in and another heart from his side will complete declarer's misery.

The deal:

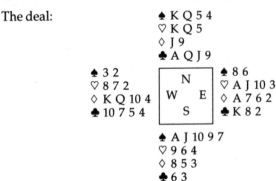

```
                        ♠ K Q 5 4
                        ♡ K Q 5
                        ◊ J 9
                        ♣ A Q J 9
    ♠ 3 2                                   ♠ 8 6
    ♡ 8 7 2            N                    ♡ A J 10 3
    ◊ K Q 10 4    W         E               ◊ A 7 6 2
    ♣ 10 7 5 4            S                 ♣ K 8 2
                        ♠ A J 10 9 7
                        ♡ 9 6 4
                        ◊ 8 5 3
                        ♣ 6 3
```

That concludes the play section for this book and, at the risk of sounding repetitive, I can only urge you to play and replay all the hands in it until you find that you are easily recognizing similar situations and it all becomes second nature. What that will save later on, when more difficult hands arrive at the table, defies calculation.

SECTION 5:

Bidding

In introducing this section, I am remembering again that my readers will fall into two categories. Those who have studied *The Expert Beginner* and *The Expert Improver* will be familiar with my approach, which is rather different to standard teaching methods. Players who have been taught traditionally and are joining me at this stage need a little introduction.

Standard books on bidding – and there are many – give long lists of rules about which suits to bid or not to bid and the point-count required to bid at particular levels. This approach gives a reasonable start but, in my opinion, is the principal cause of the very poor standard of bidding throughout the bridge world – even at the very top, alarming mistakes abound.

In the earlier books, I laid emphasis on one solitary consideration – what final contract do you have in mind? Most of the study was on the first two rounds of bidding against silent opposition. Towards the end, the opponents were allowed to enter the auction and we did a little work on the double and redouble.

In this book, we shall clear up a few odds and ends regarding bidding against silent opposition but the bulk of the study will be devoted to competitive situations, notably those in which, in my experience, players (including those reputed to be of the 'higher' echelons) seem to go continually astray.

To start the ball rolling, it will do no harm to do a short revision test in match conditions. Remember that it is not sufficient merely to write down the correct bid. You will be expected to state whether previous bids are:

1 Sign-off.
2 Invitational but non-forcing.
3 Forcing.

and into which category your proposed answer falls. Above all, you should give good reasons for your choice, with reference to how you expect the auction to proceed, and state the final contract(s) you have in mind. It will be impossible to cover the entire spectrum of the first two books, so I shall concentrate on areas where mistakes often arise. Each question should take about fifteen seconds to answer so that you should complete the hundred-question test in about twenty-five minutes.

Assume that you are sitting South and that neither side is vulnerable. Start your stop-watch.

(1) You are the dealer. What do you open on the following:

(a) ♠ K x x	(b) ♠ A K x x	(c) ♠ Q x	(d) ♠ Q 8 x x x
♡ A Q x x	♡ x x	♡ J x x	♡ Q 8 x x x
◊ A x x	◊ J x x	◊ A K 10 x x	◊ K
♣ J 10 x	♣ A J x x	♣ K Q x	♣ K

(e) ♠ K Q x	(f) ♠ A K Q J x	(g) ♠ K Q J 8 6 5 4 3
♡ K Q x	♡ A K Q J x	♡ A J
◊ A K Q x x	◊ –	◊ x x
♣ Q x	♣ x x x	♣ x

(h) ♠ x x x x	(i) ♠ K Q x	(j) ♠ J x x x x
♡ K Q J	♡ 10 x x x x x x	♡ A K Q J 10
◊ Q J x x	◊ A	◊ Q
♣ Q J	♣ x x	♣ J x

(2) Partner (North) deals and opens 1◊ and East passes. What do you reply on:

(a) ♠ K x x x	(b) ♠ A K Q x	(c) ♠ K x x x	(d) ♠ K Q x x
♡ 10 x x x	♡ J x x x	♡ x x	♡ x x
◊ K x	◊ A Q x x	◊ x x	◊ x x
♣ x x x	♣ A	♣ A x x x x	♣ A Q J x x

(e) ♠ x x x   (f) ♠ x x   (g) ♠ K Q J   (h) ♠ A K Q x x
    ♡ Q x x   ♡ A K Q x x x   ♡ x x x x x   ♡ x x
    ◊ x   ◊ A K x   ◊ K x   ◊ x
    ♣ K Q x x x x   ♣ K x   ♣ A K x   ♣ A K Q x x

(i) ♠ x x x   (j) ♠ x x
    ♡ A J x   ♡ A K
    ◊ A J x x   ◊ A K x x x
    ♣ K x x   ♣ K J x x

(3) Partner (North) deals and opens 1NT (12–14 points) and East passes. What do you reply on:

(a) ♠ x x   (b) ♠ x x   (c) ♠ K Q x   (d) ♠ K J x x
    ♡ x x x   ♡ x x   ♡ K J x x   ♡ K Q x x
    ◊ x x x   ◊ x x   ◊ K x x   ◊ x
    ♣ x x x x x   ♣ Q x x x x x x   ♣ Q x x   ♣ K J x x

(e) ♠ A K Q x x x (f) ♠ Q J x x x   (g) ♠ A K Q   (h) ♠ A K x x x
    ♡ K Q x   ♡ K x   ♡ A K x   ♡ x x x x
    ◊ A   ◊ x x x x   ◊ K x x   ◊ K x
    ♣ x x x   ♣ x x   ♣ J x x x   ♣ x x

(i) ♠ K Q x   (j) ♠ x x
    ♡ K Q x x   ♡ x x x
    ◊ J x x x   ◊ A K Q J 10 x
    ♣ J x   ♣ x x

(4) Partner (North) deals and opens 2♡ (Acol – strong) and East passes. What do you reply (assuming that you have agreed that 2♠ is the negative response) on:

(a) ♠ –   (b) ♠ K Q x   (c) ♠ x x   (d) ♠ x x
    ♡ x x x   ♡ x x   ♡ A x x   ♡ K x x
    ◊ J x x x x   ◊ A x x x   ◊ K x x   ◊ K x x
    ♣ J x x x x   ♣ x x x x   ♣ x x x x x   ♣ K x x x x

(5) Partner (North) deals and opens 2♣ (Acol – game forcing). What do you reply on:

(a) ♠ A x
♡ x x x
◊ K Q x x x
♣ x x x

(b) ♠ A x
♡ K x x
◊ x x x x x
♣ J x x

(c) ♠ x x
♡ A K Q x x x
◊ J x x
♣ x x

(d) ♠ A x
♡ Q J x x x
◊ A Q
♣ x x x x

(6) Partner (North) deals and opens 3◊ and East passes. What do you reply on:

(a) ♠ A K Q
♡ K x x x x
◊ –
♣ K Q x x x

(b) ♠ x
♡ K x x
◊ Q x x x x x
♣ x x x

(c) ♠ x x
♡ A K Q x x
◊ A J x
♣ K J x

(d) ♠ A K Q J x x x
♡ A Q J x
◊ –
♣ x x

(7) Partner (North) deals and opens 3♡ and East passes. What do you reply on:

(a) ♠ A K Q
♡ –
◊ A K Q x
♣ Q x x x x x

(b) ♠ K x
♡ K Q x
◊ A x x x
♣ K Q x x

(c) ♠ A K
♡ Q x x x
◊ x x
♣ A K J x x

(d) ♠ K Q J x x x x x
♡ –
◊ x x
♣ x x x

(8) Partner (North) deals and opens 2NT and East passes. What do you reply on:

(a) ♠ A x
♡ x x x
◊ K x x x x x
♣ x x

(b) ♠ A x x
♡ J x x
◊ A x x x
♣ A Q x

(c) ♠ x
♡ K Q x x
◊ J x x x
♣ x x x x

(d) ♠ A x
♡ K Q J x x
◊ x x
♣ x x x x

(9) You deal and open 1◊ and partner responds 1♠. What is your rebid on:

(a) ♠ x x x
♡ Q x
◊ A K Q x x
♣ K J x

(b) ♠ A x x
♡ x x
◊ K Q J x x
♣ A J x

(c) ♠ x
♡ A K x x
◊ A K J x x
♣ x x x

(d) ♠ A x
♡ A Q J x
◊ A Q J x x
♣ x x

(10) You deal and open 1♡ and partner responds 2♣. What is your rebid on:

(a) ♠ A x
   ♡ A K Q x x
   ◊ x x
   ♣ x x x x

(b) ♠ A K x x
   ♡ A K x x x
   ◊ x x x
   ♣ x

(c) ♠ A Q x x
   ♡ A K x x x
   ◊ x
   ♣ J x x

(d) ♠ A K x
   ♡ Q J x x x
   ◊ A J x
   ♣ x x

(11) You deal and open 1♠ and partner responds 2♠. What is your rebid on:

(a) ♠ A K Q J x x
   ♡ x x x
   ◊ Q x x
   ♣ x

(b) ♠ A K x x x
   ♡ x x x x
   ◊ A K
   ♣ K x

(c) ♠ A K x x
   ♡ Q x x
   ◊ A J x
   ♣ J x x

(d) ♠ A K x x
   ♡ Q J x
   ◊ A Q x
   ♣ Q x x

(12) You deal and open 1◊ and partner responds 3◊. What is your rebid on:

(a) ♠ A Q
   ♡ x x x
   ◊ K Q x x x
   ♣ A x x

(b) ♠ A J
   ♡ K Q x x
   ◊ A K x x x
   ♣ x x

(c) ♠ x x x
   ♡ K Q x
   ◊ A K J x x
   ♣ A x

(d) ♠ K J
   ♡ Q J
   ◊ A Q J x x
   ♣ x x x x

(13) You deal and open 1♣ and partner responds 2♡. What is your rebid on:

(a) ♠ J x x x
   ♡ Q x x
   ◊ K
   ♣ A K Q x x

(b) ♠ A K Q x
   ♡ x
   ◊ x x x
   ♣ A Q J x x

(c) ♠ x x
   ♡ K Q x x
   ◊ A x x
   ♣ A K Q x

(d) ♠ K x
   ♡ x x
   ◊ A Q
   ♣ A K Q J 10 x x

(14) You deal and open 3♣ and partner responds 3♡. What do you rebid on:

(a) ♠ x x
   ♡ K x x
   ◊ x
   ♣ A Q x x x x x

(b) ♠ K J x
   ♡ x
   ◊ x x
   ♣ A J 10 x x x x

(c) ♠ x x
   ♡ x
   ◊ K x x
   ♣ A Q x x x x x

(d) ♠ x x
   ♡ x x
   ◊ x x
   ♣ A K x x x x x

(15) Partner (North) deals and opens 1♡. You respond 1♠ and he rebids 2♢. What do you bid now on:

(a) ♠ A x x x   (b) ♠ A x x x   (c) ♠ K x x x   (d) ♠ A K x x
   ♡ x x   ♡ x x   ♡ x   ♡ Q x
   ♢ x x   ♢ J x x   ♢ J x x   ♢ A Q x
   ♣ Q x x x x   ♣ J x x x   ♣ K x x x x   ♣ J x x x

(16) Partner (North) deals and opens 1♢. You respond 2♣ and he rebids 2♢. What do you bid now on:

(a) ♠ A K Q x   (b) ♠ K x x   (c) ♠ x x   (d) ♠ A x x
   ♡ x x   ♡ x x x   ♡ K Q x   ♡ A x
   ♢ x x   ♢ x   ♢ J x x   ♢ x x x x
   ♣ A Q x x x   ♣ A Q J x x x   ♣ A K x x x   ♣ K J x x

(17) Partner (North) opens 1♢. You respond 2♢ and he now rebids 2♡. What do you bid now on:

(a) ♠ A K x   (b) ♠ x x   (c) ♠ K x   (d) ♠ x x
   ♡ x x   ♡ x x x   ♡ x x x   ♡ x x x
   ♢ Q x x x x   ♢ A J x x x   ♢ K J x x   ♢ A J x x
   ♣ x x x   ♣ Q J x   ♣ Q 10 x x   ♣ J x x x

(18) Partner (North) deals and opens 1♢. You respond 3♢ and he rebids 3♡. What do you bid now on:

(a) ♠ A K   (b) ♠ J x x   (c) ♠ x   (d) ♠ x x
   ♡ x x x   ♡ K x x   ♡ K x x   ♡ J x x
   ♢ K J x x x   ♢ A K x x x   ♢ A K J x x   ♢ Q J x x x
   ♣ x x x   ♣ x x   ♣ x x x x   ♣ A K x

(e) ♠ x x x   (f) ♠ –
   ♡ A   ♡ K x x
   ♢ K Q J x x   ♢ A K x x x
   ♣ x x x x   ♣ x x x x x

(19) Partner (North) deals and opens 1♠. You respond 2♠ and he rebids 3◊. What do you bid now on:

(a) ♠ Q x x x	(b) ♠ K J x x	(c) ♠ K J x x	(d) ♠ Q x x x
♡ A x x	♡ x x x	♡ x x x	♡ K J x
◊ x	◊ x x x	◊ A	◊ Q 10 x x
♣ x x x x x	♣ A x x	♣ x x x x x	♣ x x

(e) ♠ J x x x	(f) ♠ J 10 x x
♡ x x x x	♡ Q J x
◊ –	◊ x x
♣ A x x x x	♣ Q J x x

(20) Partner (North) deals and opens 2♣ and you respond 2♡. He now rebids 3♠. What do you bid now on:

(a) ♠ x x	(b) ♠ –
♡ K Q J x x	♡ K Q J x x
◊ K x	◊ x x x x x
♣ x x x x	♣ A x x

We are now going to work through the answers and you will see that I approach each problem stressing not only the absolute point-count value of the hand but also taking into account the following:

1. Quick tricks (aces and kings) are more appropriate for trump contracts and vice versa.
2. Honours are better placed in long suits (of the partnership!) rather than shorts; viz. singleton kings and doubleton queen-jacks are unlikely to pull their full weight.
3. Hands should be constantly re- or devalued as the bidding progresses.

(1) (a) With 14 points and a balanced hand, open 1NT (showing 12–14) with a view to 3NT or possibly 4♡.

(b) Another balanced hand in the correct range for 1NT but here it is preferable to open 1♣. 3NT is still the likely final or 'goal' contract but, in that case, it will be advantageous to have partner as declarer rather than face an opening lead coming round to those weak red-suit holdings. There is an easy rebid of 1♠ over a red-suit response. Goals: 3NT, 4♠ or possibly 5♣.

(c) With 15 points, open 1◊, intending to rebid no-trumps at the cheapest level. This time, it is better for our hand to be declarer, particularly as a likely spade lead should come round to Q x. Goals: 3NT, possibly 5◊.

(d) With good distribution, there may be plenty of tricks if partner can fit with either major but there are only 10 high-card points and the two singleton kings are further devalued. It is therefore best to pass, possibly intending to come in with a take-out double if the opponents bid the minors. Goals: part-score or game in either major.

(e) With 21 pts, balanced, 2NT is the standard opening bid with a view to 3NT or a possible slam in diamonds or no-trumps.

(f) Despite only 20 points, this hand needs little or nothing from partner to ensure a game in either major and is therefore worth a game-forcing 2♣. However, as long as it is agreed that 2♠ is absolutely forcing for one round (some partnerships allow a pass on a complete Yarborough), it is sufficient to open 2♠ and rebid 4♡ to show this type of hand. Goals: game or slam in either major.

(g) With seven tricks in the hand, three short of game, a preempt of 4♠, intending to play there, is ideal as, apart from the ♡A, this hand has little or no defence. There is a school of thought which considers that 11 high-card points is too strong to preempt. This is not the case when a game is bid.

(h) There are 12 high-card points but the heart and club honours are in short suits and are not pulling their full weight and it is wiser to pass.

(i) Here all the points are outside a very weak long suit. Thus the hand has plenty of defence and a preempt is both unwise and unnecessary. Pass and await further developments.

(j) This is slightly awkward in that the hearts are so much better than the spades. For that reason, some players would treat the spades as four-card and open 1♡, at least ensuring the best opening lead if West becomes declarer in a minor or no-trumps. However, the hand is not strong enough to reverse into spades if partner replies with two of a minor or 1NT and it is better to start with 1♠ to ensure bidding both suits. Goals: 4♡, 4♠.

(2) (a) Here the four-card suits are bid in the usual ascending order. Partner will bid a four-card spade suit if he has one over 1♡. If he hasn't, there will be no need to mention the spades. If we bid 1♠, a 4–4 heart fit could well be lost. Remember that with 5–5, it is correct to respond with the higher-ranking suit first. Both suits will be bid and it will be easier for partner to give preference at the same level if we bid 1♠ followed by 2♡. In this case, our goals are 3NT, 4♡ or 4♠.

(b) This is a different matter on goal-contract considerations and now it is better to bid 1♠. A heart fit may be lost but that is of little concern. We are primarily angling for a diamond (or possibly spade) slam and the last thing we want partner to do is devalue a singleton or void heart (indeed quite the opposite). Goals: five or more diamonds, 3NT, 4♠.

(c) Although the club suit is longer, the hand is not strong enough to go on to the two-level, still less make a responder's reverse (bidding 2♠ after 1♠ 2♣) so 1♠ should
                                              2◇
be preferred. Goals: 4♠, 3NT, 5♣.

(d) This has the same shape as the previous hand but now we are strong enough to go on to the two-level and make a responder's reverse so the suits are bid in natural order, starting with 2♣. Goals as before.

(e) A very awkward hand – it is not nearly strong enough for the two-level, particularly with a singleton in partner's suit. It is better to bid a non-forcing 1NT. Goals: 3NT or possibly 5♣.

(f) A slam is very likely here and, with a hand of one strong suit, we force to game with 2♡. Goals: game or slam in either red suit.

(g) Again, there is easily enough to force to game but the heart suit is very poor and a quiet start with 1♡ is in order. We shall not, however, stop bidding short of game. Goals: game or slam in hearts or no-trumps.

(h) Again, there is easily enough for a game force and both suits are good enough for a jump. However, there is much to discuss regarding choice of denomination and it is wise to start with 1♠ and jump in clubs later with a view to game or slam in either black suit. Life is awkward if the bidding goes 1◊ 2♠ as opposed to 1◊ 1♠ which is still forcing.

   3◊ 4♣   2◊ 3♣

(i) Opening bid opposite opening bid adds up to game and 3NT is hot favourite. Many players would simply bid it outright, rather than give opponents a long lecture on what to lead, and indeed a good case can be made for this. My recommendation is to discuss the final contract with partner. In this case, if partner turns up with a singleton or void spade, there could be anything up to a slam on in diamonds while 3NT is failing and, in any case, 3NT may be better played from partner's side if his spades are something like K x or A Q doubleton. I suggest a quiet 2♣. Goals: 3NT or five or more diamonds.

(j) Similar considerations apply with this stronger hand. Again I suggest 2♣, intending to follow with a forcing 4◊, initiating cue-bidding for a diamond slam. In view of the diamond support, some partnerships permit a game-forcing 3♣ on this hand but this consumes bidding space.

(3) (a) Playing Stayman, now virtually universal, a weak take-out into clubs is ruled out and it is wise to pass 1NT. This is likely to be doubled (or partner will go a few times down for 50 each undertrick while the opponents have a game on, a cheap sacrifice). Should the double come, we can then take out into 2♣, which reverts to being a natural sign-off.

(b) With such long clubs, it is worth going through Stayman with a view to playing in 3♣. We bid 2♣ now and, irrespective of partner's reply, sign-off in 3♣.

(c) With 14 points, we have little interest in any other contract but 3NT and we should sign off there now. It is usually unwise to bid Stayman (with a view to a possible 4–4 heart fit for 4♡) as this hand is so flat and partner, with an announced balanced hand, is unlikely to have much ruffing power.

(d) Here with a singleton, we should bid Stayman with a view to 4♡ or 4♠. We shall have to settle for 3NT if partner has no four-card major.

(e) Here a slam in spades or no-trumps is a strong possibility and, with a strong one-suited hand, we force to game with 3♠ and await partner's reaction. We shall make another try, even over a discouraging 3NT, with 4NT (natural rather than Blackwood as no suit will have been agreed) and finish there or in 6♠ or 6NT.

(f) With only 6 points opposite a maximum of 14, game is out of the question and we simply sign off with a weak take-out of 2♠.

(g) With 20 points and a balanced hand, a slam is on if partner is maximum in the 12–14 point range. We invite with a natural, non-forcing 4NT intending to play there or in 6NT, although partner can look for a 4–4 fit or show a five-card minor at the five-level on the way.

(h) Here game is a possibility and we invite by bidding Stayman, intending to raise 2♡ or 2♠ to an invitational 3♡ or 3♠ but to bid 2♠ ourselves if partner responds 2◊. This shows 10–11 points, invitational and non-forcing. With 12 points, we would bid 3♠ over 2◊ on the second round, again invitational and non-forcing. Goals: 3NT, 4♡, 4♠.

(i) With 12 points, a four-card major and a doubleton, we need to know partner's strength and shape. Again we use Stayman, intending to raise a heart response invitationally or bid 2NT over 2◊ or 2♠. Partner will then raise to 3NT or pass according to his strength. Goals: 3NT, 4♡.

(j) With a long running minor, it is best to sign-off in 3NT outright. Possibly the opponents may have a running suit of their own but this is a reasonable shot at game.

(4) (a) Lacking an ace and a king (or about 9 points without these controls), we must give the negative response of 2♠. This

has nothing to do with the spade suit and the void is irrelevant. We shall probably finish in 4♡ but must warn partner not to go further.

(b) Here we have a positive response and 2NT describes the hand reasonably. After the positive response to a strong two, the partnership is committed to game. Therefore the sequence 2♡ 3NT does not exist. It simply consumes unnecessary bidding space – particularly if partner has a strong two-suiter when there may be much to discuss. Goals: 3NT, 4♡ or possibly a slam.

(c) Again this is a positive response and we raise to 3♡, again game-forcing and showing at least one ace. Goals: 4♡, perhaps 6♡.

(d) Another positive response but, this time, we bid 4♡, denying an ace. Any further move is up to partner. Goals: 4♡, 6♡.

(5) (a) This is a positive response but 2◊ is the negative and nothing to do with diamonds. We bid 3◊ with a view to 3NT or perhaps a slam in diamonds or no-trumps.

(b) This time, 2NT is the more descriptive positive response on the hand. A slam is well on the cards but, particularly if partner has a strong non-diamond suit of his own, we should not want him to devalue shortage in diamonds. Goals: 3NT, possibly a slam in diamonds, if partner shows interest in the suit, or no-trumps.

(c) This is one of the rare occasions when we should make an 'unnecessary' jump. 2♡ would be positive and game-forcing but 3♡ shows a solid suit and it is worth sacrificing a round of bidding to give partner that precise information. Goals: 4♡, 6♡, perhaps 7♡.

(d) There will almost certainly be a slam on here but, this time, we proceed quietly with 2♡. The partnership is committed to game at least anyway and we shall hardly stop short of a slam. However, on this hand, the denomination is not clear and therefore we conserve bidding space. Note the contrast in mentality between this and the last hand. Goals: a small or grand slam in hearts or no-trumps.

(6) (a) We have a large point-count but a disastrous misfit and thus it is unlikely that we can improve on the current contract of 3◊. We therefore pass. If it is doubled for penalties, we still pass!

(b) This hand is at the other extreme – few points but a fantastic fit. It is clear that the opponents are almost certainly cold for at least a small slam in one of the black suits and West must have a huge hand. It is our duty to crowd him as much as possible and it is a question of how high to go in diamonds. Given that we are likely to make about eight tricks with diamonds as trumps, it depends on vulnerability. In this case, at love all, conceding 6♠ would cost 180 plus 500 for the non-vulnerable slam plus 300 for the 'value' of the game, about 1000 in all. Thus we can afford four off doubled in diamonds and should bid at least 6◊ and there is a good case for 7◊. Opponents might be cold for a grand slam or (better still) they might bid it and go off, the ♡K being badly placed for them. For completeness, it is worth discussing the position at the other vulnerabilities. At unfavourable vulnerability (vul-nerable against not), 5◊ is probably enough. At favourable, I should certainly recommend 7◊. At game all, it is more debatable, but I should recommend 6◊. All these raises are sign-offs. A preempter should never bid again unless his partner forces him to do so.

It is instructive to contrast these last two hands. On the first, I recommend a pass with 17 points; on the second, I am proposing anything up to a grand slam on 5! This illustrates the hopelessness of learning bridge, parrot fashion, without a full understanding of the scoresheet and what we are doing.

(c) Here we bid 3♡, natural and forcing. Partner now has the chance to show a spade feature with a view to 3NT, support the hearts for 4♡, or simply reject either with 4◊, which we will pass. Goals: 3NT, 4◊, 4♡.

(d) This time, partner needs no more than the ♡10 to make 4♠ a certainty so we should bid it direct as a sign-off.

(7) (a) Provided partner's hearts are of reasonable quality, there should be good play for 4♡ on this hand and it will be a certainty in the likely event of partner being short of clubs. To be fair, 3NT is also not an unreasonable shot, with a view to setting up the clubs, and indeed will be the better contract if partner has anything in clubs. But partner's hearts will be of no use in this contract so I recommend 4♡.

(b) This is the converse of the last hand. The likelihood of partner's holding the ♡A makes 3NT almost certain, played from our side of the table, while 4♡, played by partner, could well go off on a spade lead, losing two spades, a club and diamond. I therefore prefer 3NT.

Again, note the contrast between these last two hands. On the first, I recommend supporting on a void while, on the second, I advise against it on K Q x! – another illustration of the hopelessness of parrot rules.

(c) Here 4♡ will be certain but there could be a slam on if partner has first or second-round control in diamonds. I recommend 4♣, forcing. Partnership agreements vary on this point but I would allow an announced weak hand to show a second-round control in this kind of position because it is obvious that the 4♣ bidder is likely to have our kind of hand. Goals: 4♡, 6♡.

(d) This is another situation in which many players go wrong. 3♠ would be forcing and forward-going – the last impression we want to give. This hand is a misfit and the sooner we stop bidding the better. If 3♡ is doubled for penalties, we can *then* remove to 3♠, which is natural and a sign-off.

(8) (a) Although one could construct hands where 5◊ or more could be on but 3NT fails, this is most unlikely and it is best to sign off in 3NT rather than risk ending up in a diamond game which fails while 3NT is on.

(b) With 15 points, it is a question of 6NT or 7NT, according to partner's strength. We invite with a forcing 5NT, committing the partnership to at least the small slam. Partner can bid suits at the six level and we may finish in 7◊.

(c) Here we shall certainly insist on game but use Stayman 3♣

to find out whether it should be in 3NT or 4♡.

(d) Here a slam could be on and we force to game with 3♡ and see how partner reacts. Goals: 3NT, 4♡, 6♡.

(9) (a) With a good 15 points, we are strong enough to rebid 1NT. In 3NT, we shall want to be declarer so that the lead comes round to that delicate heart holding. Goals: 3NT, 4♠ or possibly 5◊.

(b) Again we are strong enough to rebid 1NT but this time, 3NT should be played from the other side to protect partner's heart holding. I therefore recommend 2♠. Goals as before.

(c) This is a good playing hand in that the points are in the long suits but the spade bid has devalued it and it is not good enough to reverse into 2♡. Rebid 2◊ quietly and partner will bid hearts if he has them. Goals: 3NT, 4♡, 5◊.

(d) This is comfortably enough for a reverse into 2♡. Goals: 3NT, 4♡, 5◊, possibly 4♠ if partner repeats the suit.

(10) This time, partner has bid two-over-one, showing 9 points or more (some partnerships insist on 10) as opposed to 6 for one-over-one.

(a) This is one of the commonest errors among weaker players. It is best not to insist on repeating that 'wonderful' heart suit. A raise to 3♣ shows a five-card heart suit anyway and is more cooperative with partner. Goals: 3NT, 4♡, 5♣.

(b) Similar arguments apply as in (9c). Despite the two-over-one, the hand is not worth a reverse. Note particularly that partner is unlikely to have four spades and, if he has, he should be strong enough to bid them over our rebid of 2♡. Otherwise he should bid 1♠ the first time. Goals: 4♡, 4♠, 3NT played from partner's side to protect his diamond tenace.

(c) This time, the club bid has improved the hand considerably and now, despite being a point or two understrength, I would recommend reversing to 2♠ here. Goals: 4♡, 4♠, 5♣.

(d) Here we are strong enough to rebid 2NT, showing 15

points. This is invitational and non-forcing though many partnerships play it as forcing. That must be discussed later. Goal: 3NT.

(11) (a) Here we have very little defence as those high spades are unlikely to stand up for more than one round. The important aim here is to keep the opponents out of the auction and we sign-off with a preemptive 3♠.

(b) Here we are aiming for 4♠ and much depends on whether partner can look after all those heart losers. We therefore make a long-suit trial bid of 3♡ (forcing) to find out. Goals: 3♠ or 4♠.

(c) Although we have a couple of points to spare on the opening bid, the hand has no distribution and the isolated honours in clubs and hearts are unlikely to pull their full weight. We therefore pass.

(d) Here we are balanced, well protected in the side suits and have only four spades. Therefore 3NT comes into consideration as final contract and we invite with a non-forcing 2NT, showing 17–18 points. Partner will now choose the final contract. Goals: 3NT, 4♠ but we might have to accept 3♠.

(12) (a) With 15 points, we are entitled to make an effort towards game and, with a minor-suit fit in an otherwise balanced hand, 3NT should be uppermost in our mind. In that contract, the major suits are most likely to be attacked, so we shall need partner to stop the hearts. In view of our spade holding, there is a good case for bidding 3NT ourselves, hoping that partner can stop hearts while ensuring that our spade tenace is protected. I prefer, however, to bid 3♠, promising the spade stop while denying the heart. Partner will then bid 3NT with hearts stopped or play in diamonds (how high depends on his length in hearts) if he cannot stop that suit.

(b) This time, despite the club weakness, it is probably best to bid 3NT direct. Partner has denied four cards in either major and although he could be 3352, he is likely to have some sort of club length. It may be vital to have our hand as declarer if partner's spades are 10 x x.

(c) This is the converse of (a) – we bid 3♡, inviting partner to bid 3NT with the spades stopped. It is likely that we shall want that contract played from his side.

(d) With only 14 points, half of which are in unprotected doubletons, we have little justification for bidding on and should pass.

(13) (a) The general guide after partner's jump in a new suit is to make the same rebid that we would have made had the response been one level lower. However, there are exceptions; here partner has specifically shown a one-suited hand. He will therefore not be interested in our poor spade suit, and indeed, we should want him to revalue rather than devalue a shortage therein. It is wise, therefore, to support hearts immediately with a view to commencing cue-bidding at once. However, it is also justifiable to repeat the clubs first and then support hearts after say

   1♣ 2♡
   3♣ 3NT
   4♡

partner will realize that we have repeated the clubs with a reason – our suit being very strong. My own preference is for 3♡, primarily because we could be stuck if partner supports 3♣ to 4♣. Now it is debatable whether 4♡ is a cue-bid or simply a support and, in the latter case, whether or not it is forcing. Goals: 4♡, 6♡ or 7♡.

(b) This is the converse of (a). We must now bid the spades, if only to show values for a possible no-trump contract. The spades are so strong that the best game or slam might be in a 4–3 fit in that suit. Goals: 3NT, 4♠, 5♣ or a slam in any non-diamond suit (partner's hearts might be solid).

(c) Here we shall almost certainly be insisting on a small slam at least but all that is necessary now is to agree hearts with 3♡ for the moment to initiate cue-bidding. Remember the sequence 1♣ 2♡ does not exist (simply taking bidding
                    4♡
space away from an unlimited partner) although some

partnerships (not unreasonably) play it to show a very minimum hand with no ace. This unnecessary rush to game, to show lack of interest in more ambitious contracts, was defined earlier as the *principle of fast arrival*.

(d) This is a rare situation where it does pay to jump 'unnecessarily' to send a definite message – here a solid club suit – with 4♣. This initiates cue-bidding. Goals: 5♣, 6♣, 7♣ or a no-trump slam.

(14) A change of suit below game opposite a preempt is forcing and asks for a further description of the hand, bearing in mind that we have already shown a one-suiter which is weak on points. Remember that it is our duty to describe our hand but the final contract should be decided by *partner*. One of the commonest mistakes, notably among weaker players (not that the experts are totally innocent!) is to keep repeating the preempt suit – partner heard it the first time.

(a) Here we have good support for partner's hearts and have no hesitation in raising to game – 4♡. But did you consider anything else? The 3♡ bid has improved this hand considerably; the trump support could hardly be better (we should not preempt in clubs with a four-card major outside) and it may well be that partner is slam-minded. Below game, it costs nothing to show what might be a vital feature with 4◇. Our opening bid showed specifically a one-suited hand and therefore this is not a second suit but a more informative raise to 4♡. As a matter of interest, even if an inexperienced partner thinks it is a suit, we can always correct to hearts. Goals: 4♡, or possibly a heart slam.

(b) This time, 3NT is a possibility and we should show our spade stop with 3♠. Partner will then bid 3NT himself or choose the final contract in hearts or clubs.

(c) Here we have to bid 3NT, promising a diamond stop but denying a spade stop. Partner will then pass or choose the final contract on the information we have given.

(d) Here we have nothing to offer outside clubs and must say so with 4♣. Partner will then choose the final contract or force again with another change of suit. Goals: 4♣, 5♣.

(15) In this sequence, partner has shown two suits and asked for preference.

   (a) With equal length in the two suits, we prefer the first, guaranteed, in principle, to be five-card. We bid 2♡, hoping to play there in what is likely to be a misfit.

   (b) Where we are one card longer in the second suit, the position is more debatable but partner is considerably more likely to be 5–4 than 5–5 in the red suits. 5–2 fits tend to play better than 4–3 fits because declarer is less likely to lose trump control. It therefore pays to give false preference to 2♡, hoping to play there.

   (c) This is a poor misfit and with a majority of two in favour of the second suit, it is best to settle for 2♢ and pass.

   (d) With 16 points, we must certainly insist on game but any non-club denomination is possible. We need to ask partner for more information about his hand and do so with a fourth-suit-forcing 3♣. Goals: 3NT, 4♡, 4♠, 5♢ or possibly a slam.

(16) (a) Here we must insist on game and make a forcing responder's reverse of 2♠. We shall want a no-trump game to be played from his side if he has a tenuous heart stop like K x. Goals: 3NT, 4♠, 5♣.

   (b) This hand appear to be a misfit. Styles vary on the meaning of the sequence 1♢ 2♣. In days gone by it used to be an

2♢ 3♣

attempt to play in 3♣ (as might be appropriate here). Nowadays it is played as forward-going. In the latter case, it is probably best to pass 2♢ as the best of a bad job.

   (c) Here we should look towards game and, with 3NT favourite, we must show our good heart feature with 2♡ (responder's reverse and forcing). This may or may not be a suit and, if partner has four cards (and was not strong enough to reverse), the sequence 1♢ 2♣ is forcing and, when

2♢ 2♡
3♡

we return to diamonds, partner should realize that we meant the heart bid as a feature for no-trumps rather than a suit. Goals: 3NT, 5♢ although 4♡ could be best, even on a 3–4 fit.

(d) Here we are worth a try for game but, if partner has vulnerable holdings like Q x in one of the majors, it may be necessary to have him as declarer in the likely goal of 3NT. The best try therefore is 3◊, invitational but non-forcing. Let partner take it from there. Goals: 3NT, 5◊.

(17) In this sequence, we have denied a four-card major and partner is showing stops in the non-diamond suits with a view to 3NT.

   (a) Here we reply with 2♠ (forcing) and hope partner will be able to bid no-trumps with his (possibly broken) club and heart stops protected. If he bids 2NT, we shall raise to 3NT as we are maximum in the 2◊ range. Note, however, that it is not necessary to bid 3♠ on this round as 2♠ is forcing. It could be that the partnership has to stop in 3◊.

   (b) This time, we show our club feature with 3♣ (forcing). Partner will now be able to bid 3NT or stop in 3◊. In this situation, he does not know our strength but that cannot be helped.

   (c) Here we have stops in both black suits and a maximum so we are pleased to sign off in 3NT. We shall want to be declarer to protect that ♠K.

   (d) We have a club feature of sorts but the hand is so poor that it is probably wisest to try to sign off in 3◊.

(18) Here we have less bidding space and it is therefore wise to confine the discussion to the major-suit stops.

   (a) With the spades well stopped, we sign off in 3NT.

   (b) With a half-stop in spades, we bid 3♠, inviting partner to bid 3NT with another half-stop or play in 4◊ or 5◊ otherwise.

   (c) This time, 3NT is ruled out but the singleton spade (with partner known to be weak in that suit) could be a tremendous bonus in a diamond contract and we are happy to play in game. Rather than bid 5◊ direct, it costs nothing to show our heart feature with 4♡ on the way. Partner now may be able to bid 6◊.

   (d) This time, the spade holding isn't so good but there is still scope for discussion between 4◊ and 5◊. Our top clubs could be a useful feature so we bid 4♣. Partner must now choose between 4◇ and 5◇.

(e) This hand is disastrous and there could easily be three spade losers. It is best to sign off in 4◇.

(f) Now the void of spades is priceless in a diamond contract and we are soon going to learn something new – the splinter bid. We very briefly mentioned this in *The Expert Improver*. An unnecessary jump in an unbid suit shows a void in that suit. Here we bid 4♠ to show the void. We shall play at least 5◇ but this bid may pave the way for 6◇ or 7◇.

(19) This time, with a major suit agreed, the discussion is on whether we are going to play in 3♠, 4♠ or even a slam.

(a) Here, with a singleton diamond and four trumps, we have the ideal hand to go straight to 4♠ despite the minimum point-count.

(b) The diamond holding could not be worse and despite 8 points, we should try to sign off in 3♠.

(c) This is a dream of a hand, certainly worth game, but partner might have made the trial with a view to a slam so it costs nothing to show the ideal diamond holding with a raise to 4◇.

(d) This one is more debatable. We have some help in diamonds and much may depend on the position in the other two suits. We do not have to commit ourselves at this stage but can show a doubtful diamond position and values in hearts with a forcing 3♡. Partner can now decide on 3♠ or 4♠, crediting us with this sort of hand.

(e) Again the diamond position is ideal and we should insist on game despite the low point-count. On the way, just in case partner was thinking of a slam, it will cost nothing to show our ♣A with 4♣.

(f) Here we have some help in diamonds in the doubleton with four trumps. However, the position in hearts and clubs could hardly be worse with our low honours prob-ably facing doubletons or singletons in partner's hand and therefore of little, if any, worth. We should therefore sign off in 3♠.

(20) Partner has shown a solid suit and has initiated cue-bidding. We are obliged to show our aces, irrespective of our attitude to spades.
   (a) We have no ace and must bid 4♠.
   (b) We show the ♣A with 4♣.

This covers a reasonable cross-section of the first two rounds of bidding and I hope new readers understand and appreciate my approach, particularly noting the emphasis on the consideration of final contract. Points and distribution are servants rather than masters.

Our first new sequence concerns the responder's handling of very weak distributional hands of about 5–8 high-card points which are too strong to pass the opening bid but not strong enough to bid at the two-level. Suppose we hold:

   ♠ x
   ♡ K J x x x x
   ◊ Q x x
   ♣ x x x

and partner opens 1♠. Although this is hardly an accurate description of the hand, we are forced to bid 1NT. If partner follows with two of a minor, our bid of 2♡ is a sign-off. Even if partner is very short of hearts, he should pass (unless, perhaps, he has eleven or more cards in his two bid suits) as our hand will be completely useless unless those hearts are trumps. The same applies even if our bid has to be at three-level. On

   ♠ x
   ♡ x x
   ◊ Q x x
   ♣ K J x x x x

the sequence 1♠ 1NT is again a sign-off and should not be dis-
              2♡ 3♣
turbed. If partner carries on bidding because he dislikes clubs, he will be simply asking for a double which is likely to be expensive.

We are now going to consider the third round of bidding and summarize a cross-section of the possible scenarios. On the first two rounds, the partners will normally have suggested denominations and either agreed on one of them or still be debating the issue. Let us look at few example sequences:

(1)1♡ 1♠   (2)1♡ 1♠   (3)1♡ 1♠   (4)1♡ 1♠   (5)1♡ 1♠
    2◊ 2♡   2◊ 3◊   2◊ 2♠   2◊ 2NT   2◊ 3♣

In the first four of these, both partners have limited their hands. The opener failed to open at the two-level and limited his hand further by the 2◊ bid, which was passable. The responder's 1♠ bid was forcing and therefore unlimited but, once he had shown his preference or made a limit-bid in no-trumps, he too had limited his hand. In (5), while opener is limited, responder has forced again, asking for more information, and is therefore still unlimited.

It will be impossible to cover every possible combination, so we shall consider a few common ones in each case. What I should like you to do is simply to state what you would understand by the next bid by opener in the following cases, clarifying as far as possible:

1 The shape and strength he is trying to show.
2 Whether the bid is forcing, invitational or sign-off.
3 The likely final contract(s) anticipated.

Each example should take about fifteen seconds and you should complete the twenty-question test in a maximum of five minutes. Start your stop-watch.

(1) After the sequence 1♡ 1♠   what do you understand by
                        2◊ 2♡
    (a) 3♣   (b) 3◊   (c) 2♠   (d) 3♡ ?

(2) After the sequence 1♡ 1♠   what do you understand by
                        2◊ 3◊
    (a) 3♡   (b) 3♠   (c) 4♣   (d) 3NT ?

(3) After the sequence 1♡ 1♠   what do you understand by
                        2◊ 2♠
    (a) 2NT   (b) 3♣   (c) 3◊   (d) 3♡ ?

(4) After the sequence 1♡ 1♠   what do you understand by
                        2◊ 2NT
    (a) 3♣   (b) 3◊   (c) 3♡   (d) 3♠ ?

(5) After the sequence 1♡ 1♠   what do you understand by
                        2◊ 3♣

  (a) 3◊   (b) 3♡   (c) 3♠   (d) 4◊ ?

Let us work through the answers:

(1) (a) The first point to emphasize in this sequence is that
    responder has only given preference to, rather than
    supported, the hearts and therefore has promised no more
    than a doubleton and no more than his original 6 points. By
    bidding a fourth-suit-forcing 3♣, opener has committed
    the partnership to the three-level with no more than
    6 points guaranteed opposite him and therefore he should
    have of the order of 17:

    (i) With genuine heart support, responder may treat the
    bid as a long-suit trial and bid 3♡ or 4♡ accordingly.

    (ii) If he has given false preference to hearts, typically with
    three diamonds and two hearts, he may now clarify
    this with 3◊.

    (iii) With a club stop, he may bid 3NT although point-
    count is relevant here. Partner failed to jump over 1♠
    and is unlikely to have much more than 18 points.
    Thus with a minimum 6 points concentrated in the
    black suits, the hand will be a hopeless misfit and the
    no-trump game will have little chance. With 8 or more
    points, however, it is in order to bid 3NT with ♣ Q x or
    better.

  (b) This time, opener has confirmed at least 5–5 in the red suits
    and this bid is non-forcing, allowing responder to pass if
    he has given false preference. He may however, go further
    if he has useful cards in the red suits. In the blacks, only
    aces are likely to be of any value at all and then only for one
    trick each.

  (c) Here opener has shown 3541 and the bid is non-forcing.
    Responder should now choose the final contract
    dependent on his shape and strength. Club honours other
    than the ace will be of little value opposite an announced
    singleton.

  (d) This is a positive try for game, almost certainly guaranteeing a six-card or longer heart suit as only two were promised by responder – non-forcing.

(2) (a) Here opener is likely to be 6–5 in hearts and diamonds and he is offering final contracts of 3♡ (the bid is non-forcing) or 4♡, while being prepared for 4♢ or 5♢.

(b) As in (1c) above, opener has promised 3541 and is prepared to play in 3♠ (the bid is non-forcing) or 4♠, 4♢ or 5♢ or even possibly 4♡ on a 5–2 fit.

(c) This is a rare example of a long-suit trial (obviously forcing) with a minor suit agreed as trumps. The fact that opener has made no attempt to play in 3NT implies that his clubs are *weak* and he needs help to play in 5♢. His shape is likely to be 1543 or possibly 0553. Therefore, when considering his reply, responder should not only consider his club holding but also devalue any low spade honours.

(d) This promises a good club stop and, in principle, is a sign-off. However, can you think of a situation in which it would be right for responder to take it out? Opener is likely to be 1543 and responder is very weak in spades; 5♢ may have a better chance. A typical hand might be one such as ♠x x x x ♡A ♢K Q x x ♣K x x x where the potential ruffing values on both sides make the trump contract preferable – it will be hard to establish tricks for no-trumps.

(3) In this sequence, responder has expressed a wish to play in his suit despite being offered two others. The first point to emphasize therefore is that the hand is likely to be a misfit and, in that case, opener should pass rather than take the bidding higher, which is just asking for trouble. In the vast majority of circles, 2NT in this sequence is almost invariably a mistake! Players do it on hands like: ♠x ♡A K x x x ♢Q x x x ♣A Q x. Well, I had 15 points and a double club-stop, partner! Very true, but where are those eight tricks coming from when partner puts down ♠K Q J x x x and little else? There will be two club tricks and two hearts but little more – and that presumes a club lead. It could be even worse. Any move over 2♠ implies either a willingness to play at least in 3♠ (if partner turns up with a load of spades without a side entry) or a very

distributional hand in the red suits with which opener thinks that it is worth raising the level of bidding to avoid playing in spades.

(a) This would show about 17 plus points with typically a double stop in clubs and tolerance for spades (a doubleton or singleton honour), say ♠ Q ♡ A K x x x ◊ K x x x x ♣ A Q. Responder now chooses the final contract.

(b) This is fourth-suit-forcing and offers contracts in any non-club denomination at the three-level. Again opener must be strong with tolerance for spades.

(c) Here opener is at least 5–5 in the red suits and wishes to play there or in 3♡. Responder should not repeat his spades unless he considers his suit worth having as trumps opposite a void.

(d) Here opener promises at least six good hearts and probably more and he should therefore have five diamonds. Responder should pass or raise to 4♡ but should only correct to diamonds (which involves going to the four-level) with a majority of three in favour. It is probably not worth doing it with one heart and three diamonds as there may only be minimal advantage in a possible 5–3 fit against a 6–1 heart fit.

(4) (a) This is one of the rare occasions where the fourth suit is non-forcing. The reason is that responder has completed a description of his hand and shown some club interest with his 2NT bid. Opener therefore has no further questions to ask and is probably 0544.

(b) Here opener has shown at least 5–5 in the red suits and wishes to play in one of them. Responder should pass or correct to 3♡ accordingly.

(c) This time, opener has at least six hearts and similar considerations apply as in (3d) above.

(d) Here opener is likely to be 3541 and responder can choose the final contract, 3NT or 4♠ on that basis. After 2NT, 3♠ is forcing.

(5) Here responder has forced another bid out of opener and therefore the opener guarantees no more, in either strength or

shape, than he promised by his first two bids. Some partnerships insist that a fourth-suit-forcing bid guarantees a further bid (unless opener bids game) and this has advantages in respect of bidding space on big hands. However, I do not recommend this.

(a) Here opener would ideally be 5–5 in the red suits but, if he is 2542 or 1543 with no club stop, he has to bid either 3◊ or 3♡ and, in this situation, he is advised to repeat the stronger suit.

(b) Again, ideally opener should have six hearts but similar thoughts apply as in (a).

(c) Here opener is 3541.

(d) This is a big red two-suiter, 5–5 at least, and strong but denying a club stop. The bid is forcing on the grounds that the 3♣ bidder has taken responsibility for 3NT with no extra values from the opener and should have about an opening bid. The partnership should therefore have a combined point-count at least in the high twenties and is committed to game.

This should give you the idea and we are now going on to further study of sequences involving fourth-suit-forcing. We shall see that it can be put to a number of uses and introduce the concept of the advanced cue-bid.

Let us look at a few sequences:

(1)	1◊	1♠	(2)	1◊	1♠	(3)	1◊	1♠	(4)	1◊	1♠
	2♣	2♡		2♣	2♡		2♣	2♡		2♣	2♡
	3♣	3NT		3♣	3◊		3♣	3♠		2♠	3♣

(5)	1◊	1♠	(6)	1◊	1♠	(7)	1◊	1♠	(8)	1◊	1♠
	2♣	2♡		2♣	2♡		2♣	2♡		2♣	2♡
	3♣	3♡		2NT	3♣		2NT	3◊		2NT	3♠

(9)	1◊	1♠	(10)	1◊	1♠	(11)	1◊	1♠	(12)	1◊	1♠
	2♣	2♡		2♣	2♡		2♣	2♡		2♣	2♡
	2NT	4♣		2NT	4◊		2NT	4♡		2NT	4♠

We could go on for hours but this is a good cross-section. In the first place, the fourth-suit-forcing bid should be considered a probe for no-trumps. We then distinguish between the cases where opener is unable to bid no-trumps and those where he can indeed do so.

In the first group (1–5), no-trumps may be ruled out as the final denomination and the discussion centres around which suit to choose. In the second (6–12), responder has effectively 'contradicted himself' by asking for no-trumps and then taking out the affirmative response. This apparent contradiction sends a message of extra strength and usually a control (at least second-round) in the fourth suit bid. For that reason, all sequences in that second group are forcing unless game is bid.

Let us go through each sequence in detail, distinguishing between those given above and the corresponding sequence in which the fourth-suit forcing bid and its response were omitted:

(1) Contrast with 1◇   1♠
                    2♣   3NT

Here the responder has chosen a final contract, suggesting that he wants no further discussion. Where he bids the fourth suit, he is less sure. He may have a five-card spade suit and he is giving opener (who may be 3154) a chance to support with a view to 4♠. Alternatively, responder may have a tenuous heart stop like K x x or A x x and would wish to be dummy if opener has Q x.

(2) Contrast with 1◇   1♠
                    2♣   3◇

where responder could not even suggest no-trumps. With the fourth-suit forcing, he was prepared to play at least 2NT, but when opener was unable to produce at least a half-stop in hearts, he had to settle for 3◇. This is non-forcing and opener is only likely to go further if he is very short of hearts.

(3) Contrast with 1◇   1♠
                    2♣   3♠

which is an invitational jump. Where the fourth-suit-forcing bid is used, the sequence is forcing. Responder must have a very good hand and be prepared to play in 4♠ or at least the four-level in one of the minors.

(4) Contrast with   1◊   1♠
                        2♣   3♣

which is an invitational raise with no interest in no-trumps. With the fourth-suit-forcing bid, responder was interested in no-trumps, but when opener supported spades, presumably with something like 3154, responder returned to clubs, indicating only four spades and at least four clubs. The sequence is non-forcing.

(5) Here the repeat of the fourth suit is natural and forcing. Responder has insisted on keeping the bidding open despite a likely misfit. He has preferred to bid and repeat hearts rather than bid 2NT over 2♣. He probably has a big major two-suiter and is asking for preference but must at least be prepared to play in 3NT.

(6) As in (4) above 1◊   1♠
                     2♣   3♣

is an invitational raise. The 2♡ bid followed by the raise after hearing no-trumps is much stronger and is likely to show heart control. 3NT is still possible as final contract but 5♣ or even a slam are now in the reckoning. The sequence is forcing for one round.

(7) The same applies as in (6) except that diamonds is now agreed.

(8) This is similar to (3) above – forcing for one round.

(9) This has gone past 3NT and is therefore forcing to game and is slam-minded. Contrast with 1◊   1♠
                                  2♣   4♣

Here there are two schools of thought. Some insist that this sequence should also be forcing for the same reason. Others suggest that the fourth-suit bid is available if responder wants to insist on game and that therefore this should only be invitational, opener being allowed to pass if he is seriously short on top tricks, when 5♣ is likely to fail. I have to admit that I prefer the second approach. However, to play both sequences as forcing has one big advantage. It can now be specified that the 2♡ bid guarantees at least second-round control in hearts, while the direct raise denies it. Opener is now far better informed as to whether to start cue-bidding or just give up in 5♣. This is something on which a partnership has to agree.

(10) This is similar to (9) above except that diamonds are now agreed.

(11) The opener has shown some values in hearts with the 2NT bid and therefore this is a sign-off.

(12) Contrast with   1◇   1♠
                       2♣   4♠

which shows a good hand but expresses a desire to to play in 4♠ on the information given so far. With the fourth-suit-forcing bid preceding it, a slam is suggested and cue-bidding invited. The bid, however, is not forcing and opener should understand that the spades, while being long enough to stand up on their own, will probably not be rock solid in the absence of an immediate jump to 2♠ over 1◇.

We are now going to introduce the *splinter* bid. The word literally suggests that infuriating little foreign body which gets stuck under the skin and is hard to remove. Its contribution to bridge jargon derives from its uniqueness – one alone – a singleton. Here we extend the use to cover a void. The showing of a shortage in a side-suit is very useful when considering the possibility of a small or grand slam in a suit contract.

We briefly mentioned the possibility earlier on in the sequence

     1◇   3◇
     3♡   4♠

where the opener was, in the first place, looking for 3NT but expressing weakness in spades. Responder's announcement of a void paved the way for a possible diamond game or slam. Let us look at a few more sequences we have not yet used:

(1) 1♠   4♣   (2) 1♡   4◇   (3) 1♡   1♠
                                             4◇

(4) 1♠   2♠   (5) 1♡   3♡   (6) 1◇   3◇
     4♣   4♠   4♡

In each case we note that, had the last bid been at the level below, it would still have been forcing and therefore the jump is, in principle, 'unnecessary'. Remembering that a round of bidding has been lost, it can only be justified if a specific message is being sent.

Partnership agreements vary on the exact meaning. Some allow a splinter on a singleton or void. Others insist on a void only. A good case can be made on both sides. The advantage of allowing a singleton or void is in frequency of occurrence – voids are very rare. The advantage of restricting it to the void lies in accuracy. The partner will find it difficult to value an ace accurately when it might be facing a singleton (useful) or a void (unnecessary). Where a singleton or void is allowed, the splinter suit will have to bid twice to confirm the void as first-round control. This is something on which a partnership has to agree. For the moment, let us simply talk about 'shortage'.

Let us look through those sequences in detail:

In (1) and (2), responder has enough to support the opener's major suit at least to game (the partnership is already on the four-level) and is showing shortage in the bid minor suit in addition to at least four trumps.

In (3), opener guarantees at least a raise to game in spades, therefore at least four trumps, and a diamond shortage.

In (4), spades are agreed and opener has enough for at least game and has slam aspirations – he shows his club shortage.

In (5), hearts are agreed and the opener, again looking for a slam and prepared to play at least at the five-level, is showing spade shortage.

In (6), diamonds are agreed and opener, prepared to play at least in game, is showing heart shortage.

The partner of the splinter bidder can now cue-bid, if possible, with a view to a slam. Note that, with voids around, Blackwood is out of order and 4NT should be used to cue-bid the ace of trumps.

Let us look at a few pairs of hands in which the accuracy of slam bidding is enhanced by the use of the splinter. For simplicity, we shall assume that, for the rest of this section, only the void is allowed.

(1) ♠ A Q J x x   ♠ K x x x   (2) ♠ —   ♠ Q x x x
    ♡ K J x   ♡ A Q x   ♡ A K x x   ♡ Q x x x x x
    ◊ J x x x   ◊ —   ◊ A K x x x ◊ Q x
    ♣ Q x   ♣ K J x x x   ♣ K x x   ♣ A

1♠	4◊		1◊	1♡
4NT	5♡		3♠	4♣
5♠	6♠		4◊	4♡
Pass			4NT	5♣
			5◊	5♡
			6♣	6◊
			7♡	Pass

In (1), East's void of diamonds is just what West needs opposite his poor suit. He shows his ace of trumps (denying the ♡A) and East shows his ♡A (denying the ♣A). The slam must now be a good bet.

In (2), despite East's complete lack of aces and kings, West's splinter, showing the void of spades, improves the hand considerably. Admittedly the ♠Q is worthless but the length in trumps is priceless in what will clearly be a crossruff situation and he is therefore justified in making a positive move (4♡ would be a rejection). The 4♣ bid shows a first-round control. Note, however, that it has been mentioned that, with good trumps in an announced weak hand (typically opposite a two-opener) it is sometimes justified to waive the rules in this respect in cue-bidding a second-round control.

West cue-bids his ◊A and now East signs off in 4♡, having done as much as he could to date. With a king in partner's bid suit, diamonds, he would have been justified in bidding 4◊ (no cost below 4♡).West cue-bids his ace of trumps with 4NT and East shows that he also has second-round control in clubs with 5♣. West shows his ◊K with 5◊, having no more to show at this stage. West knows he is worth a small slam at least and investigates a possible grand by showing his second club control. Despite partner's announced singleton, this may be useful if he turns up with three small diamonds. East can now show his diamond feature (again no cost below 6♡) and with his excellent trumps, West can confidently bid the grand slam.

(3)	♠ A Q J x x x	♠ K x x x	(4)	♠ A K x	♠ Q x x
	♡ Q x x x	♡ x x x		♡ –	♡ J x x
	◊ A K J	◊ x x		◊ A K x x x x	◊ Q J x x x
	♣ –	♣ K Q x x		♣ x x x x	♣ A J

1♠	2♠
4♣	4♠
Pass	

1◊	3◊
4♡	5♣
5♠	6◊
Pass	

In (3), after 1♠ 2♠, West could adopt two approaches. He could reasonably try 3♡, a long-suit trial, asking for help in hearts. The club void, however, is more specific. This is the last thing East wants opposite his club values and he signs off in 4♠, showing no further interest.

In (4), West's void of hearts is ideal for East and he cue-bids his ♣A (denying ♠A). For West, a grand slam is a possibility, so he bids 5♠, confirming his ♠A and inviting East to bid 6♣ to show second-round control of clubs, if he has it. East signs off in 6◊.

These should be enough to give you the idea and we shall learn later when we allow the opponents to enter the auction, that, while a bid of their suit is an unassuming cue-bid or directional asking bid as we learnt in *The Expert Improver*, a jump in it shows a shortage, as in this section.

We shall conclude the section on bidding against silent opposition with a revision test in match conditions. Again, you should be able to do each example in under fifteen seconds, completing the twenty-four questions in well under six minutes. In each case, state what you have learnt about partner's hand from the auction so far, whether his last bid was forcing, invitational or sign-off and the same regarding your proposed answer. Most important of all, you should indicate the final contract(s) anticipated.

(1) Partner deals and the bidding goes   1♠   1NT
                                            2◇

What do you rebid now on:

(a) ♠ J x   (b) ♠ x   (c) ♠ x   (d) ♠ x x
    ♡ K J x x x   ♡ Q J 9 x x x x   ♡ A x x x x   ♡ x x
    ◇ J x   ◇ x x   ◇ x x x   ◇ Q x
    ♣ x x x x   ♣ K x x   ♣ Q x x x   ♣ K J 10 x x x x

(2) You deal and the bidding goes   1♡   1NT
                                      2◇   3♣

What do you bid now on:

(a) ♠ A x x   (b) ♠ A Q x   (c) ♠ x
    ♡ K J x x x   ♡ K Q x x x   ♡ K Q J 10 x x
    ◇ K J x x   ◇ J x x x x   ◇ A J 10 x x x
    ♣ x   ♣ —   ♣ —

(3) You deal and the bidding goes: 1♡   1♠
                                      2◇   2♠

What do you bid now on:

(a) ♠ x   (b) ♠ —   (c) ♠ Q
    ♡ A K x x x   ♡ K J 10 x x   ♡ A K Q x x
    ◇ A 10 x x   ◇ K J 10 x x   ◇ A Q x x
    ♣ K Q x   ♣ A J x   ♣ x x x

(4) You deal and the bidding goes: 1◇   1♡
                                      1♠   2♣

What do you bid now on:

(a) ♠ A J x x   (b) ♠ A J x x   (c) ♠ K J x x   (d) ♠ K Q J x
    ♡ K x x   ♡ K x   ♡ J x   ♡ K x
    ◇ A K x x x   ◇ K Q J 10 x   ◇ A Q J x x   ◇ A Q J 10 x
    ♣ x   ♣ J x   ♣ K x   ♣ x x

(5) Partner deals and the bidding goes: 1♡   1♠
                                          2♣

What do you bid now on:

(a) ♠KQJxxx   (b) ♠KQ109xxx (c) ♠KQxxx
    ♡x   ♡xx   ♡Qx
    ◇Axx   ◇Ax   ◇J10x
    ♣Jxx   ♣Ax   ♣Axx

(d) ♠KQxxx
    ♡Kx
    ◇Kx
    ♣AKxx

(6) Partner deals and opens 1♠. What do you reply on:

(a) ♠KQJx   (b) ♠Kx   (c) ♠Axx
    ♡AQxx   ♡AQJ10xxx   ♡Kxxx
    ◇–   ◇Qx   ◇–
    ♣Kxxxx   ♣xx   ♣AKQxxx

(7) You deal and the bidding goes   1♠   2◇
                                    2♠   4♣

What do you bid now on:

(a) ♠AKJxxx   (b) ♠KQ10xxx (c) ♠AQJxxx
    ♡xxx   ♡AKx   ♡KJ
    ◇Jx   ◇x   ◇Jx
    ♣Ax   ♣xxx   ♣xxx

Let us work through the answers.

(1) (a) There is a school of thought that believes that it would be
        beneficial to bid 2♡ on this hand, offering it as an alterna-
        tive contract to 2♠ and so indeed it would be if partner's
        shape proves to be 5341. However, the 2♡ bid needs to be
        reserved for hands with longer heart suits, i.e. in which
        responder's hand will be of little use unless those hearts
        are trumps. In these cases, it would be disastrous for
        opener to return to 2♠, which could well be doubled for a
        heavy penalty. With this hand, therefore, it is wise to
        ignore the relatively poor heart suit and give preference to

2♠, hoping to play there.

(b) This hand is only useful in hearts and now we do bid 2♡, hoping to play there.

(c) The argument here is similar to that in (a) but now we prefer diamonds to spades and are therefore wise to pass.

(d) This hand will be worth a lot of tricks if those clubs are trumps but very few if they are not. We therefore bid 3♣, hoping to play there.

(2) We now see the above situation from the other side of the table and we should not disturb 3♣ without a very good reason.

(a) There is no reason to bid.

(b) Arguing with partner on this type of hand is likely to bring even more serious trouble than we are in already. If 3♣ is doubled, it is probably still best to pass.

(c) We can make plenty of tricks with either red suit as trumps, standing alone. Despite partner's discouraging bidding, game could still be on, particularly in 4♡. Now it is reasonable to bid 3◊ and partner should choose the final contract from there, crediting us with this type of hand.

(3) (a) We have 16 points but the hand is a disastrous misfit and we should pass. Players reaching this stage should have conquered the temptation to bid a hopeless no-trump contract long ago.

(b) Here the same applies and I strongly recommend a pass. Partner could have a three-card diamond support (when 3◊ may well be a superior contract) but if he hasn't, the opponents, clearly informed of a misfit, could start doubling, with the result that a modest undoubled penalty in 2♠ could become a huge doubled penalty one level higher. The winning bridge player is not one who must be successful on every hand but one who ensures that his failures are minimized.

(c) Despite the singleton spade, this is quite a good hand with all the points in the long suits of the *partnership*. If game is to be reached, it would have to be in 4♠ and I would suggest that this is worth an invitation to 3♠.

(4) Here we have been forced to speak again and have been asked for a further description of the hand, primarily considering the club position for no-trumps.

(a) Here we can support partner's hearts but with 15 points and partner having taken responsibility up to 2NT (remember that, with a club stop, we should bid it with extra strength), this hand is easily worth a raise to 3♥, forcing for one round. Any non-club game is possible but, knowing our shape almost exactly, it is for partner to decide.

(b) Here there is nothing to do but repeat our excellent diamond suit with 2◊ – non-forcing. Partner will take it from there.

(c) With a club stop, we are entitled to bid no-trumps and, with a hand well above minimum for the opening bid, we should bid 3NT with a view to playing there. If partner wishes to bid on, that is up to him and he may be planning a slam in a non-club suit.

(d) Here we have no club stop but an above-minimum opening and we can show this with 3◊ – forcing for one round as in (a).

(5) (a) Here we are worth a game try and can invite with 3♠, showing a good six-card suit. Partner will probably raise to 4♠ with tolerance of the suit and/or a point count in excess of what he has shown so far.

(b) This hand is easily worth game but, with plenty of top controls, a slam could easily be on. Rather than bid 4♠ direct, it costs nothing to bid a fourth-suit-forcing 2◊ now and then, irrespective of partner's reply, bid 4♠. Partner can then pass or investigate a slam, knowing that we have a bit to spare including diamond control.

(c) Here we are contemplating game but there are several candidates: 3NT and 4♠ are favourites but neither 4♥ nor 5♣ are yet ruled out. This hand is ideal for a fourth-suit-forcing 2◊ to find out more about partner's hand. Let us work out the next round of bidding.

   (i) If partner bids 2NT, he is likely to have a singleton spade in a 1534 shape and it will be wise to pass.

   (ii) If partner merely bids 2♡ or 3♣, again game is unlikely
        and it is probably wise to pass.

   (iii) If partner bids 2♠, we can invite game by asking for
        help in diamonds with a long-suit trial bid of 3◇. This
        should prove a success as partner is likely to be 3514.

   (iv) If partner bids 3♡, 3♠ or 4♣, we will be happy to raise
        to game in the respective suit.

(d) Here it is a question of game or slam but there is no need to
    rush. Our first duty is to find out more about partner's
    hand with a fourth-suit-forcing 2◇.

   (i) If partner bids 2NT, we can then bid 3♣ (forcing after a
       fourth-suit-forcing bid has been answered by no-
       trumps) and see if partner is interested. We shall finish
       in 3NT, 5♣ or 6♣, dependent on partner's shape and
       wealth in top controls.

   (ii) If partner bids 3NT, we bid 4♣, agreeing the suit as
        trumps and initiating cue-bidding with a view to a
        club slam.

   (iii) If partner merely bids 2♡, the position is less clear as
        3NT, 4♡ or 5♣ could be best. With the bulk of the
        points in aces and kings, I suggest pushing for the club
        slam with 4♣ (forcing and initiating cue-bidding),
        prepared to play in 5♣ which should at least be as
        good as 4♡.

(6) (a) Here a slam is very likely and a good start will be a splinter
        bid of 4◇. Partner will reject with 4♠ or, if he is interested,
        cue-bid in the non-diamond suits.

   (b) Here we shall almost certainly want to play in 4♡. The
       meaning of the sequence 1♠ 4♡ is something that a
       partnership must agree on and it has to be said that most
       people play it as natural. However, it seems a pity to lose
       the splinter when the void is in hearts and there is no need
       to preempt with a good hand opposite an opening bid. We
       can reach 4♡ easily by bidding 2♡ now and 4♡ over
       partner's response. The further advantage of this approach
       is that, if partner is strong, it will be much easier to find a
       slam.

(c) Although a slam is well on the cards, there is no guarantee that spades is the best trump suit and, even with ♠ A x x x, it is advisable to start by showing the principal feature of the hand with a game-forcing jump to 3♣. We can then have a quiet chat with partner afterwards. Note that the splinter option has not necessarily been lost. We could still bid 5◊ after partner's rebid of 3♡, 3♠ (when spades are now likely to be a playable trump suit) or even 4♣.

(7) This time, partner has promised a void of clubs and spade agreement.

(a) Here our ♣A is useless and with a minimum hand and plenty of red-suit losers, we should try to sign off in 4♠.

(b) Now the club void is just what the doctor ordered and we shall almost certainly be insisting on a small slam at least. For the time being, however, there is no need to do more than show our first-round heart control with 4♡, simultaneously denying the first-round diamond control (as we have by-passed 4◊). On the next round, our bid of 5◊ will promise second-round control. Many partnerships discourage cue-bidding voids and singletons in partner's bid suit and it must be said that such features are often more of a liability than an asset. However, when there are plenty of trumps, it is usually permissible. In this case, a good grand slam is likely to be missed if partner has something like ♠ A J x x ♡ Q x x ◊ A Q J x x x ♣ – and he fears the loss of a diamond trick.

(c) This hand is not as good as that in (b) but every card is likely to be useful and we should be able to underwrite 5♠. It is therefore worth cue-bidding the ♠A with 4NT.

Competitive Bidding

We are now going to allow the opponents to enter the auction and, again remembering my two categories of reader, it will do no harm to have a revision test on what we have, or should have, learnt so far. Keeping the same time limit, about fifteen seconds per example, I should like you to try and complete the hundred-question test in under twenty-five minutes. Again, it will be impossible to cover every possible situation, not to mention that 'expert' style recommends competing on weaker hands than I do, so I shall concentrate on areas where I find that less experienced players are continually erring. As usual, state the information available from the bidding so far, whether, where relevant, bids are forcing, invitational or sign-off and what final contract(s) you envisage. Assume you are sitting South at love all. Start your stop-watch.

(1) East deals and opens 1♡. What do you bid on:

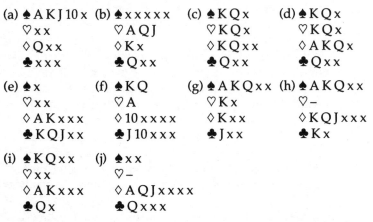

(a) ♠ A K J 10 x
    ♡ x x
    ◊ Q x x
    ♣ x x x

(b) ♠ x x x x x
    ♡ A Q J
    ◊ K x
    ♣ Q x x

(c) ♠ K Q x
    ♡ K Q x
    ◊ K Q x x
    ♣ Q x x

(d) ♠ K Q x
    ♡ K Q x
    ◊ A K Q x
    ♣ Q x x

(e) ♠ x
    ♡ x x
    ◊ A K x x x
    ♣ K Q J x x

(f) ♠ K Q
    ♡ A
    ◊ 10 x x x x
    ♣ J 10 x x x

(g) ♠ A K Q x x
    ♡ K x
    ◊ K x x
    ♣ J x x

(h) ♠ A K Q x x
    ♡ –
    ◊ K Q J x x x
    ♣ K x

(i) ♠ K Q x x
    ♡ x x
    ◊ A K x x x
    ♣ Q x

(j) ♠ x x
    ♡ –
    ◊ A Q J x x x x
    ♣ Q x x x

(2) Partner (North) deals and opens 1♡; East overcalls 1♠. What do you bid now on:

(a) ♠ A J 10 x x
    ♡ x
    ◊ Q x x x
    ♣ Q x x

(b) ♠ K J x
    ♡ J x
    ◊ Q x x x
    ♣ x x x x

(c) ♠ A Q x
    ♡ x x
    ◊ Q x x
    ♣ J x x x x

(d) ♠ K Q x
    ♡ Q x
    ◊ A x x x
    ♣ x x x x

(e) ♠ x x   (f) ♠ Q x x   (g) ♠ –   (h) ♠ x x
    ♡ x x   ♡ A x   ♡ K Q x x   ♡ Q x
    ◊ A K x x x   ◊ A K Q x x   ◊ K Q x x   ◊ A K J x x
    ♣ Q J x x   ♣ x x x   ♣ K x x x x   ♣ K Q J x

(3) Partner deals and opens 1♡; East doubles (obviously for take-out). What do you bid now on:

(a) ♠ 10 x x   (b) ♠ x x   (c) ♠ K x   (d) ♠ x
    ♡ K Q x   ♡ A Q J x   ♡ K Q x x   ♡ K Q x x x
    ◊ x x   ◊ Q x   ◊ K x x x   ◊ x x x
    ♣ x x x x x   ♣ x x x x x   ♣ J x x   ♣ x x x x

(e) ♠ K x   (f) ♠ K Q x x   (g) ♠ x x   (h) ♠ K Q J 10 x x x
    ♡ x x   ♡ x   ♡ J x x x   ♡ x
    ◊ K x x x   ◊ A J x x   ◊ x x   ◊ x x x
    ♣ J x x x x   ♣ J 10 x x   ♣ A K J x x   ♣ x x

(i) ♠ 10 x x   (j) ♠ A Q x
    ♡ –   ♡ x x x x
    ◊ Q 10 x x x x x   ◊ K x x x
    ♣ x x x   ♣ A x

(4) West deals and opens 1♡; partner doubles and East passes. What do you bid now on:

(a) ♠ x x x x   (b) ♠ x x   (c) ♠ Q x x   (d) ♠ x x
    ♡ x x x   ♡ Q x x x   ♡ K Q x   ♡ x x x
    ◊ x x x   ◊ x x x   ◊ Q x x x   ◊ A K Q x x
    ♣ x x x   ♣ Q x x x   ♣ x x x   ♣ x x x

(e) ♠ A Q x x   (f) ♠ K Q x   (g) ♠ x x   (h) ♠ x x
    ♡ x   ♡ K Q x   ♡ K Q J 10 x   ♡ A J x x x
    ◊ A Q x x   ◊ x x   ◊ Q x x   ◊ J x x x
    ♣ J x x x   ♣ Q 10 x x x   ♣ J x x   ♣ x x

(5) West deals and opens 1♠; partner doubles and East redoubles. What do you bid now on:

(a) ♠ K J 10 x x   (b) ♠ x x x   (c) ♠ x x x x   (d) ♠ x x
    ♡ x x   ♡ x x x x   ♡ x   ♡ x
    ◇ x x x   ◇ x x x   ◇ Q x x x x   ◇ Q x x x x
    ♣ x x x   ♣ x x x   ♣ Q x x   ♣ x x x x x

(6) West deals and opens 1♡; partner bids 1♠ and East passes. What do you bid now on:

(a) ♠ x   (b) ♠ K x   (c) ♠ K Q x   (d) ♠ x
    ♡ K Q x x   ♡ A Q J   ♡ x x   ♡ x x x x
    ◇ x x x x   ◇ x x x x   ◇ Q x x x   ◇ x x x
    ♣ x x x x   ♣ x x x x   ♣ x x x x   ♣ A K Q x x

(e) ♠ K x   (f) ♠ K Q   (g) ♠ K Q x   (h) ♠ K Q x x x
    ♡ x x   ♡ A x   ♡ x x   ♡ –
    ◇ K x x x   ◇ A K x x   ◇ x x x   ◇ J x x x x
    ♣ K Q J x x   ♣ J 10 x x x   ♣ A K J x x   ♣ x x x

(i) ♠ K Q x x x
    ♡ –
    ◇ A Q x x x
    ♣ J x x

(7) Partner deals and opens 1NT; East doubles (obviously for penalties). What do you bid now on:

(a) ♠ 10 x x   (b) ♠ x x x x x x   (c) ♠ K Q x   (d) ♠ K Q J x x x x
    ♡ x x x x   ♡ J x x   ♡ K Q x   ♡ x
    ◇ x x x   ◇ x x   ◇ Q x x x   ◇ x x x
    ♣ x x x   ♣ Q x x   ♣ x x x   ♣ x x

(e) ♠ x   (f) ♠ x x
    ♡ x x   ♡ x x
    ◇ A J x x x   ◇ x x x x
    ♣ K J x x x   ♣ 10 x x x x

(8) West deals and opens 1NT; partner doubles and East passes. What do you bid now on:

(a) ♠ J 10 x x   (b) ♠ x x x x x   (c) ♠ Q x x   (d) ♠ x
     ♡ x x x   ♡ x x x   ♡ –   ♡ x x
     ◊ x x x   ◊ x x x   ◊ K Q x x x x x   ◊ K x x x x
     ♣ x x x   ♣ x x   ♣ x x x   ♣ K x x x x

(e) Would any of your answers alter if East redoubles?

(9) West deals and opens 1♡; partner bids an unusual 2NT, showing at least 5–5 in the two minors. East passes. What do you bid now on:

(a) ♠ J 10 x x x   (b) ♠ x x x x x   (c) ♠ K Q x   (d) ♠ K Q J x x x
     ♡ x x   ♡ x x x   ♡ K J x   ♡ Q x x
     ◊ x x x   ◊ A Q   ◊ A K x x   ◊ x
     ♣ x x x   ♣ Q J x   ♣ Q x x   ♣ x x

(e) ♠ x x x x x
     ♡ K Q x x
     ◊ x x
     ♣ x x

(f) Would any of your answers alter if, on (a), (d) and (e), East had doubled for penalties?

(g) Would any of your answers alter, in all five cases, if East had bid 3♡?

(10) East deals and the bidding goes:

W	N	E	S
		1♡	2◊
Pass	3◊	Pass	?

What do you bid now on:

(a) ♠ K J 10   (b) ♠ K x   (c) ♠ x x
     ♡ x x   ♡ J x x   ♡ K Q x
     ◊ A K Q x x   ◊ A K Q x x   ◊ K Q J x x
     ♣ x x x   ♣ Q x x   ♣ x x x

(11) West deals and the bidding goes:

	W	N	E	S
	1♠	2♣	Pass	3♣
	Pass	3♠	Pass	?

What do you bid now on:

(a) ♠ Q x x
♡ A x
◊ Q x x
♣ K x x x

(b) ♠ x x x
♡ A J x
◊ K x
♣ Q x x x x

(c) ♠ x
♡ K Q x
◊ Q x x x
♣ A x x x x

(d) ♠ x
♡ Q x x
◊ A x x x
♣ A x x x x

(12) Partner deals and opens 1♡; East overcalls with 2♠. What do you bid now on:

(a) ♠ J 10 x
♡ Q J x x
◊ Q x
♣ K x x x

(b) ♠ x x x x x x
♡ A J x
◊ J x
♣ J x x

(c) ♠ K Q x x
♡ x
◊ K Q x x
♣ Q x x x

(d) ♠ K J x
♡ K Q x
◊ Q x x x
♣ x x x

(13) West deals and opens 1♡; partner overcalls with 2♠ and East passes. What do you bid now on:

(a) ♠ K J 10 x
♡ x x
◊ A Q x
♣ x x x x

(b) ♠ K x x x
♡ –
◊ A K x x
♣ Q x x x x

(c) ♠ K x x
♡ x
◊ A Q x x x
♣ K Q x x

(d) ♠ K
♡ J x x
◊ A K Q x x x
♣ Q x x

(14) West deals and opens 1♡; partner bids 2♡ and East passes. What do you bid now on:

(a) ♠ x x x x
♡ x x
◊ Q x x x
♣ x x x

(b) ♠ x x x
♡ A Q x x
◊ x x x
♣ Q x x

(c) ♠ K Q x x x
♡ Q
◊ K Q x x x
♣ x x

(d) ♠ x x
♡ J x
◊ A K Q J 10 x x
♣ x x

(15) Partner deals and opens 1♡; East bids 2♡. What do you bid now on:

(a) ♠ x x x
♡ A Q
◊ Q x x x
♣ J x x x

(b) ♠ x x
♡ Q J x x x
◊ x x
♣ Q x x x

(c) ♠ x
♡ K x x x
◊ K Q J x x
♣ x x x

(d) ♠ K Q x x
♡ x
◊ K x x x
♣ Q x x x

(16) West deals and opens 1♡; partner overcalls 2♣ and East doubles for penalties. What do you bid now on:

(a) ♠ 10 x x x   (b) ♠ K J x x x   (c) ♠ x x x x   (d) ♠ x x
    ♡ K Q x x x   ♡ J x x   ♡ A K Q x   ♡ K Q J 10 x x x
    ◊ Q x x x   ◊ K J 10 x x   ◊ x x x x   ◊ x x
    ♣ –   ♣ –   ♣ x   ♣ x x

(17) East deals and the bidding goes:

	W	N	E	S
				1♠ 2♣
	Dble	2♡	Dble	?

What do you bid now on:

(a) ♠ J 10 x x   (b) ♠ K Q x x x   (c) ♠ K x
    ♡ –   ♡ –   ♡ Q x
    ◊ A x x   ◊ Q x   ◊ Q x
    ♣ K J 10 x x x   ♣ K Q 10 x x x   ♣ K Q J x x x x

(18) East deals and the bidding goes:

	W	N	E	S
			1♠	2◊
	Dble	Rdble	Pass	?

What do you bid now on:

(a) ♠ K J x   (b) ♠ Q J x
    ♡ x x   ♡ x x
    ◊ K J 10 x x x   ◊ K Q J x x
    ♣ K x   ♣ Q x x

Let us work through the answers:

(1) (a) This is not a hand on which we should normally open the bidding but, with an excellent spade suit, it is in order to overcall with 1♠. It is most unlikely that we shall run into an expensive double and would welcome a spade lead should West become declarer at no-trumps or one of the minors. If partner has a good hand, we might reach 4♠.

    (b) This is the converse. We have 12 points, as opposed to 10 last time and, although we would consider opening the bidding, we should refrain from overcalling. The spade suit is nowhere near good enough and we do not want it led. If partner touched it from a broken holding like A Q or

K x, it could be very expensive. With all our points in short suits, the hand is better suited to defence and we therefore pass, hoping to defend a heart contract.

(c) With 17 points, balanced, and a good heart stop, we are entitled to overcall with 1NT, showing 15–17 points (some partnerships insist on 16–18). We are hoping to end in 3NT.

(d) With 21 points balanced, we are too strong to overcall 1NT and (unless we have agreed to play it as natural) 2NT would show a minor two-suiter. It is preferable to play it this way as it is very rare that one picks up a natural 2NT opener when an opponent has enough to open the bidding. With balanced hands above the 1NT overcall range, it is advisable to make a take-out double first and then bid no-trumps to show the extra strength. A reasonable guide is that a double plus a no-trump bid at the cheapest level allowed by partner's response shows about 18–20 and, with 21 or more, we double and then jump in no-trumps. Again we are hoping to finish in 3NT.

(e) This is the type of hand suitable for an unusual 2NT. Many players do it with this shape, almost irrespective of strength, because of the considerable preemptive value. Against this has to be weighed the chance of a heavy penalty and the mine of information regarding distribution given away if the opponents do finish in game or slam in a major. Obviously, vulnerability is highly relevant because we are primarily aiming for a sacrifice in five of a minor but experience shows that bidding on poorish hands tends to give away too much information to be worthwhile and I recommend that a near-opening bid should be considered minimum and it is important to have points in the long suits implied, as here.

(f) This shows the other side of the coin. The two minors are very poor and the points are in the short suits, suggesting better suitability for defence. We therefore pass.

(g) This hand is good enough for an intermediate jump overcall of 2♠, hoping to reach 4♠. Partnerships vary in the requirement for a jump overcall. Many nowadays, notably in America, prefer to play them weak for preemptive value and, on this type of hand, they would double first and then bid spades to show the extra strength. The jump overcall is non-forcing. With stronger hands, where we might wish to force, there are the options to double, then cue-bid the opponents' suit and bid spades later; or (stronger still) cue-bid the first time and then bid spades.

(h) This is a case in point where we have a near-certain game in our own hand. A take-out double should be avoided here for two reasons. With two long strong suits, we prefer to play rather than defend and do not want partner to be tempted to stand 1♡ doubled. Also we almost certainly want to play in spades or diamonds and we do not want partner to go flying with a string of clubs, expecting support from us. On this type of hand, we want a long discussion so we set up a forcing situation with a cue-bid of 2♡, forcing at least to suit agreement, after which we shall hope to finish in 4♠, 5♢ or a slam in one of those suits.

(i) With two suits, particularly when they include the other major, it would be a pity to have to commit ourselves to one of them by overcalling 2♢ when the spade fit might be lost. The best procedure is to make a take-out double and 'correct' partner's likely club reply to diamonds, offering diamonds or spades with a view to 5♢ or 4♠. It is more difficult with a 4225 shape when the hand is not really strong enough to double and then correct 2♢ to 3♣. Doubling and then bidding spades would imply longer spades than clubs – again misleading. In that case, it is better to overcall 2♣, hoping that partner can find a bid to give us the opportunity to show the spades next round. Some pairs, however, fearing that the most likely game, 4♠, will be missed, waive the rules with this type of hand, either doubling, intending to stand 2♢, or by overcalling on a four-card suit. There are pros and cons to all these approaches and it is largely a question of style.

(j) It is not unreasonable to overcall with 2♢ on this hand but it has little if any defence and a preempt is much more appropriate. We cannot bid 3♢ because that would be a simple jump, showing a much stronger hand, primarily orientated towards 3NT. To preempt over an opening bid, we must make a double jump, bidding on the three-level over a lower-ranking suit (e.g. 1♣ 3♠) or, as in this case, at the four-level over a higher-ranking suit. As we have a heart void, it is unlikely that opponents will have a serious misfit and will double for a heavy penalty. Exchange our club and heart holdings and I should recommend 2◇ because now an opponents' misfit is much more likely.

(2) (a) Here, with a heavy spade stack and a dislike of hearts, we have an ideal penalty double and we shall treat a withdrawal to the minors with equal contempt. Note that, if partner repeats his hearts, he will be doing so in the expectation of a singleton or void opposite and we must respect his decision and pass. We refrain from flying into no-trumps with such a misfit. Removing the double will be a sign of weakness from partner and there will be no game.

(b) A no-trump response over a one-level opener *without interference* would show 6–8 points (many say 6–9). Once opponents interfere, partner has another chance to bid and now there is little point in bidding at the lower end of the range, particularly with the majority of our points in opponents' suit (albeit well placed). Some would recommend valuing up the well-placed spade honours and treating it in the 8–10 point range for 1NT, and indeed a good case can be made for this. I prefer a pass, intending to bid no-trumps if partner reopens. We then might reach 3NT.

(c) Here we are in the 8–10 point range and, with a double spade-stop, 1NT, hoping for 3NT, is ideal.

(d) This time, we are strong enough for 2NT, again hoping for 3NT.

(e) Here, in the absence of the spade overcall, we were going to bid a natural and forcing 2◇ and there is no reason to change that here. We are looking for five of a minor but 3NT may be on if partner can stop the spades.

(f) This is strong enough for a game-forcing 3◇, looking for

3NT or 5◊, or a possible slam.

(g) This is easily strong enough for game in hearts but rather than commit ourselves to that immediately there is no harm or cost in telling partner about the spade void with a splinter bid of 3♠. If partner has two useful (i.e. non-spade) aces, 6♡ is likely to be on.

(h) Here we have another game-forcing hand but, at the moment, five of a minor or even four hearts on a 5–2 fit could be on. We express our strength with an unassuming cue-bid of 2♠, inviting partner to describe his hand further. This forces to suit agreement and we shall not let the bidding die below game. If partner is strong and has at least second-round control of spades, a slam could be on in any non-spade denomination.

(3) Styles vary in respect of treatment of opponents' take-out double. Some recommend ignoring it completely and bidding as though the opponent had passed and this certainly has an advantage in terms of ease of memory. However, with (i) opponents, in principle, being in a forcing situation; (ii) the (admittedly rare) possibility that the double could be left; (iii) the availability of the redouble; there are far more options and it seems a pity not to take advantage of them.

I therefore explained that responder should place his hand into one of six possible categories, according to strength, attitude to partner's suit and whether points are concentrated in our outside partner's suit. The six categories are therefore (drawing the line between weak and strong at about the 9–10 point mark):

1 Weak with a misfit.
2 Weak with a fit and most of the points in partner's suit.
3 Weak with a fit and most of the points outside partner's suit.
4 Strong with a misfit.
5 Strong with a fit and most of the points in partner's suit.
6 Strong with a fit and most of points outside partner's suit.

The approach is that the greater the fit and the more points we have in partner's suit, the more we want to play rather than defend and vice versa. Where we want to play, we bid up, trying to prevent opponents from finding their fit. Where we are happy to defend, we keep the bidding low, allowing opponents to bid. Let us consider our examples in that light and discuss it further afterwards.

(a) Here we have a fit and no defence outside the heart suit so we must bid up, trying to cramp the opponent's bidding space and suggesting a possible sacrifice. We bid 2♡ and a case can be made for 3♡.

(b) This time, we are slightly understrength for a normal raise to 3♡ but, for that type of hand, the 2NT bid is available so we do bid 3♡ here.

(c) This is a good raise to 3♡ and we show it with 2NT (forcing), hoping to finish in 4♡.

(d) With a massive heart fit and no defence outside, we should preempt to the limit with 4♡, making life as difficult for opponents as possible and suggesting a possibly profitable sacrifice if they do bid game over it.

(e) Here we have all our points outside hearts and with partner having an opening bid, we are happy to defend. It is unlikely that 1♡ doubled will be left and we have plenty of points (the kings are probably well placed) if it is. We therefore have little reason to bid.

(f) This time, we have a similar hand to the doubler and we have opponents in terrible trouble. Now, and in my opinion, only now, is the time to redouble. This effectively says to partner that we think we can make 1♡ by sheer strength of high cards and that, if opponents run, we shall double for a huge penalty. Many redouble on 10 points or more, irrespective of shape, but then opener has little idea what final contract (playing or defending) is anticipated. Remember that, if opener has very poor hearts, he must remove the redouble and then we shall play in one of the other suits.

(g) Here we have a good fit for hearts and enough to raise to the three-level but the points are outside and my recommendation for showing this hand is to pass and then bid 3♣ (forcing) next round to show the suit and the heart fit in one breath. Partner is then well informed as to whether to play 3♡, 4♡ or even more!

(h) This time, despite the misfit, the hand being worth six tricks in spades on its own, it is worth preempting. How high depends on vulnerability, but I would recommend 2♠ vulnerable, 3♠ non-vulnerable. Partner should appreciate that we have this type of hand and have bid spades despite East's likely interest in the suit.

(i) The diamond suit is poor this time and preempting, particularly with a void in partner's suit, is out of order. The big danger is that 1♡ doubled will be left and, as the hand may be worth up to five tricks more with those diamonds as trumps, it is worth raising the level of bidding with 2◇, which should be treated as a sign-off, partner realizing that we have this type of hand and only bid with a diamond fit.

(j) Here we have enough to insist on game but, with the points outside trumps, I recommend passing now to force West to bid and then 4♡ next round. Partner will then know what to do if the opponents decide to sacrifice. In this kind of situation, West is bound to have a very poor hand and I am a great believer in forcing people to bid when they do not want to! Almost certainly, he will have to bid a poor suit and the following kind of scenario often happens. Suppose hearts are trumps and East, having doubled, is on lead. The bidding goes:

```
W    N    E    S
     1♡   Dble Pass
2♣   Pass Pass 4♡
end
```

and the club situation is:

```
        Q x
x x x x         K J x x
        A x x
```

East dutifully leads his partner's 'suit', presenting us with an unmakeable contract. I can assure readers that I have benefited from this situation countless times through this tactic, including one classic occasion when my partner, after gross overbidding, was handed an unmakeable slam by two experts – you should have heard the post-mortem!

I have gone into this question at some length because it epitomizes the need to understand what we are doing with a view a to final contract. Few people adopt these tactics but, for me, they have yet to fail.

(4) (a) Here we have been forced to speak and must bid our longest side-suit, 1♠. Remember this promises 0–7 points and that a pass, converting the take-out double to penalties, is a *strong* bid.

(b) The same applies and, with the ♡Q badly placed, we are down to an effective 2 points but must still bid our longest non-heart suit, 2♣. If we had two four-card non-heart suits, we normally bid in the usual ascending order.

(c) This time, we have a good stop in hearts and can respond 1NT, showing 8–10 points (limited and non-forcing). However, we should not be too excited about this hand. The one thing partner does not want is points in hearts, badly placed under the opener and probably facing a singleton. If partner is strong, we might reach 3NT.

(d) Here we have enough to jump to 3◊, showing about 8–11 points, again limited and again non-forcing. 3NT might be on if partner can stop the hearts. If he is void or singleton, we might reach 5◊.

(e) Here we have a big hand with all the points outside hearts – just what partner wants. We certainly have enough to insist on game with 4♠ being hot favourite. For the time being, however, there is no need to rush into decisions. All we need do is establish a forcing situation by cue-bidding 2♡ and let partner describe his hand.

(f) With 12 points, we are strong enough to bid 2NT (showing about 11–13 and non-forcing; remember partner, with a good shape, may be below 12 points). We are primarily looking for 3NT rather than 5♣ and this is a more descriptive bid than 3♣.

(g) Here, with the very strong heart suit, there is every chance of defeating 1♡ heavily and we pass, converting the double to penalties. Partner should realize that our trumps are long and solid and should lead one if he has one. We are aiming to draw declarer's trumps early to prevent him from scoring tricks by ruffing.

(h) This is an unpleasant situation – the hearts are not strong enough to stand the double and the point-count not high enough to bid 1NT. We must simply answer the double with 2◊. If partner shows a strong hand, we shall be happy to look for 3NT.

(5) The redouble has removed the force and we shall now see that, although we are in some trouble, bidding is very often much easier. That is why I tend to avoid the redouble unless I have the opponents well collared as in (3f) above.

(a) This is a classic example. We would have been debating whether to stand the double or bid a poor three-card minor on the two-level had East passed – a horrible decision. Now we can pass and leave partner to rescue himself into his longest suit.

(b) Same again – we would have had to bid 2♡ without the redouble – now we can pass and await developments. At the worst, we can always bid 2♡ later – nothing has been lost.

(c) This time, we have a definite choice in diamonds and should bid 2◊ (intending to play there), making it clear to partner that this is a long suit.

(d) Here we can offer two suits and do so with an 'unusual' 1NT. Note that, with opponents having announced the balance of the points, it can make no sense to play in 1NT, which will be doubled for an enormous penalty. Here it shows two suits, minors in the first place, but we can also do it with two red suits, intending to correct 2♣ to 2◊ (or redouble for SOS) to show this type of hand.

(6) (a) This hand is a disaster – our few points are badly placed and of little, if any, use and we should pass.

(b) This time, we can bid 1NT showing about 8–11 points

(remember partner, with good spades, can be well below opening-bid strength) with good hearts and at least tolerance for spades (which will be the source of most of the tricks). We refrain from flying into no-trumps with a misfit – the suits may all be stopped but we will have nowhere to go for tricks.

(c) Here we have a fit with points in partner's suit and we are keen to prevent West from reopening. We bid 2♠ (preemptive rather than constructive) and some would even recommend 3♠.

(d) It may well be that the hand plays better in clubs than spades but 2♣ would be a forward-going and constructive bid (angled towards 3NT, 4♠ or 5♣) and that is the last impression we want to give. It is best to pass. The three top clubs will help to make 1♠. If West reopens, we shall be delighted to defend with a singleton in partner's suit.

(e) Here, with an opening bid and good tolerance for the spades, we are entitled to make a constructive move forward with 2♣. This is invitational but non-forcing and looks for 4♠ or 5♣. 3NT may be on if partner has a good double heart stop.

(f) Here we have easily enough for game but any non-heart denomination is possible. To clarify this to partner, we establish a forcing situation with an unassuming cue-bid of 2♡ (forcing to game or suit agreement), after which we will discuss the denomination.

(g) A game is likely to be on here but, before committing ourselves, we should describe our hand with 3♣, forcing one round and implying willingness to go to at least 3♠ (or 4♣ in the case where we have a self-supporting suit and are looking for 3NT).

(h) Here we have a fabulous fit and no defence and should preempt to the limit with 4♠. If West wants to reopen with an obviously strong hand, let him do it at the five-level!

(i) This is a stronger hand and, if partner can control the clubs, a small or even grand slam could easily be on. Admittedly, the splinter bid of 3♡ allows West more space to bid but with 7 points outside the spade suit, it is probably worth it.

We shall insist on at least 4♠.

(7) (a) This is a nightmare come true but there is nothing to be gained by moving to the two-level (remember we would need an extra trick to break even and *two* extra tricks to show a profit). We pass and take our medicine.

(b) Here it is probably worth raising the level of bidding to have those spades as trumps – they will be useless otherwise. We sign off in 2♠.

(c) With 12 points, our partnership has the balance and we redouble, intending to double any rescue by opponents.

(d) Here we have a stronger hand than in (b) and it may well be that opponents are cold for a game in a non-spade denomination. We therefore preempt to 3♠ (some would recommend 4♠). This is non-forcing.

(e) Here we want to play in a suit contract but are not sure which minor to choose. We bid 2NT (unusual and forcing) showing, in the first place, two minors, but we can do it on any two adjacent suits, using the SOS redouble if partner picks a lower-ranking suit in which we are short.

(f) This is similar to (b) and we rescue to 2♣. Remember that, after the double, constructive bidding is out of order and this reverts to a weak natural sign-off.

(8) A good guide in this situation is to treat partner as though he had opened a strong no-trump (say 15 points or more), bearing in mind that Stayman does not now apply. Occasionally, it will become obvious that he has doubled on a long running suit.

(a) Here we have nowhere to go and should pass, respecting partner's decision.

(b) Here it is worth making a weak take-out into 2♠ to have that weak suit as trumps in an entryless hand. If partner makes a further move, we respect it and pass.

(c) This time, we have a lot of points and are delighted to defend 1NT doubled. If game is on in diamonds, what will happen to 1NT doubled? Shudder the thought!

(d) The same thing applies – why move?

(e) If East redoubles, then on (a), we still pass (with one more point than we might have had!) and let partner decide whether to rescue or take them on. Remember that, wherever possible, the decision should be taken by the *strong* (and therefore more knowledgeable) hand rather than the weak partner, i.e. the dog should wag the tail.

On (b), we have a definite escape and should bid 2♠ as before. On (c) and (d), it is likely that partner has doubled on a long running suit rather than on points and we have certainly no reason to bid. The penalty should be considerable. Thus the answer is 'No' in all four cases.

(9) (a) Here we are asked for our choice of minor and, with equal length, it is usual to choose the lower-ranking, i.e. 3♣, hoping to play there. Remember this promises neither strength nor length in clubs.

(b) We have a lot of points here, just where partner wants them, and are therefore worth a game try. 4♣ is highly invitational (but not forcing – the only forcing bid is 3♡) and partner should bid game if he can avoid three losers in the majors.

(c) We should be able to run nine tricks in the minors and, even though the hand will be played from the 'wrong' side in 3NT, partner can ensure a heart stop by just covering whatever East leads. 3NT is a sign-off and partner should only move with twelve or more cards in his suits, when a minor-suit slam could be on.

(d) Here we can bid 3♠ despite the misfit as the hand is probably worth six tricks more if those spades are trumps. Partner's minor-suit tops should contribute a trick or two and 3♠ may well be made.

(e) This is a nightmare but all we can do is to bid 3♣ and hope to be able to play it undoubled. It would be folly to pass 2NT and advertize that we are in trouble. Opponents are less likely to double if we bid with apparent confidence.

(f) If East doubles for penalties, we do not have to commit ourselves on (a) and (f). We pass and let partner make the choice or redouble with equal length in the minors. In (d), the position is less clear. The chances are that East intends to double either 3♣ or 3◇. But it may be that he can only double one of them. I should recommend bidding 3♣ now and moving to 3♠ if it is doubled. Some would suggest 3♠ at once.

(g) If East bids 3♡, then we will obviously pass on (a), (d) and (f) and still bid 3NT on (c). (b) is less clear as 4♣ should be taken as merely competing rather than invitational. I should suggest a confident 5♣ and they may well decide (rightly or wrongly) to sacrifice. We will, of course, double 5♡ if East bids it, hoping to make top tricks in the minors and to warn partner not to go any further.

(10) (a) This hand is worth a try for 3NT and we bid 3♠ to show spade values. If partner can stop the hearts, he may be able to bid 3NT; otherwise we shall have to settle for 4◇.

(b) Again, with 15 points, we are worth a try for 3NT but we will need help for partner in hearts and make a directional asking bid with 3♡, again prepared to play 4◇ if partner cannot oblige with a half-stop.

(c) Here, despite the good heart stop, we are minimum and short of top controls and therefore should pass, content to play in 3◇.

(11) Here partner has made a directional asking bid, angling for 3NT but prepared to play in clubs if we disappoint.

(a) ♠ Q x x is ample and we bid 3NT, intending to play there.

(b) Here we cannot stop the spades and have a disastrous holding and so must be content to try to sign off in 4♣.

(c) Again, we cannot oblige with a stop but the singleton spade and long clubs make it worthwhile to try for game and we bid 5♣.

(d) This is similarly worth 5♣ but it does no harm to cue-bid our ◇A on the way with 4◇. Partner needs have no more than something like: ♠ J x x ♡ A K x ◇ x ♣ K Q J x x x for the slam to be cold. In any case, the 4◇ bid costs nothing.

(12) (a) This is worth no more than a good raise to 2♡. However, one should be prepared to be pushed up one level to com-

pete and on this hand, we can bid 3♡. Partner, however, must take into account the fact that we have been pushed and not be too keen to raise to game unless he is worth at least a trial over 1♡ 2♡ without interference. He will take his badly-placed spade holding into account.

(b) This hand would also have raised to 2♡ but the spade holding is disastrous and it is wise not to bid at this stage in case West is very short of spades, when 4♡ doubled could go badly down. If partner can reopen, i.e. he is the one who is very short, we will be happy to raise to game.

(c) Here we have a misfit and a very unpleasant trump stack and are delighted to double for penalties.

(d) Here, with a good double-stop and the correct point-count, we can bid 2NT (non-forcing), hoping to finish in 3NT or 4♡.

(13) (a) We have excellent trump support and no wasted heart values and are delighted to sign off with a raise to game in 4♠.

(b) Here a slam could easily be on and we show our (probably crucial) heart void with a splinter bid of 4♡. Partner can sign off in 4♠; otherwise cue-bidding will follow.

(c) Here again, a slam is possible and there are two approaches. One is to bid 3◊ (forcing), intending to follow with 4♠. However, I prefer to bid 3♡ (which partner will take as directional asking in the first place) and then remove 3NT to 4♠. Partner will realize that the 3♡ bid was an advanced cue-bid, showing at least second-round control, and pass or look for a slam accordingly.

(d) Here we are primarily looking for 3NT, hoping to make it by cashing those solid diamonds. Over 3◊ (forcing), we hope that partner will be able to make a directional asking bid.

(14) Partner has shown a huge hand and has forced to suit agreement. Therefore, there is no need to rush unless we have a specific message to send. This is one rare occasion where we need not worry too much about final contract as partner will be taking that decision.

(a) In the first place, we have been asked to bid our suits and we simply answer with 2♠ and await partner's reaction.

(b) With a good double heart stop, we bid 2NT. Should partner raise to 3NT, we can bid a *quantitative* 4NT as this is a stronger hand than it might have been.

(c) Here we will almost certainly be bidding up to the slam zone but, for the moment, there is no need for more than a quiet 2♠. We will show our diamonds later and keep the bidding open, hoping for a small or grand slam in one of our suits.

(d) This is the one exception where we have a solid suit and should clarify it at once with a jump to 4◊. Cue-bidding will follow and we shall probably end in 6◊ or 7◊.

(15) This time, opponents are in a forcing situation and are likely to reach game at least. It is up to us to give information to partner regarding whether we wish to sacrifice or defend.

(a) Here we can show our values in hearts, indicating a safe lead, by doubling the cue-bid. Partner can bid up in the suit if he has length.

(b) Here we have little or no defence and should preempt to the limit. Vulnerability is obviously relevant but we should bid at least 4♡ – at favourable vulnerability, a case could be made for 5♡.

(c) Here we show our diamond suit in addition to heart support with 3◊. Partner will then be better placed to decide whether to defend or sacrifice against a likely black-suit game or slam.

(d) With excellent defence against all three non-heart suits, we are happy to pass and let opponents get on with it. The last thing we want to do is to warn them that there is trouble ahead before it is too late. We should be able to double any game contract.

(16) (a) This is a nightmare but any attempt to move to another contract is likely to increase the penalty. We pass and take our medicine.

(b) With two good five-card suits to offer as alternative, an SOS redouble is in order. Partner will now remove to 2◊ or 2♠.

   (c) Here the same applies as in (a). We are not tempted to bid 2NT which will be even worse than 2♣. As a general rule, it is seldom right to take a doubled suit contract out into no-trumps.

   (d) This time, our hand will be worth several more tricks with those hearts as trumps and we should bid 2♡, which partner should respect.

(17) (a) Another nightmare but we have no better contract to offer and must respect partner's move to 2♡. We pass gracefully.

   (b) Here 2♠ might be a better contract but partner's hearts will be useless and the chances are that it is better to pass 2♡.

   (c) Here we have a fabulous surprise for partner in our heart support and are again happy to pass. We do not want to play 3♣ (a level higher anyway) with ♣ A 10 9 x x or all six outstanding clubs offside.

(18) Here partner has asked us to choose between hearts and clubs. In (a), we have no length preference and prefer 2♡, being a level lower. In (b), we bid our longer suit, 3♣.

We have spent considerable time on misfit hands and must now turn to those where both sides have fits and the bidding is likely to progress to a high level. Eventually a stage is reached where we have to decide whether to compete further or defend (doubled or undoubled). Often, little is known about a hand. Consider this kind of sequence which occurs all too often.

Suppose East deals at Love All:

W	N	E	S
		1♡	1♠
4♡	4♠	5♡	?

So East has opened 1♡ and we have overcalled 1♠. Nothing much to worry about so far but how about West's 4♡ call? He could have made it preemptively, on a long string of hearts and little or no defence – trying to make it difficult for us to find the correct level in spades – or he could have a reasonable hand, intending to make it.

There is similar doubt regarding partner's 4♠ bid. Does he think we can make that game or does he believe that 4♡ will be made and that this will be a cheap sacrifice, or that both contracts will be made? It is anybody's guess and the 5♡ bid from East thickens the plot further. Is that a sacrifice against 4♠ or does he believe that 5♡ will be made and that the penalty from 4♠ will be minimal, or does he think that both contracts will be made? He does not know what his partner's 4♡ bid was based on!

The whole position is little more than a guessing game and there is no better proof than two well-known tips from the 'experts' applicable to situations of this kind. One says 'If in doubt, bid one more'; the other 'The five-level belongs to the opponents.' Most lamentable and, justice being what it is, countless rubbers, matches and tournaments are won and lost in this area. Good judgment is therefore beyond price.

At this stage, all we can do is to make a list of the factors to be taken into account when considering the options available.

1 The state of the auction. Here we have three options:
   (a) compete by bidding 5♠;
   (b) double, firmly discouraging partner from competing;
   (c) pass and let partner decide.
   There will, however, be positions where the hand on our left has made the last bid and partner has passed it round to us. The three options are then:
   (a) compete:,
   (b) double and defend – partner should not overrule this – having left the decision to us, he should accept it;
   (c) pass and allow the opponents' contract to be played undoubled.

2 The potential gain and loss through competing, passing or doubling. Vulnerability is obviously highly relevant, but let us consider the position at Love All as illustration. Suppose we compete with 5♠, are doubled and go two off, finding afterwards that 5♡ doubled would have suffered a similar fate. We have lost 300 instead of gaining 300, the mistake therefore costing 600. At the other extreme, suppose we double 5♡ and they make it and find that 5♠ would also have been made, then we lose (counting the non-vulnerable game as being worth 300)

650 + 450 = 1100 or 650 + 650 = 1300 if 5♠ would have been doubled. As you see, the mistake through failure to compete is about twice as costly as that through competing and this is the mentality behind the 'If in doubt, bid one more' philosophy.

However, experience shows that, more often than not, bidding in this kind of situation has been stretched by one or both sides and once the probabilities of the above contingencies have been taken into account, the case in favour of electing to defend becomes much stronger. It is therefore usually right, once an opposing pair has been pushed up one level (here from 4♡ to 5♡), not to compete further but let them play. This is the rationale behind the 'Five-level belongs to the opponents' mentality.

3 The risk that, if we compete, we might push opponents from part-score to game, or from game to slam, or from small slam to grand slam – a serious loss in all three cases.

4 The degree to which we have bid our hand already. Have we already stretched, bid accurately, or do we have a bit to spare? In the last case, is that surplus better employed offensively or defensively?

5 The length and strength of the suit we have agreed with partner. Obviously the longer and stronger we are in that suit, the less chance we have of making a defensive trick in it and the more suited we are to competing as opposed to defending, and vice versa.

6 The length and strength of the suit that opponents have agreed. From the point of view of competing, the worst holding is undoubtedly the doubleton. The opponents are likely to have nine cards between them and if we have a doubleton, partner is likely to be similarly endowed and the opponents may be pleasantly surprised to take two tricks in defence. A void or singleton is obviously preferable, and trebleton or more implies shortage with partner.

7 The honour holdings in the side suits. The more and the higher we have there, the better placed we are for defence and vice versa.

8 The length in the side suits. Two-suiters, particularly with

honours in the long suits, are better for declaring and vice versa.

Quite a mouthful – and we haven't even considered the human element. Some players are more competitive than others; some are more likely to double than others, and so it goes on. For the time being, all we can do is to work through a few examples. Before doing so, however, allow me to offer a word of warning. There is no absolute right and wrong in these situations – what follows are merely my suggested answers, with which many top-class players would, I am sure, agree, and just as many, I am equally sure, would disagree. It is anybody's guess.

With the kind of sequence we have been discussing, it is usually right to pass and leave the decision to partner. He knows whether his 4♠ bid was serious or sacrifice and we do not. Also, he is probably better placed to judge the merits of West's 4♡ bid. Let us look at six hands:

(a) ♠ Q J 10 x x   (b) ♠ K Q J x x   (c) ♠ A K J x x   (d) ♠ K Q J x x x
     ♡ A x   ♡ Q x   ♡ x x x   ♡ A x
     ◇ K Q x   ◇ K Q x x   ◇ K x   ◇ Q x x
     ♣ x x x   ♣ J x   ♣ x x x   ♣ x x

(e) ♠ K J 10 x x x   (f) ♠ A K Q x x x
     ♡ K x x   ♡ –
     ◇ Q J x   ◇ K Q x x x
     ♣ x   ♣ x x

In (a), most of our points are outside the spade suit, we have a doubleton heart and do not want to play 5♠. I recommend warning partner with a double. In (f), we are very strong in playing strength in this three-loser hand and there is no guarantee that we have any defensive tricks at all. Spades will certainly not provide more than one trick (and then only if we are lucky) and diamonds are unlikely to provide more than one, if any. I recommend competing with 5♠. On all the others, it is not clear-cut and I should recommend passing, allowing partner to decide.

But now let us go to the other side of the table and consider the position where the decision has been left to us. Now we are North and the bidding has gone:

```
W     N     E     S
            1♡    1♠
4♡    4♠    5♡    Pass
Pass  ?
```

Here we are better placed in that we know whether our 4♠ bid was a sacrifice, fearing that 4♡ was going to be made, or serious, thinking that we would make 4♠. Again, let us look at six hands.

(g) ♠ K Q x x	(h) ♠ 10 x x x	(i) ♠ K Q x	(j) ♠ J 10 x x x x
♡ –	♡ K x x	♡ x x	♡ –
◇ Q J x x x	◇ K Q J x x	◇ A x x	◇ J 10 x x x
♣ x x x x	♣ x	♣ Q x x x x	♣ x x

(k) ♠ K J x x	(l) ♠ A x x x
♡ x	♡ J x
◇ K x x x	◇ Q x x x x
♣ x x x x	♣ J x

On (g), it is anybody's guess how many tricks we shall make in spades but it is unlikely that we shall make eleven. If partner is short of diamonds, our honours may provide some defence and it is possible that opponents will find the bad heart split inconvenient. It is no certainty that 5♡ will be made but it will not be going down heavily – I recommend a pass.

On (h), our points are all outside spades and partner may well provide one spade trick. It is clear that opponents are sacrificing and I recommend a double.

On (i), for a hand that has raised to game, we are 'short' of spades and two tricks there are by no means ruled out. The ace of diamonds is a near-certain trick and the ♣Q may also help in defence. We have 11 points and opponents are likely to be sacrificing. I recommend a double.

On (j), we have a playing hand with no defence and partner's failure to double 5♡ (and it is not clear-cut that we should stand it if he had!), it is clear that 5♡ is almost certain to be made, costing 450. There is every chance that we can escape for two off (300) or less in 5♠ and I recommend competing. The risk of pushing opponents into a makeable slam is small. West could have made a more constructive bid over 1♠ than 4♡, had he been interested in a discussion and equally, East could have made a cue-bid (or Blackwood) over 4♠ if he had been interested. It is therefore most unlikely that they will risk looking silly by going down in 6♡ when a good penalty is available in 5♠ doubled. However, if we bid 5♠, East does bid 6♡ and partner is unable to double, leaving the decision to us, we must be prepared to bid 6♠, settling to lose another 200 or 300 rather than risk losing an almost certain extra 500.

On (k), we are unlikely to make 5♠ and, with some defensive prospects in the two kings, I recommend a pass.

On (l), again 5♠ is most unlikely to be made and could go badly down. We have already stretched with the 4♠ bid. The two doubleton jacks might have some value in defence if partner can produce honours in those suits and I recommend a pass.

This sample dozen should give you a good idea of how to think about the most delicate – but often most crucial – decisions in the game. But remember, we worked them all out at Love All. Change the vulnerability, and there are four possibilities, and the decision could well be different – notably on (k).

We will conclude the book with another one-hundred question test on competitive situations and again I shall be concentrating on positions where, in my experience, even the better players tend go wrong. In each case, I shall want you to give your choice of bid, stating detailed reasons with reference to the considerations listed above. Assume in all cases that you are sitting South and that the score is Love All but state what modifications, if any, there would be to your answers if you were:

(i)   non-vulnerable against vulnerable;
(ii) vulnerable against non-vulnerable;
(iii) at Game All.

As there is much to discuss on each question, I shall allow up to a minute to answer each one, but you should attempt to finish the test in under an hour-and-a-half. Start your stop-watch.

(1) You deal and the bidding goes:

W	N	E	S
			1♡
1♠	2♡	2♠	?

What do you bid now on:

(a) ♠ Q J x
♡ A K x x x
◇ K x x
♣ x x

(b) ♠ x x x x
♡ K J x x x
◇ A x x
♣ A

(c) ♠ K Q x
♡ J 10 x x x x
◇ A x
♣ Q x

(d) ♠ –
♡ A K Q x x
◇ A x x x
♣ Q x x x

(2) Partner deals and the bidding goes:

W	N	E	S
	1♡	1♠	2♡
2♠	Pass	Pass	?

What do you bid now on:

(a) ♠ K J x
♡ J x x x
◇ Q x x x x
♣ x

(b) ♠ x x x
♡ K x x x
◇ A x x x
♣ x x

(c) ♠ K Q x x
♡ Q 10 x x
◇ –
♣ x x x x x

(d) ♠ –
♡ Q x x
◇ J 10 x x x
♣ Q x x x x

(3) You deal and the bidding goes:

W	N	E	S
			1♠
2♣	2♡	3♣	?

What do you bid now on:

(a) ♠ Q J 10 x x
♡ K x x
◇ K x
♣ K J x

(b) ♠ A K x x x x
♡ J x x x
◇ A x x
♣ –

(c) ♠ K Q J x x
♡ Q x x
◇ A
♣ x x x x

(d) ♠ A K x x x
♡ x x x
◇ Q x x
♣ K Q

(4) Partner deals and the bidding goes:

W	N	E	S
	1♠	2♣	2♡
3♣	Pass	Pass	?

What do you bid now on:

(a) ♠ Q J x
♡ K Q x x x
◇ K x x
♣ x x

(b) ♠ x x x
♡ K J x x x
◇ Q x
♣ K J x

(c) ♠ K x x
♡ K Q J x x x
◇ A x x
♣ Q

(d) ♠ J x x
♡ A Q x x x
◇ K
♣ J x x x

(5) East deals and the bidding goes

W	N	E	S
		1♡	2◇
2♡	3◇	3♡	?

What do you bid now on:

(a) ♠ Q J x
♡ x
◇ A K Q x x
♣ x x x x

(b) ♠ x x x x
♡ K J x
◇ A J 10 x x x
♣ –

(c) ♠ K Q x x
♡ x x
◇ A K x x x x
♣ Q

(d) ♠ –
♡ x x x x
◇ A K Q x x x
♣ A x x

(6) West deals and the bidding goes:

W	N	E	S
1♡	2◇	2♡	3◇
3♡	Pass	Pass	?

What do you bid now on:

(a) ♠ x
♡ x x x
◇ K x x x
♣ K Q x x x

(b) ♠ x x x x x
♡ –
◇ K x x x
♣ K x x x

(c) ♠ x x x
♡ K J 10 x
◇ K Q x x
♣ x x

(d) ♠ Q x x
♡ A x
◇ Q x x x
♣ K x x x

(7) West deals and the bidding goes:

W	N	E	S
	1♠	2♣	3♣	?

What do you bid now on:

(a) ♠ Q J x x
♡ x x x
◇ K x
♣ A x x x

(b) ♠ x x x
♡ J x x x
◇ x
♣ A Q x x x

(c) ♠ x x x x
♡ x x x x
◇ A
♣ K Q x x

(d) ♠ –
♡ x x x
◇ A K x x x
♣ A Q x x x

(8) East deals and the bidding goes:

W	N	E	S
		1♠	2♣
3♠	4♣	4♠	?

What do you bid now on:

(a) ♠ J x x
♡ A x x x
◇ x
♣ K Q J x x

(b) ♠ x x x
♡ x x
◇ A K
♣ A J 10 x x x

(c) ♠ x x x x
♡ K J 10
◇ –
♣ A K J x x x

(d) ♠ K Q 10
♡ A x
◇ x x
♣ Q J 10 x x x

(9) West deals and the bidding goes:

W	N	E	S
1♠	2♣	3♠	4♣?
4♠	Pass	Pass	?

What do you bid now on:

(a) ♠ Q J x	(b) ♠ K J 10 x	(c) ♠ K x	(d) ♠ -
♡ x x	♡ x x	♡ x x x x	♡ K x x x
◊ K x x x	◊ x x	◊ A x	◊ K x x x
♣ K Q x x	♣ A x x x x	♣ A x x x x	♣ Q x x x x

(10) You deal and the bidding goes:

W	N	E	S
			1♡
1NT	3♡	3NT	?

What do you bid now on:

(a) ♠ J x x	(b) ♠ x x x x	(c) ♠ Q x x	(d) ♠ x x x
♡ A K x x x	♡ K J x x x x	♡ A 10 x x x x	♡ Q J 10 x x
◊ K x x x	◊ A K x	◊ A	◊ A K Q x x
♣ Q x	♣ -	♣ Q x x	♣ -

(11) Partner deals and the bidding goes:

W	N	E	S
	1♡	1NT	3♡
3NT	Pass	Pass	?

What do you bid now on:

(a) ♠ Q J x	(b) ♠ x x x x	(c) ♠ Q x	(d) ♠ -
♡ K x x x	♡ J x x x x x	♡ Q x x x x	♡ K Q x x x
◊ K x x x x	◊ A x x	◊ Q x	◊ J 10 9 x
♣ x	♣ -	♣ Q J 10 x	♣ J 10 9 x

(12) You deal and the bidding goes:

W	N	E	S
			1♡
1♠	2♡	3NT	?

What do you bid now on:

(a) ♠ Q J x	(b) ♠ x x x x	(c) ♠ x	(d) ♠ x x x x
♡ A Q x x x	♡ K J x x x	♡ K Q J 10 x x	♡ K Q x x x x
◊ Q J x	◊ A x x	◊ A x	◊ A Q x
♣ x x	♣ A	♣ J 10 x x	♣ -

(13) You deal and the bidding goes:

W	N	E	S
			3♡
3♠	4♡	4♠	?

What do you bid now on:

(a) ♠ x x x
♡ A Q J x x x x
◇ x x
♣ x

(b) ♠ A x
♡ K Q x x x x x
◇ x x
♣ x x

(c) ♠ x
♡ Q J 10 x x x x x
◇ x x
♣ J x

(d) ♠ x x x
♡ K J 10 x x x x
◇ –
♣ J x x

(14) Partner deals and the bidding goes:

W	N	E	S
		3♡	3♠	4♡
4♠	Pass	Pass	?

What do you bid now on:

(a) ♠ Q J x
♡ Q x
◇ A K Q J x
♣ x x x

(b) ♠ x
♡ K x x
◇ A Q x
♣ x x x x x x

(c) ♠ –
♡ K 10 x
◇ A x x x x
♣ K 10 x x x

(d) ♠ x x x
♡ A
◇ A Q x x
♣ A J x x x

(15) What do you bid on these same four hands if partner doubles 4♠?

(16) West deals and the bidding goes:

W	N	E	S
3♡	3♠	5♡	?

What do you bid now on:

(a) ♠ Q J x
♡ Q x
◇ x x x x x
♣ x x x

(b) ♠ A x x x
♡ x x x
◇ A K x x x
♣ A

(c) ♠ A x x x
♡ x x
◇ A x
♣ A J 10 x x

(d) ♠ K Q x x x
♡ x
◇ J x x x x
♣ x x

(17) What do you bid on these same four hands if East had bid 6♡?

(18) What do you bid on these same four hands if East had bid 7♡?

(19) You deal and the bidding goes:

W	N	E	S
			1♡
Dble	3♡	4♣	?

What do you bid now on:

(a) ♠ K J x
♡ A Q x x x
◇ K J x
♣ x x

(b) ♠ x x x x
♡ K Q J x x
◇ A x x
♣ K

(c) ♠ x
♡ Q J 10 x x x
◇ A x
♣ K J x x

(d) ♠ x x x
♡ J 10 x x x
◇ A Q J x
♣ A

(20) Partner deals and the bidding goes:

W	N	E	S
	1♡	Dble	3♡
4♣	Pass	Pass	?

What do you bid now on:

(a) ♠ Q J x x
♡ A Q x x
◇ x x x
♣ x x

(b) ♠ x x x
♡ K J x x x
◇ x x
♣ K Q x

(c) ♠ x x
♡ K J x x
◇ A x
♣ x x x x x

(d) ♠ J x x x
♡ K J x x
◇ Q x x x x
♣ –

(21) Partner deals and the bidding goes:

W	N	E	S
	1♡	Pass	Pass
Dble	2♣	2♠	?

What do you bid now on:

(a) ♠ Q J x x
♡ Q x x
◇ x x x x
♣ x x

(b) ♠ x x x x
♡ J x x x
◇ K x x
♣ x x

(c) ♠ x x x
♡ Q x x
◇ x x x
♣ Q J x x

(d) ♠ x x x
♡ –
◇ x x x x x
♣ Q J x x x

(22) You deal and the bidding goes:

W	N	E	S
			1♡
Pass	Pass	Dble	Pass
1♠	2♡	2♠	?

What do you bid now on:

(a) ♠ A J x
♡ A Q x x x
◇ J x x
♣ x x

(b) ♠ x x x x
♡ K J x x x x
◇ A K x
♣ –

(c) ♠ –
♡ K J x x x x
◇ A x x
♣ K 10 x x

(d) ♠ K Q x x
♡ K Q x x x
◇ A x x x
♣ –

(23) You deal and the bidding goes:

	W	N	E	S
				Pass
	1♠	2♡	3♠	?

What do you bid now on:

(a) ♠ Q x	(b) ♠ x x x x	(c) ♠ J x x x	(d) ♠ –
♡ A Q x x	♡ K J x x	♡ Q J 10 x x	♡ K Q x x x
◇ J x x x	◇ x x	◇ –	◇ A x x x x x
♣ x x x	♣ A K x	♣ A 10 x x	♣ x x

(24) Partner deals and the bidding goes:

	W	N	E	S
			Pass	1♡	1♠
	2♡	3♣	3♡	?

What do you bid now on:

(a) ♠ A K Q J x	(b) ♠ K Q x x x	(c) ♠ A Q x x x x	(d) ♠ K Q 10 x x
♡ x x x	♡ J x x x	♡ J 10 x x	♡ K Q J x
◇ Q J x x	◇ x	◇ –	◇ x x x x
♣ x	♣ A Q x	♣ K J 10	♣ –

(25) You deal and the bidding goes:

	W	N	E	S
				Pass
	1♠	2◇	2♠	2NT
	3♠	Pass	Pass	?

What do you bid now on:

(a) ♠ Q J x	(b) ♠ K x	(c) ♠ K Q 10	(d) ♠ J 10 x x
♡ K x x	♡ x x x	♡ Q 10 x x	♡ K x x
◇ Q J x	◇ A x x	◇ A x	◇ A Q x x
♣ Q x x x	♣ A x x x x	♣ 10 x x x	♣ J x

Let us work through the answers.

(1) (a) The bidding has devalued the hand considerably and those spade honours will be worth little. Partner has another chance to speak and to compete now is likely to give the wrong impression. I recommend a pass.

    (b) This illustrates the other side of the coin. We have only 12 high-card points, as opposed to 13 last time, but the whereabouts of those points and the suit distribution are a very different story. Partner is most unlikely to have more than a singleton spade and could well be void, in which case there could be a tremendous crossruff on, particularly if partner has plenty of trumps. However, one word of warning is appropriate. In cases where we have length in a suit bid and supported by opponents, implying that partner is very short, he will have taken this into account in his bidding and we must be careful about counting it twice. I certainly recommend competing and suggest a long-suit trial with 3◊.

(c) Most of our points are in short suits, notably spades, suggesting preference for defence, but it is unlikely that we shall be able to take six or more tricks with spades as trumps, particularly if partner's few points are in hearts. However, with those hearts as trumps, assuming that partner has a doubleton spade, we are likely to take one top spade trick and a spade ruff and there is every chance that we could make 3♡. I therefore recommend competing. Note that this is purely competitive. If we wanted to invite game, we should make a trial in one of the minors. Another important consideration in these competitive situations is to decide *now* what we are going to do if opponents compete further – that would be with 3♠ here, but the consideration will be several times more important later on in the game and slam zones. In this case, we intend to pass 3♠.

(d) The void of spades is ideal and a case could be made for bidding game outright. However, partner is not exempted from having points in spades himself and I recommend a long-suit trial with 3♣.

(2) This is the auction in (1) taken a stage further as seen from the other side of the table. We have to consider whether we are minimum or maximum for our original raise and the way in which the spade competition has re- or devalued our holding in that suit.

(a) There are two good features and one bad about this hand. The extra trump combined with the singleton club strongly suggest competing. On the other hand, the presence of 4 out of 7 points in spades, probably well placed over the overcall, suggests defence. Much depends on whether partner's minor-suit honours are in clubs, in which case we should pass, or diamonds, in which case we should compete. Vulnerability could be relevant here. At Love All, we would lose 90 + 60 plus the value of the part-scores if we pass and both 2♠ and 3♡ are making. This is more serious than the loss (50 + 50 = 100) if we compete and both 2♠ and 3♡ are defeated by one trick. At Game All, however, the loss is 100 + 100 = 200, and that arguably swings the odds in favour of defence. As there is also the chance that, if we do compete, opponents might decide to go to 3♠ which we will be happy to defend, I suggest competing with 3♡.

(b) Here again, we have an extra heart with an outside doubleton and no wasted points in spades and I therefore suggest competing with 3♡.

(c) This is similar to (a) but more extreme, in that partner may now be void of spades, and much depends on his length in trumps and whether opponents find the necessary trump lead. Again, I am inclined to recommend competing with 3♡.

(d) Here the first comment is that it is surprising that the bidding has died so low with both sides having found fits in a very distributional hand. It is likely that partner has four spades, which will probably include honours. We are very short on top tricks and I would recommend a pass as it is most unlikely that 3♡ will be made, especially on a trump lead.

(3) The 2♡ bid is forcing but, once the 3♣ bid has come in, the force is lifted as partner has another chance. Thus, with hands of minimum opening strength and/or relatively useless points in clubs, we can warn partner that our hand has been devalued by passing.

(a) This is a case in point. We have heart support but are aceless and the club honours will be of little, if any, use. I recommend a pass.

(b) This time, despite the minimal 12 points, the bidding has improved the hand considerably. Anything up to a grand slam could be on in either major and I recommend showing the club void with a splinter of 4♣. Partner can take it from there.

(c) This time, partner is certain to be short of clubs and we have no wasted points there. With the solid spade suit and no diamond loser, I would suggest 4♡, but it is certainly worth at least 3♡.

(d) This is bigger, point-wise, but the club holding is worth only one trick and the rest of the hand is minimal. I recommend a pass.

(4) Here the auction in (3) is looked at a stage further from the other side of the table. Partner has left the decision to us, suggesting that he is not very keen on what has happened so far.

(a) Here we have no wasted points in clubs and I would recommend competing with 3♠ (non-forcing) rather than sell out in 3♣. Partner may be able to bid game in one of the majors or (less likely) 3NT with a double club-stop.

(b) Here, with club honours, we are better suited to defence so I recommend a pass.

(c) Here we have easily enough for game and the best way to make the choice is the cue-bid of 4♣, asking partner to describe his hand further. If he bids 4◊, we shall correct to 4♡, offering 4♡ or 4♠ as final contract.

(d) Partner almost certainly has a singleton or void club but was unable to bid. This surely rules out the void and a useless singleton honour is a strong possibility. Even now, he might well have raised our hearts and his failure to do so suggests a doubleton or less. That leaves ten cards for spades and diamonds in which case our singleton ◊K will be very welcome. I recommend competing with 3♠, which partner is likely to be able to raise to 4♠.

(5) As indicated earlier, it will be particularly important to decide, in advance, what we are going to do if we compete and opponents go to 4♡. That may well be a stretch but, if we have no defence, the contract will be made.

(a) Here, with most of our points in diamonds, our defensive prospects are poor and I would recommend a pass. 4◊ is unlikely to be made anyway.

(b) This is another matter and we have every prospect of defeating 4♡. The hand is not strong enough to invite game so I should recommend merely competing with 4◊, intending to pass 4♡.

(c) The defensive prospects here will very much depend on the opponents' spade holdings and who has the ♠A. However, this hand has considerable playing strength with 12 points in the long suits. If partner can manage a heart stop, 3NT could be on and I should recommend 3♠, showing spade values, inviting 3NT or 4◊ or 5◊, according to partner's hand.

(d) The bidding has improved this hand considerably and, with partner marked with a singleton or void heart, anything up to a grand slam could be on in diamonds. There are a number of possible approaches. One is to bid 4♣, as a long-suit trial, and see how partner reacts. We shall go to 5◊ at least. However, I prefer the splinter of 4♠ to show the void – partner can then assess the value of all his black-suit honours. Vulnerable against not, there is a case for bidding 6◊ or even 7◊ outright and leave the opponents to guess what to do. For all they know, a sacrifice could be well worthwhile but they could find that it is a phantom.

(6) This is the auction in (5) taken a stage further and seen from the supporter's viewpoint. We have to weigh up the chances of defeating 3♡ with those of making 4◊ and of pushing opponents in 4♡, which may or may not be made.

    (a) This hand is more suited to playing and its defensive prospects largely depend on opponents' club holdings. It is interesting that nobody bid spades and partner is likely to have four. On that assumption, it is noteworthy that he did not make a take-out double. The implication is that he is very short of clubs, possibly 4261, and our defensive prospects are now very good. I would take the view that opponents are unlikely to make 4♡ and compete with 4◊, prepared to defend 4♡.

(b) Here partner will have some length in hearts and should realize that we are short – yet he did not compete. The implication is that he has heart honours. With a number of black-suit losers, 4◊ is unlikely to be made and we shall not know what to do if they go to 4♡. On the other hand 3♡ is unlikely to be defeated and 4◊ will almost certainly not be doubled. With a bad trump split guaranteed for opponents in 4♡, I should take the view that it is worth competing with 4◊, intending to allow 4♡ to play.

(c) Here there is every prospect of defeating 3♡ and many black-suit losers in 4◊. With weak trumps, it is most unlikely that opponents will persist with 4♡ over 4◊ and I recommend passing now.

(d) With scattered honours and little playing strength, we have little to add to what we have already bid and I recommend a pass.

(7) The important distinction between this hand and the last is that, while in (6) opponents bidding had died, here West is still unlimited, except to the degree that he did not open with a forcing bid at the two-level. Therefore preparation for action against 4♠, or even a slam, should be uppermost in our minds.

(a) Here partner will be very short of spades and will probably sacrifice at the slightest provocation – the last thing we want. I do not therefore recommend competing with 4♣ but prefer a pass.

(b) This time, the opponents are likely to be cold for at least 4♠ and may have a slam on. Partner is likely to be short of spades and so a sacrifice should be cheap. In this kind of situation, it is usually good tactics to make the sacrifice *in advance* with 5♣. This has a number of advantages: if West is slam-minded, he will be debarred from Blackwood and must start cue-bidding at the five-level. On the other hand, if West is at the weak end of the opening range, it may not be clear to him who is sacrificing against whom. He may be wise to pass, leaving the decision to his partner, but East may not know what the situation is either. If opponents do reach the slam zone, the decision to, or not to, sacrifice will depend on vulnerability but, particularly as opponents will have had to bid it with reduced bidding space, it is unlikely to be worthwhile going to the seven-level except at favourable vulnerability.

(c) Partner is now very likely to be void of spades and much depends on his heart holding. The difference between this hand and the last is that here we have considerable defence. As long as neither opponent is void of clubs, we can defeat 5♠ with a diamond lead, club returned to partner's assumed ♣A and a diamond ruff. For that reason, I recommend a cue-bid of 4◊. Note that, as this commits the partnership to 5♣, it is *not* a long-suit trial as opposed to the sequence 1◊ 3◊ which can be played as a long-suit trial,
     4♣
the partnership being able to stop in 4◊. It has to be admitted that this bid may warn opponents off bidding 5♠ and leave them room to cue-bid in 4♡ or 5♣, while a direct 5♣ would leave them guessing and take up more space and this problem illustrates the clash of styles. Many top-class players prefer to make life difficult for opponents even if partner also has to suffer. I prefer to make life easy for partner, even if it means opponents may benefit. I leave it to you, but the most important thing at this stage is to appreciate the con-siderations involved.

(d) Here we have a tremendous supporting hand and there are a number of approaches: a direct 5♣; cue-bids of 4◊ or 4♠; or even a direct 6♣. The fate of that contract will depend on partner's hearts but, if we bid it direct, we might well get a spade lead and make the contract despite the heart losers. The direct slam bid also has the advantage that it is will not be clear who is sacrificing against whom. Let us consider the hand further. Partner has bid on a broken suit and is unlikely to have many points in spades or diamonds so it would appear that he ought to have first or second control in hearts and, in the former case, 7♣ could be on. I would suggest that, if we are vulnerable, it is a question of 6♣ or 7♣ and would go slowly with 4◊, intending to bid 4♠ if partner shows a heart control. Non-vulnerable, partner is likely to be weaker and I would now prefer a direct 6♣, willing to forego a possible grand slam to keep the opponents guessing.

(8) Here we have the same auction at the next stage from the other side of the table. The first point to note is that partner should have decided what he is going to do if 4♠ is passed round to him. It is thus a question of whether we should bid in front of him, i.e. whether we have extra vital information.

(a) We have nothing beyond our overcall, no surprises, and therefore no reason to bid. I recommend a pass.

(b) We have an extra club (important for playing but likely to work against us in defence as an opponent could be void) and two top diamond tricks which could be crucial in defence. However, partner's length in spades is unknown and either defending 4♠ or persisting with 5♣, making or as a cheap sacrifice, could be right. I suggest leaving it to partner and again recommend a pass.

(c) This time, partner is likely to be void of spades and we have a lot of points in clubs, no losers in diamonds, and we might hold our losers in hearts to one even if partner lacks the ace. If he has the ♡A, the grand slam in clubs could be on but I should recommend simply bidding 6♣, intending to double 6♠. We will then be faced with the problem of whether or not to lead a low club, hoping to find partner with the ♣Q for a diamond ruff. The risk of disaster is probably too great and we may well be ruffing what will be partner's trick anyway. A high club or trump is probably safer.

(d) Here we have most of our high cards outside clubs and, with the strong trump holding, are better suited to defence. We should warn partner to that effect with a double. If he takes it out, that is his responsibility.

(9) This is the same auction a stage further as seen from the supporter's point of view. We should have already decided what to do over 4♠ before bidding 4♣ and thus should have little to think about.

(a) We are happy to defend and pass.

(b) It is interesting that partner did not go to 5♣ despite a likely void of spades. He probably has some useful defensive red honours. We are happy to double.

(c) Here we probably have two or three defensive tricks and certainly do not want to sacrifice. We are happy to pass.

(d) This is less clear. It could well be that both games are making but they could both go down. The loss through failure to compete is likely to outweigh that through competing and I recommend 5♣. This gives the additional chance that opponents may go to 5♠ which we shall be happy to defend.

(10) Here West has guaranteed at least one stop in hearts but, on the bidding, is unlikely to have more than that. Very often in this sequence, East will try 3NT hoping to run a long minor suit after the stop has been knocked out.

(a) We have nothing beyond our opening bid and no reason to bid again. Partner has another chance and I suggest a pass.

(b) East is likely to have a long club suit and his defensive prospects, at least, are poor against a heart contract. Whether 4♡ will be successful, of course, depends on partner's spade holding but I certainly recommend bidding it, irrespective of vulnerability, as 3NT will probably be made.

(c) This is a much better hand for defence as we are likely to be able to stop both minors. It is possible that West has a double heart stop, but unlikely. He could well have ♡ K J x with partner having the ♡Q over him. Our black-suit holdings are most unsuitable for play and I recommend a double. If opponents run to four of a minor, let them play it undoubled. The important aim is to stop partner from sacrificing in 4♡, which could be very expensive.

(d) It is likely that a diamond lead will defeat 3NT but partner will surely never find it. This hand is much more suited to playing than defending and it could well be that we can avoid a heart loser if West has the ♡K and partner the ♡A. The fate of 4♡ depends on the spade position but we should certainly compete at any vulnerability. However, there is no need to rush into 4♡. A better bid is surely 4◇. With hearts the agreed suit, this is surely lead-directing against a possible 4NT contract. It can hardly be a cue-bid with a view to a slam with a strong no-trump sitting over us. However, even if it were, we could clarify the meaning by bidding on over partner's enforced 4♡. A slam try implies confidence in making eleven tricks.

(11) Here we have the same auction, taken a stage further and seen from the supporter's angle.

    (a) We have nothing further to say and I recommend a pass.

    (b) It is most unlikely that we shall defeat 3NT and, if partner is short of spades, 4♡ could well be made. I recommend competing with 4♡.

    (c) This is a poor hand for both playing and defending but there is no reason to bid any more.

    (d) This is more debatable and we have an unpleasant surprise for opponents in both minors. With plenty of points, I recommend a double. If East runs to 4♣, we can be confident that partner is short of the suit and now 4♡ is likely to be made and we can bid it. Partner might decide to double 4♣ if his hearts are very poor.

(12) This again may be bid on a long minor with a heart stop.

    (a) With a minimal opening bid, we have nothing further to say. I recommend a pass.

    (b) The same applies but there is every chance of defeating 3NT if partner has a heart honour. Nevertheless, we do not double. West may well have a singleton heart and there is no guarantee that we can defeat 4♣.

    (c) This time, we are confident of defeating 3NT as we have a very unpleasant surprise for East in clubs. Partner has raised us on poor hearts and is likely to have spade length and all his honours outside hearts. Again a double risks a removal to 4♠ but, as the penalty could be heavy, I suggest that it's worth the risk.

    (d) This time, partner is likely to be short in spades; we have little defence against 3NT and I would recommend competing at any vulnerability. Our intention is to double 4♠ and partner should realize that we want a club lead – if we bid 4♣ now! As before, this can hardly be a slam try and is a bid made with final contract considerations in mind!

(13) The golden rule regarding preempts is to refrain from bidding again unless forced to do so. The exception arises when there is an unexpected defensive prospect when a double (bearing in mind that the preemptive bid has expressed little or no defence) is in order.

    (a), (b), (c), there is no reason to bid. Partner must make the decision and he should have decided what to do over 4♠ before bidding 4♡.

    (d) This is a different matter. Partner is on lead and his choice could be crucial. A double here indicates an 'unexpected' lead as opposed to the 'expected' heart. It should be obvious to partner what is required.

(14) Here we have the same auction a stage later as seen from the other side of the table. We should have decided what to do over 4♠ before bidding 4♡ and ought to have our answer ready.

    (a) 4♠ might well be made but could go up to two down if partner is short of diamonds and I recommend a double.

    (b) Here it is unlikely that we can defeat 4♠. Partner is unlikely to have many clubs and 5♡ should be a worthwhile sacrifice. At worst, there will be a small loss at adverse vulnerability and we have the chance that they may go to 5♠ (particularly at that vulnerability) rather than risk accepting a small penalty, not to mention the chance that, for all they know, 5♡ might be made. Against 5♠, we might make two diamonds tricks and a heart for a great gain.

    (c) Here we bid 5♡, hoping to be successful. Again we are happy to defend 5♠.

    (d) Here, if partner is very short of spades, we might make 5♡ but there is no guarantee and I recommend doubling 4♠, intending to cash the ♡A and then switch to trumps as we are well covered in all three side-suits.

(15) Where the preempter has doubled, he is indicating a minor-

suit void and now the picture could change markedly.

(a) It is likely that the void is in diamonds and now 4♠ will be heavily defeated. Even if it is in clubs, all is not lost. As long as the opponents can follow to one round of diamonds, there is still time to switch and we shall take at least four tricks. We obviously pass.

(b) Now the void is almost certainly in clubs and we can review the position. If we decide to defend, we shall lead our lowest club, indicating a preference for a diamond return, and could well take up to six tricks if East, as is likely, has the ◊K. On the other hand, in hearts, we have only one black-suit loser and could well make up to twelve tricks if partner has ◊K or ◊ J 10. The danger of playing in hearts lies in a likely trump lead – and continuation when we give up a spade. We might now be held to ten tricks even if the diamond finesse is right. I recommend standing the double.

(c) Here we do not know where the void is but can find out by cashing the ◊A. However, once we give the ruff, we are relying on the ♡K as reentry, i.e. partner needs to have the ♡A and underlead it *and* both opponents must follow. Against this, in 5♡, we are guaranteed at least two spade ruffs (even on a trump lead). This now looks a very good contract and I recommend 5♡.

(d) Now the penalty should be something to write home about! Pass without a trace of a smile.

(16) The first point to realize is that the 5♡ is merely extending the preempt rather than inviting the preempter to a slam. It is common practice in many sequences to play a bid of five of a major as invitational to a slam dependent on trump quality, but this is not one of them. Partner is likely to have a strong hand as both opponents have demonstrated their reluctance to defend.

(a) We are not strong enough to bid and therefore pass, leaving any further action to partner.

(b) Partner is very likely to be void of hearts and, in that case, a grand slam is only likely to be defeated if he turns up with three small diamonds. The conservative-minded might settle for the small slam but I recommend bidding the grand and hoping for the best.

(c) The heart holding is not so good this time and there could be a minor-suit loser. Nevertheless, I would recommend 6♠. Particularly if we are vulnerable against not, opponents might well decide to sacrifice in 7♡, which we shall be happy to double.

(d) This is a rare situation with three hands at the table clearly weak but partner unable to bid game. It is now likely that both the 3♡ preempter and his partner have a good card or two outside their suit so a slam is ruled out. I would merely compete with 5♠.

(17) Now the situation is less clear. Once East bids a slam, he may be intending to make it or merely offering an advance sacrifice. It should be obvious from our hand which it is.

(a) This is a very poor hand and we have no reason to take a decision either way. Pass and let partner decide.

(b) The void of hearts with partner is now even more likely than before. East is obviously terrified of defending and I now recommend 7♠ with confidence.

(c) Partner is now more likely to have a singleton or void heart and I recommend 6♠, intending to double 7♡.

(d) Here it is more likely that East's slam bid is serious and now we have to consider whether to sacrifice and it is a close decision. First of all, how certain is the slam to make? East has simply shut his eyes and bid it with only approximate knowledge of his partner's hand. Partner should have some values outside spades to justify entering the bidding at all at the three-level. If we compete, we are likely to go at least three off, losing 500 (non-vulnerable) or 800 (vulnerable). On the other side, the slam, counting a non-vulnerable game as worth 300, is worth 980 (non-vulnerable) and if they are vulnerable, we lose 180 + 750 = 930 plus 500 for the rubber if we are vulnerable, 700 if we are not. I should suggest taking out insurance and competing if we are non-vulnerable but passing if we are vulnerable.

(18) (a) Here 7♡ has obviously been bid seriously and we can see no defence as East is likely to be void of spades. Partner is likely to be void of hearts and have long spades so we could escape for four or five off in 7♠, a good sacrifice at any vulnerability. However, a word of warning indicated earlier – it is a well-known tactic to bid vulnerable grand slams with a certain loser in this type of sacrifice situation when opponents will find it irresistible to take out cheap insurance. I think it best to pass. Partner will realize that we have not doubled for lack of a defensive trick and that East is likely to be void of spades, implying that we have some support. Let *him* take the decision in that knowledge.

(b) This is obviously an attempted advance sacrifice. I recommend 7♠ without further comment.

(c) This is more difficult as partner could have a big hand but with a singleton heart. We cannot pass now; partner may think that East's bid is serious and work on that mistaken assumption. My view is that, this time, we should take out insurance by doubling at any vulnerability as there is no guarantee that 7♠ will be made even if partner is void of hearts.

(d) Again, I would recommend taking out insurance by sacrificing, except at adverse vulnerability where the profit will, at best, be minimal. They haven't yet made 7♡.

(19) Here partner has shown a weak raise to 3♡ – a full-strength raise to 3♡ would have been shown by 2NT.

(a) Our spade and diamond tenaces are badly placed under the doubler and the club holding could hardly be worse. I recommend a pass.

(b) This is a slight improvement in that we are now down to a singleton club – albeit a likely wasted king – and there are no wasted honours in spades or diamonds. However, East's preference for clubs over spades implies shortage in spades and therefore length in that suit in partner's hand. This does not augur well for 4♡. We are down to an effective 10 points and again I recommend a pass.

(c) This is another story. Partner is likely to be short of clubs and we have an extra trump for an obvious crossruff situation. Despite only 11 points including club honours (possibly well-placed but hardly 'working'), I recommend competing with 4♡.

(d) Now there is no club loser but the diamond finesse is likely to be wrong and the spade holding is unattractive. We are low on points anyway and I recommend a pass. Note that, in all the 'pass' cases, partner has another chance.

(20) This is the same auction a stage further, as seen from the supporter's angle, after opener and the doubler have stated that they have nothing more to say.

(a) We have no reason to bid again.

(b) With the club honours now reduced to defensive status, we have less reason to bid than in (a).

(c) Now partner is likely to be short of clubs and we have a possible crossruff position. Against that, the two doubletons in spades and diamonds are not good features. We note that partner did not persist over 4♣ and it may well be that East doubled on a spade-diamond hand, with only tolerance for clubs. Therefore, if we allow 4♣ to play, a forcing game (persistent heart leads) may cause West to lose control. I recommend passing as it is unlikely that 4♡ will be made.

(d) With the void of clubs, the case of competing with 4♡ is much stronger but the spade and diamond holdings are uninviting. We also have to consider what happens if we bid 4♡ and they go to 5♣. Can we be confident of defeating them? Much will depend on the opponents' heart split but I would take the view that, with 7 high-card points opposite an opening bid, there is more to be gained than lost by competing and that it would be feeble to allow 4♣ to be played. I recommend 4♡ but accept that there is a case for passing.

(21) Here partner has shown a big two-suiter (5–5 at least) and has been keen to get both suits in before opponents get together.

(a) Here, despite acceptable heart support, 3 of our 5 points (admittedly maximum for the range of our pass) are facing a shortage and therefore useless. I recommend a pass – partner has another chance.

(b) One point less this time but the bidding has improved things on two counts. The extra heart combined with the doubleton club suggests good ruffing potential and the likely 4–4 spade fit found by opponents suggests that the ◇K may not be wasted opposite a likely doubleton or trebleton in partner's hand. I recommend competing with 3♡.

(c) In the pass range, this hand could hardly be bigger, with every point working overtime. We prefer clubs but game there would involve going to the five-level and partner may have three losers in the other two suits. I recommend 4♡.

(d) Now we have a big crossruff situation but no guarantee of game for the same reason as above. I recommend inviting with 4♣ and partner should realize that we have this type of hand.

(22) This time, partner has competed in hearts and should be just under a normal raise to 2♡.

(a) With a minimum opening bid and 5 points in opponents' suit, we have no reason to bid.

(b) Partner is likely to have a singleton or void spade and now the prospects are far better. We can confidently bid game but note that a slam is out as partner would need a spade void and ♡ A x x x, good enough for 2♡ the first time and, even now, a trump lead will break the slam.

(c) Here again, it is worth competing but we need to know where partner's few points are. Many would be content merely to compete with 3♡ but I would suggest a long-suit trial of 3♣. Give partner ♣ A x and four small hearts or ♣ Q J and ♡ Q and 4♡ is an excellent contract.

(d) Partner is now certain to be singleton or void in spades and, if his honours are in diamonds, 4♡ will have good chances. Against that, if partner has values in useless clubs and only three trumps, a trump lead could defeat 2♡, never mind more! Nevertheless, I would take the view that, if partner cannot help in diamonds, it is most unlikely that we will be doubled in 3♡ (particularly as we are obviously thinking about 4♡!) and risk a long-suit trial of 3◇.

(23) In all these cases, as indicated before, we have to decide what we are going to do over 4♠ if we do decide to compete.

(a) This hand is disastrous on a number of counts, particularly the spade holding. 5♡ will probably go several down and is unlikely to be a profitable sacrifice, even at favourable vulnerability and we should not want to tempt partner to bid on. The only point of bidding 4♡ is that it indicates a safe lead. On lead against 4♠, partner will be reluctant to touch his broken heart holding. Against that, we have 8 points and West may decide to pass 3♠ and we have a spectacular gain. On balance, I recommend a pass.

(b) This time, our playing prospects have improved spectacularly as partner will not have more than one spade and could well be void. We are certainly happy to play up to 5♡ but it costs nothing to bid 4♣ (forcing) on the way, indicating where our defence is if they compete in spades and suggesting a possible slam if partner has top tricks in diamonds.

(c) Here partner needs at least ♠ – ♡ A K x x x x ◇ x x x x ♣ K x x for a small slam to be cold and a slightly stronger hand could guarantee the grand. What do we bid now? Arguably, 5◇ would be ideal as a splinter bid but it could be misunderstood as a long diamond suit, trying to play there. This particularly applies if our hand has not passed originally. Here we have passed and there should be no ambiguity. However, it is a dangerous bid to make and it is safer to keep it simple. A reasonably practical bid is an outright 6♡ – let the opponents guess whether to defend or sacrifice. An alternative approach is to bid 4♣ now and, if partner cue-bids 4◇, bid 4♡ and see if partner carries on. If partner fails to cue-bid 4◇ and tries to sign off in 4♡, then we will bid 5◇ and hope partner will realize that we are missing second-round control in clubs.

(d) Here we could have anything up to a grand slam on and we should start by cue-bidding the spade control with 4♠. Let partner continue cue-bidding from there.

(24) With partner having passed originally, he should not bid 3♣ without spade support; i.e. willing to play at least 3♠.

   (a) Even giving partner the ♣A, we may lose four tricks in the red suits in 4♠ and there could even be three diamond losers through a ruff. However, we must also consider opponents' point of view. East has merely competed (3◊ would have been a try for game) so it is unlikely that they will bid 4♡ over 3♠ but, particularly if we are vulnerable against not, they may well decide to sacrifice in 5♡ over 4♠. Now our singleton club will ensure a crushing defeat. I suggest gambling 4♠ but there is a case for stopping in 3♠.

   (b) Now our club holding is a dream and we have no hesitation in insisting on game. However, with partner marked with a shortage in hearts, there could be more on. It costs nothing to bid 4♣, enabling partner to cue-bid in hearts, after which 6♠ might be reached.

   (c) This is even more sensational and now even a grand slam is possible. We splinter with 4◊ and again partner can show his heart control. We are likely to reach at least 6♠.

   (d) Here with so many points in hearts, we want to defend despite the spade fit and we pass. There is a case for doubling but I would not recommend it with an aceless hand.

(25) (a),(b),(c) We have bid our hand to the limit and have no reason to bid again.

   (d) Here partner is clearly very short of spades and now it is worthwhile competing in diamonds with all except one of our points working. I suggest 4◊ and partner, with a void of spades, should realize that we have this type of hand and may well push on to 5◊.

We have concentrated on major-suit hands in this test and, where minor-suits are involved and 3NT comes into the reckoning as final contract, the position tends to be more complicated and an intensive study is, perhaps, best left to a later date. But, for the time being, that will do. I emphasize the use of the one-closed hand exercise and its application in the bidding and urge you to redo all the examples and tests over and over again until they become second nature. You will then be ready for the next stage – *The Expert Club Player* – where we shall be learning more advanced plays and defences and introduce duplicate bridge and the further bidding and scoring complications involved. It will be the graduation stage in becoming a competent and much sought-after partner.

Index

Bidding
  Advanced cue-bid 219
  Advanced sacrifice 268
  All or nothing theory 122
  Blackwood (use and abuse of) 43,
    136, 203 seq.
  Competitive bidding test 258 seq.
    answers 264 seq.
  Convention 9
  Cue-bidding (see also advanced
    and unassuming) 72–3, 99, 101,
    159, 224, 269
  Directional Asking Bid 225, 249
  Double – revised score 10
  False preference 211, 216
  Final or 'goal' contract 8, 11, 20,
    43, 78, 96, 193 seq.
  Force 194 seq.
  Fourth-suit forcing 216, 219, 220
  Grand-slam force 72–3
  Invitation 194
  Language or sytem 8
  Long-suit trial 85, 93, 216, 230,
    264, 269
  Negative response 196
  Overcall 237
  Preempt 239 seq.
  Principle of fast arrival 56, 210

  Protective position 41
  Redouble – revised score 10
  Reverse 30, 96, 201 seq.
  Sacrifice (see also advanced) 253,
    279
  Sign-off 8, 194 seq.
  SOS redouble 245 seq.
  Splinter 213, 222, 279
  Stayman 24, 203 seq.
  Suppressing majors 123
  Take-out double 65–6
  Trial bid 208, 213, 250
  Unassuming cue-bid 135
  Unusual no-trump 188

Blockage 13, 49, 55, 157
Bluff and double bluff 120
Broken holding 83, 161

Captain's privilege 190
Controls 13
Covering (or not) an honour 36,
  39, 71
Cutting out suit 119

Daisy picker 23
Deception 119
Declarer play at no-trumps 13

Problems 16, 24, 32–3, 41–3
Solutions 17–20, 24–6, 33–5, 44–51
Declarer play at trumps 53
  Problems 56–7, 65, 68, 70, 72, 76, 81, 85, 90, 93, 96, 98–102
  Solutions 66, 68, 70–2, 73–5, 76, 81–2, 86–8, 90, 94, 96–7, 102, 115
Defence at no-trumps 117
  Problems 120–2, 128–9, 134–6, 141–3
  Solutions 122–6, 129–32, 136–141, 144–150
Defence at trumps 151
  Problems 153–4, 158–9, 163–4, 169–70, 177–8, 182–4
  Solutions 154–6, 159–62, 165–7, 170–3, 179–81, 184–91
Defensive signalling
  encouragement 168
  count 117, 122seq.
  McKenney suit preference 137, 172
Desperate measures 167
Discarding 117 seq
Drop or finesse 20–23
  (combining chances) 54, 72 seq. 102
Dropping on air 40
Doubling for lead 24
Duplication of values/pattern 48, 89

Elimination 91, 103, 108, 113, 115
Endplay 83 seq.
Entries and entry problems 13, 26, 27–9 seq., 110

Familiarization with pack 8, 10
Free finesse 158 seq.

Going as near to card as possible 152

Holding up 13 seq.

Inferences 19,184
  negative 124
Insurance 275

Master hand 94
Middle-card lead 128 seq.

One-closed-hand exercise 281

Parrot rules 9, 205, 206
Partial elimination 91
Passive defence 190
Percentage calculations 23, 25–6, 54, 59, 92, 102, 133
Peter 122, 174
Platform of knowledge 8
Principle of fast arrival 56, 210

Quick and slow tricks 122

Race 13, 21, 132
Refusing to overruff 176

Religious adherence to signals 156
Research 93, 107
Reverse dummy 94 seq., 110
Ruff and discard 84, 89 seq., 108, 160 seq.
Ruffing finesse 64
Ruffing high 108

Safety play 48–9, 81
Sacrificing a trick 34, 62
Scoring – revision 9–10
Second hand low 33, 104, 144, 148
Short-hand first 31

Signalling 117
Skew distribution 133
Smoking out 91 seq., 107
Solid holdings (shown by discard)
    152 seq.
Squeeze play 137
Stop 53, 57, 61, 73, 78, 184, 212, 217
    seq.
Stayman 24, 202 seq.

Tap on shoulder 110
Tenace 40, 88, 151, 187, 188, 207
Three-card position 55, 60, 67, 70,
    82, 91, 105, 107, 109, 127, 157,
    160, 189

Trial run 58
Trump promotion (also see
    uppercut, refusing to overruff)
    174 seq.
Two-card position 17, 36, 49, 53,
    63, 67, 82, 91, 175

Unnecessary losses 62, 63
Uppercut 175, 189

Weakness through strength to
    strength 67, 81
Working cards 155

Yarborough 200